Guided Affective Imagery

Mental Imagery in Short-Term Psychotherapy

The Basic Course

Prof. Dr.med. Hanscarl Leuner
Department of Psychotherapy and Psychosomatics
Center of Psychologic Medicine
University of Göttingen
West Germany

Translated by Elizabeth Lachman

Edited by William A. Richards, Ph.D.

1984
Thieme-Stratton Inc.
New York

Georg Thieme Verlag
Stuttgart • New York

Library of Congress Cataloging in Publication Data

Leuner, Hanscarl.
Guided affective imagery—the basic course.

Translation of: Katathymes Bilderleben—Grundstufe.
Bibliography: p.
Includes indexes.
1. Imagery (Psychology)—Therapeutic use.
2. Psychotherapy, Brief. I. Richards, William A.
II. Title. [DNLM: 1. Fantasy. 2. Psychotherapy,
Brief—methods. WM 420 L653g]
RC489.F35L4813 1984 616.89'14 84-16456
ISBN 0-86577-132-4

This work was previously published in German as *Katathymes Bilderleben—Grundstufe.* Copyright © 1982 by Georg Thieme Verlag, Stuttgart, West Germany.

Printed in the United States of America

GUIDED AFFECTIVE IMAGERY
Prof. Dr.med. Hanscarl Leuner

TSI ISBN 0-86577-132-4
GTV ISBN 3-13-653101-9

5 4 3 2 1

Table of Contents

Preface to the Third German Edition

The second edition of this volume concerning the elementary level of guided affective imagery was out of print shortly after the end of one year. From this, one can appreciate the great interest in our method in psychotherapeutic circles and by those interested in psychotherapy. To date, it has not been necessary to supplement or expand this volume appreciably. New findings concerning theory and practical psychotherapy with guided affective imagery only indirectly affect the theme of this book, the "elementary level," and are therefore to be published elsewhere.

The text of the third edition has been carefully revised again. This book has in the meantime found surprising response among Anglo-American readers, so that an English translation is planned.

I sincerely thank all of those colleagues, who, through their critical comments, have contributed to the correcting of the text.

Göttingen, March 1982 *Hanscarl Leuner*

Preface to the Second German Edition

This volume about the elementary level of guided affective imagery was out of print for a long time. After careful consideration, it is again appearing in the seminar format of the first edition. The many positive comments, which I have received from readers, suggested that this lively and easily comprehensible style of presentation be maintained. It evolved from my introductory seminars at the large psychotherapeutic advanced training congresses, such as the Northern German Psychotherapy Days in Lübeck and the Lindau Psychotherapy Weeks, as well as those in Aachen and in Langeoog. This is realized in part by dispensing with an overly systematic organization of the material.

The manuscript was not only completely revised, but was also augmented by subtly examining therapeutic-technical details with examples from practice. In this way I have tried to do justice to the rapid development of guided affective imagery in the therapeutic-practical area (see H. Leuner, 1980) since the founding of a number of national associations, which regularly conduct central and regional seminars (Appendix II).

Nevertheless, this volume remains restricted to the *introduction to the elementary level* (formerly lower level) of guided affective imagery.

The intention to make this seminar the basis for training as a therapist in guided affective imagery, as was expressed in the preface of the first edition, had to be abandoned. When I wrote the manuscript for the first edition well over ten years ago, the very broad experience in the training of therapists in guided affective imagery was not yet available. Today we have a much clearer view of the difficulties and problems that arise when advanced education in general psychotherapy and depth psychology is lacking and empathic therapeutic guidance on the regressive level of mental imagery has not been adequately provided. The use of the mental imagery technique, with clinical cases of neuroses and psychosomatic illnesses, is in no way indifferent. To be able to do this, the therapist must gain a high degree of experience and confidence.

The necessary skills are acquired through participation in the multilevel self-awareness seminars in the course of training as a GAI therapist. Partly in the role of therapist, partly in that of the patient and through the supervision of his treatment cases, the future therapist receives broad feedback and important corrections of his therapeutic behavior. By this means, all of those mistakes ought to be avoided, which usually burden autodidactic treatment attempts. In addition, it is absolutely necessary to acquire the psychodynamic concept of depth psychology underlying the procedure and to assimilate it for perceiving the patient's and the therapist's behavior as well as for drawing conclusions.

This book is not only intended for readers who want to become acquainted with the procedure, but is meant to supplement the seminar training as a detailed presentation of the elementary level of guided affective imagery by reproducing extensive clinical experience. I examined the theoretical depth psychological connections only to the extent that seems necessary to understand the technical steps described. They have been dealt with elsewhere, in part (Leuner, 1980), and I also present them in seminars, of which a summary is planned in a separate volume.

Göttingen, January 1981 *Hanscarl Leuner*

Session One: General Orientation

Purpose of this Course

This course provides basic knowledge of Guided Affective Imagery (GAI). Above all, it is directed to those interested persons who want to become familiar with this approach to psychotherapy, in terms of both theory and technique, in order to understand it and to become able to integrate it within the current framework of psychotherapeutic procedures. An introduction to GAI, such as this, transmitted for ease of reading through the transcription of course sessions, has recently become all the more important, now that GAI has been accepted by the medical association of the Federal Republic of Germany as a recommended procedure under the supplemental categories *Psychotherapy* and *Psychoanalysis.* Even beyond this, however, in the past 5 years, as GAI has become known in professional circles, at least by name, an increasingly large readership has manifested the desire to become informed about it. Beginning with this session, this course is intended to fulfill this need.

As already emphasized in the Preface, the objective of this course is not to train therapists, since psychotherapy can neither be learned from books nor acquired without the necessary self-awareness; above all, the guidance of qualified teachers (training therapists) along with the regular supervision of tape-recorded cases in treatment is necessary. If I repeat myself on this point, it is solely because this basic rule of psychotherapy is, in fact, too easily violated. GAI is in no way a neutral procedure. Here, errors in therapy weigh much more heavily due to the greater intensity of the therapeutic alliance in comparison with exclusively verbal treatment.

History of Guided Affective Imagery

The history of GAI goes back to 1948. At that time, my attention was drawn to an unsystematic attempt by Happich (1932) to focus on imaginings in psychotherapy. It was published and remained without further consequences. Happich, who was apparently unfamiliar with depth psychology, applied his imaginal exercises in the area of religious meditation. My main interest was first of all directed toward attempts to subject depth psychological symbolism and the symbolism of dreams to experimental verification. My intention was to convey this, in my opinion, very important area of psychic self-representation to the skeptics among my colleagues in accordance with their own espoused scientific standards. My diverse, in part, systematic experiments with mental imagery led to the first programmatic publication 6 years later (1954). Here I gave the procedure the scientific designation "experimental guided affective imagery" (EGAI; in German, "Experimentelles katathymes Bilderleben" [EkB]. This term, which is somewhat awkward for practical purposes, seemed necessary to procure serious academic consideration of my discovery, especially since connected with it was a basic psychotherapeutic principle that had been subjected neither to prior theoretical nor applied investigation. It was the first introduction of an experimental means of verifying symbolism and its significance in the field of psychodynamics.

Concepts and Name of the Approach

A change of the name seemed necessary, after I later discovered that mental imagery additionally may bring with it a surprising therapeutic effectiveness, which until then had not been systematically demonstrated. As the experimental approach necessarily interferes with therapy, it therefore had to be put aside. For therapy, the free unfolding of spontaneously arising emotions and the imaginal contents dependent on them are much more desirable. For this reason, since approximately 1964 I have spoken simply of "guided affective imagery," at the suggestion of close colleagues, and of "symboldrama." In the meantime the latter term has gained acceptance in Sweden and, in part, in the United States. These are convenient names, which in their concepts at the same time express something about the essence of the procedure. The dependence of the images upon the affective world is apparent in both names mentioned. The encounter with symbols during the unfolding of an experiential drama is well captured in the term *Symboldrama.*

Position within the Range of Psychotherapeutic Approaches

The attempt to integrate GAI into the framework of the well-known psychotherapeutic approaches does not appear to be easy. Although the effect of overall bodily relaxation and internal shifting (*Umschaltung,* to use the term coined by J.H. Schultz) is an important component, which will be discussed in greater detail later, GAI cannot be included among the previously so-called "concealing," "training," or "supportive" procedures. In the narrower sense, however, it does not belong to the purely verbal approaches either, as, for instance, Rogers' person centered therapy, or to psychoanalysis, in which the chief technique is to uncover conflicts, which are then to be verbalized. Nevertheless, the approach does have an uncovering component of its own, which, however, first presents itself in the form of the symbolic imaginal contents, and only at a later point in the therapeutic process transcends the relatively difficult threshold from experiencing symbols to verbalizing the conflict. I myself have never been able to conceive of GAI in its total concept as anything other than a psychoanalytically oriented method. It becomes effective upon the basis of a controlled regression, that is, a regression of the ego in the sense of a regression induced by the therapist to earlier emotional levels and ways of functioning. In this respect and in conformity with depth psychological dream theory, GAI proceeds on the assumption of the existence of unconscious drive impulses, motivations, defensive processes, and thus, naturally, the dynamic significance of dream symbols. Nor could GAI deny the significance of mobilizing emotions for the therapy and the recognition of transference and countertransference relationships between patient and therapist. In the meantime one of our renowned psychoanalysts has tagged GAI as a "legitimate child of psychoanalysis" (Ehebald, 1979).

GAI as a System

GAI represents a system of differing approach techniques, which are in part arranged in polar fashion and are graduated in higher stages as management models and therapeutic strategies of intervention. The system, as a whole, is based upon man's fundamental experience that he can create imaginings using his fantasy. Although this has always been known, not only in dreams (as first dealt with by Freud) but also in daydreams, it has never actually been investigated thoroughly, that is, systematically and scientifically. Using this imaginal capacity, man is able to design anew, over and over again, and can thus confront himself in a strange, subtle dialectical process. I drew up the hypothesis that the daydream obeys certain rules and laws of its own. Step by step, I attempted to prove these empirically, aided by simple experiments to render them therapeutically useful. A series of individual works arose from this, which are listed in Appendix III.

Teachability

I have divided GAI into three levels to make it easy to teach and to do justice to the differing training levels of prospective therapists. The basic level, to which this seminar is dedicated, offers a therapeutic repertory providing sufficient help to perform a fully defined and qualitatively superior short-term therapy. At this level, the therapist's basic orientation still remains somewhat pragmatic. The follow-up intermediate level is only hinted at, but cannot be included in this course. It offers an additional wide array of therapeutic tools, including motifs and therapeutic strategies, and, discusses to a greater extent than the basic level, the problem of transference and countertransference and how they are dealt with in GAI. With these means, the experienced therapist is also put in the position of acquiring the techniques to work through personality disorders. Finally, the advanced level of GAI follows as a specific supplement. In it are combined a range of especially powerful interventions, some of which are active and some clearly psychoanalytically-oriented. The two supplementary levels are briefly outlined in Appendix I so that the reader of this course will not be narrowly limited to the basic level.

Requirements

The reader who wants to obtain an introductory survey of GAI and its effects will not be able to comprehend the unique characteristics of the approach or be able to make comparisons to other methods unless he/she is acquainted with the fundamentals and has some practical experience in psychotherapy. In this regard it would be desirable for the reader to have a basic orientation in general depth psychology and psychosomatic medicine and to be personally experienced in relaxation procedures, such as autogenic training. If he wants to approach the study of GAI more thoroughly, I recommend personal experience with mental imagery, even if only for a short time, preferably conducted by a therapist, but possibly in the form of group GAI.

Intensity

However, there is one thing of which those interested in GAI should be fully aware. Although implementing the method may at first seem very easy, and as tempting as it is to explore and apply it, thereby releasing the fascinating and strange images of the unconscious, an important warning must be made. GAI is an intensive and powerful therapeutic procedure. Only those who have been psychotherapeutically trained in GAI and have experience with it can determine whether the application of GAI is indicated and know the necessary introductory steps for obtaining and evaluating the clinical history. Experience is needed to be able to assess the patient's capacity for stress and to estimate in the individual case the dangers involved in using mental imagery, if the ego is weak.

Qualification as a GAI Therapist

The fact that this mental image technique is a potent therapeutic device has meant that, thus far, only professionally competent groups have been admitted to the training program for therapists: physicians with previous psychotherapeutic training, clinical psychologists, therapists for children and adolescents, and, if these basic requirements are not present, fully trained psychoanalysts. However, the first two groups are also required to have assimilated the fundamental content and methodology of depth psychology through supplementary training in order to become certified as GAI therapists. This usually has not been imparted to them during their course of study, which has had a primarily scientific orientation. To illustrate this point I refer to Appendix II, in which the current advanced training schedule of the AGKB* is reproduced. This association offers lectures, seminars, and practical courses dealing directly with GAI. The foundations of general depth psychology, as required of physicians and psychologists within the scope of the training as psychotherapists are taught at specific institutions and psychoanalytic institutes.

Training Analysis?

Occasionally, I am asked whether a training analysis is desirable or even recommended for the use of symboldrama. In principle, this is not the case. It is, now as ever, undisputed that a training analysis, or even a psychoanalysis for therapeutic purposes for those persons who have to struggle with personality problems, can be extremely productive for their training as a therapist. As is generally known, it is the fate of the therapist to regularly bring his own person and natural patterns of response, as they were developed, into the psychotherapy unintentionally. The old view is still valid that a therapist cannot advance his patient further than he/she has developed in his/her personality. That is the reason why potential therapists are very strongly urged to undertake a period of training analysis or even better a

---

* Association for Guided Affective Imagery, headquarters: Friedlander Weg 30, 3400 Göttingen, Federal Republic of Germany.

Training Therapy

more extensive training therapy with GAI with a training therapist authorized to do this (from his association). An additional, very productive program, which goes beyond this, is to participate in GAI group therapy. The experience of the last 5 years has shown that this procedure, which I will not cover in this course, can accomplish decisive things in the unfolding and harmonizing of the personality, particularly with regard to improving the perception of the self and others, as well as the empathic capacity for therapeutic regression. These are categories that are demanded all the more of the psychotherapist conducting GAI as a regressive method.

Depth Psychological Training

In addition to instruction in psychoanalytic thought, it is also important to have a knowledge of depth psychological symbolism, which should be as broad and subtle as possible. Previously I published a comprehensive survey on this subject (Leuner, 1978) and also developed a technique with which the therapist, trained in the basic level, can learn to decipher not only the collective but also the specific symbolism of a particular patient. In his progress through the AGKB's advanced training program, the therapist gains practical experience with regard to this. In no other method does the comprehension of symbols and the vivid emotional representation of unconscious conflicts address the therapist as directly as in GAI.

Therapeutic Goals

If one considers psychotherapeutic procedures from the point of view of their objectives, hypnosis and autogenic training to a greater extent, as well as behavioral therapy, limit themselves predominantly to treating symptoms and are less concerned with resolving the psychodynamic causes of these symptoms. One might say that psychoanalysis very decisively deals with this resolution and the maturation of the personality in diverse respects. Its goal is to effect changes in the personality structure. The objective of GAI is likewise predominantly directed to the adjustment of the unconscious pathological psychodynamics. In contrast to psychoanalysis, the restructuring of the personality remains in the background at the basic level and is only conducted when it appears necessary and then with the help of techniques from the intermediate and advanced levels. In the process of reaching that point, however, it was discovered through GAI that a broad intermediate field in which processes of adjustment and compensatory mechanisms of the ego—overly restricted by neurotic maladjustments—become possible with the help of symboldrama. I will go into greater detail about this later in connection with the presentation of the therapeutic components of GAI.

Returning to the initial question concerning the position of symboldrama in the range of psychotherapeutic procedures, in my opinion it stands closest to psychoanalysis. However, GAI neither sets the high claim of having a personality-changing effect nor does it need to do this for a large percentage of chronically neurotic and psychosomatic cases. In this respect

GAI remains more modest in its objectives but in spite of this accomplishes, in comparison, something substantial viewed from clinical standpoints. In my opinion it closes a broad gap between the symptom-centered procedures, on the one hand, and the great psychoanalytic cure, on the other. Furthermore, GAI is also indicated for the wide selection of persons, who are not or not yet accessible to a therapy that uncovers conflicts: strongly intellectualized patients and those whose categories of thought are fixated on operative thinking within the scope of the psychosomatic syndrome. But I also count straightforward persons of the simpler social strata especially those who are unaccustomed to use introspection among this broad spectrum of patients who can be reached with GAI.

As we will realize later, one focal point of GAI lies in stimulating certain self-regulating tendencies of the ego and to thereby mobilize the often cited "self-healing powers of the psyche."

Diagnostics

As one of the basic requirements of every psychotherapy, the therapist must gain diagnostic points of reference covering a certain range before beginning the therapy. He does not so much need to know the kind of existing pathological disorders, as to be able to clarify the question of whether he can treat the patient using the method supported by him in a really meaningful and productive way.

Prognostics

This means therefore that the prognosis must be sufficiently favorable to institute the respective procedure, in our case, for example, the basic level of GAI. Only by doing this can the therapist avoid unsuccessfully treating an especially complicated chronic case, for instance, or a neurosis reaching into the depths of the person, a borderline or even a particularly unstable (depressive) patient with a weak ego, or even triggering unpleasant, anti-therapeutic reactions. Then the therapy can be more damaging than useful and is thus contraindicated. The experienced therapist gains this diagnostic information only by

Intake Interview

recording a comprehensive depth psychological case history and by considering the well-known prognostic indicators. The contents of GAI itself can also give him quite concrete information on to his/her patient's current pattern of response. From this he can ultimately conclude whether GAI can be introduced immediately or only later in therapy, after way by dealing with pressing conflicts verbally for a longer period of time.

At the close of this hour, I would like to familiarize you

Accomplishments of GAI

with examples of the accomplishments of symboldrama. I am of the opinion that the initiator of a new therapeutic approach has the obligation to show whether his methods accomplish more than others and to show specific aspects of these accomplishments in the treatment of patients. Experience has painfully taught that a comparison of the therapeutic successes of various methods according to strict scientific standards can be gained only with difficulty or, in actuality, not at all. In the past years my colleagues and I have spent much effort and methodological work in treating patients with GAI under controlled conditions. We wanted to discover what the procedure accomplishes with an unselected group of patients when the treatment is restricted from the outset to 15 sessions in one case and 20 in the other. Both the first study by Wächter and Pudel (1980) and the second by Kulessa and Jung (1979, 1980), including the follow-up studies, have demonstrated exceedingly encouraging results. In both studies the patients came from the general clinic of the university psychiatric hospital in Göttingen and were randomized. Two-thirds of the patients had chronic neurotic symptoms for a duration of 5 to more than 10 years.

Effectiveness Controls

In this course I do not want to trouble you with methodological questions and statistics. Both studies have been published in various places. Several studies also exist about the treatment of psychosomatic syndromes, generally acknowledged as difficult, which are only accessible to psychotherapy in the analytic sense with great difficulty, if at all. I mention the investigation by Klessmann and Klessmann (1978) on the outpatient treatment of pubertal anorexia nervosa, by Wilke (1980) on the therapy of a group of patients with ulcerative colitis, and by Roth (1980) on a group of women and men with functional genital and sexual disorders.

Psychosomatic Syndromes

For the purpose of this course I will limit myself to recounting four cases from medical practice. For reasons of space, I have condensed the presentation a great deal and reproduced even important case history information only sketchily. In actual fact, both cases 1 and 3 dealt with very poorly educated persons for whom a depth psychological intake interview in the customary form could not be conducted. That sometimes conforms to the realities in practice, but nevertheless does not prevent one from making use of GAI in a therapeutically effective way.

Examples of Individual Cases

Case 1 (1)*

The 35-year-old master mechanic at a Volkswagen service station had a banal accident at work 1 year before starting treatment. It was connected with a terrifying situation. Immediately afterward dizziness, general weakness and exhaustion, episodes of profuse sweating, a tendency to collapse and anxiety attacks appeared in connection with heart palpitations. Thus, the picture of a cardiac neurosis was in evidence. Attempts to work after temporary rest intensified these complaints. Ultimately, the patient was whiny, could not read any more or leave the apartment, and feared that he would die of his cardiac symptoms. Finally, there existed a depressive

Cardiac Neurosis

---

* The numbers in parentheses refer to the Index of Case Studies in Appendix IV.

syndrome with psychosomatic complaints with clearly hysterical structural elements of the personality. A little less than a year after these complaints began, which, as mentioned, led to an incapacity to work, the patient entered treatment as an outpatient. The psychogenic cause quickly became clear, supported by a negative physical examination. The therapy encompassed 26 individual sessions in symboldrama conducted once a week. Although the patient was a very poorly educated person and not even the slightest idea was expressed by him in response to what he experienced in GAI, he nevertheless passed through the essential phases of a typical treatment on the basic level, lost his symptoms to a large extent toward the end, and began working again. Above all, he was capable of giving up his passive attitude of expectancy and was able to demand his rights and to assert himself successfully to his own advantage. During the follow-up questionnaire survey 8 years later, he reported that he had not become ill again. Neither the known nor new symptoms had appeared. He had been capable of working without interruption.

Case 2 (2)

Depression

A 52-year-old well-educated housewife became ill 2 years before admission to therapy with what appeared to be a reactive depression, after she had been informed that a close cousin of hers had died. Shortly afterward, it became necessary for her to begin caring for her ill and frequently nagging husband, which put excessive strain on her. Then spells of dizziness also appeared. Nothing abnormal was discovered in an otological examination. However, following the suboccipital puncture performed at the same time, the patient decompensated with psychogenic symptoms. She complained of intense headaches and could not take care of the household any longer. She became increasingly nervous and soon stomach pains appeared. A neurasthenic picture developed with inner restlessness, tension, trembling of the limbs, exhaustion, irritability, and cardiac palpitations. A 5-week stay in a hospital and a cure at a health resort were unsuccessful. Finally, she had to be admitted to our psychiatric hospital. Here the patient showed a pronounced agitated, depressive state with a strong hypochondriacal accent. Her personality structure was clearly hysterical with compulsive traits. The typical treatment with neuroleptics and imipramine accompanied by discussions led to only a slight improvement during the 7-week hospital stay. Shortly before she was discharged from the hospital, the patient had a relapse. To make one final therapeutic attempt with this case, which seemed unsuited for psychotherapy to begin with, I ultimately referred her for further treatment with the basic level of GAI to a young woman colleague, who had practical experience in GAI as a part of her training. In 10 days, nine sessions of 45 minutes' duration were conducted. The patient temporarily abreacted very strongly in association with biographical material, which seemed to be important. Although still unstable, she had improved considerably and, accompanied by her husband, she could now be discharged home. Her depression and the hypochondriacal complaints had disappeared. The neurasthenic picture, which had impaired the patient, had also receded to a large extent. Undoubtedly, she was still not "cured," and following this an extended outpatient psychotherapy, lasting a total of 160 hours with the advanced level of GAI, was necessary. Nevertheless, after the brief treatment of nine sessions, the patient had stabilized enough to be able to confront the, in reality, burdening situation of her marriage. With the help of the basic level of GAI it had therefore become surprisingly possible to compensate for the pathological picture, which had in the meantime become subchronic and was inaccessible to other therapies, enough for the patient to be able to manage herself to a large extent. The patient was followed-up after 2 years and continues to be free of depression; she succeeded in changing her behavior toward her partner and her life situation.

Case 3 (3)*

Phobia

A 38-year-old employed woman had been unable to work for over a year due to attacks of agoraphobia accompanied by tachycardia and a tendency to collapse, which soon led to a general phobic syndrome. She was admitted to a psychiatric hospital abroad, presenting an emotionally labile picture and hypochondriacal complaints. Perspiring, numbing of the hands, cardiac palpitations were among the accompanying psychosomatic symptoms. A former colleague of mine treated the patient with the basic level of symboldrama. After only eight sessions within 4 weeks, some of the patient's symptoms disappeared and with them some of her neurotic expectations of failure. Until then she had only been barely managing to function.

With a good transference, she soon began to exercise physically, to fight her anxiety, and she enrolled in a school for gymnastics. During this physical training, she overcame the remainder of her symptoms and requested her discharge from the hospital to begin working again. In this case, one succeeded within relatively few sessions in removing very disturbing symptoms, which had already existed for a year, and the directing was left up to the patient's own initiative. Today such possibilities of compensating the neurosis are also known in psychodynamic short-term therapy. It is definitely legitimate to

---

*** I thank Prof. Dr. G. Barolin, then at the City Psychiatric Hospital "Rosenhügel" in Vienna, for kindly contributing this case history.**

designate GAI as a short-term psychotherapy, although it is also possible with this technique to carry out extensive treatments in cases that are less easy to compensate.

Case 4 (4)*

Obsessive-Compulsive Neurosis

A 19-year-old confectioner complained of being severely handicapped in his profession because he could not assert himself with his colleagues, was easily ridiculed, had great difficulty in making social contacts, and had no relationships whatsoever with the opposite sex. According to his descriptions and his behavior, he had an extremely restricted, anxious personality with a clearly obsessive-compulsive structure. Compulsive thinking, as his almost constant companion, disabled him most of all. In these compulsive thoughts he had to curse God and call those persons closest to him abusive names, which ultimately triggered his guilty conscience. He had had these symptoms from the age of 13 on, or for approximately 6 years.

The psychotherapy with GAI, which was conducted by the author, required a total of 45 sessions. As the therapy progressed, the main motifs of the panorama of the basic level, the motif of climbing a mountain, of the course of a brook, of the house, developed step by step, proceeding in part in dramatic and also strongly regressive symboldramatic stretches. They symbolized the breakthrough of aggressive impulses, the vehement separation from the maternal image, and the constructing of a new ego ideal with a relaxation of the authoritarian conscience.

At the end of treatment, all of these motifs showed not only pronounced phenomena of change, but also a development to relatively harmonious and unobtrusive scenes, which were largely free of fixated images. From this the author assumes a deeper structural change in the person of the patient. Clinically, the patient developed a pleasant readiness for making social contacts. He established a steady relationship to a girlfriend, left his mother and moved to Munich, where he took the master confectioner's examination and took over a well-paid position in a widely known confectionery. The compulsive thinking had practically disappeared. The follow-up examination 4 years later showed that the immediate success of the therapy had been maintained and that beyond this he had continued to develop socially on his own, both personally and professionally.

Focus of Indications

To summarize, one can now say something about the *focus of the indications* for the basic level of symboldrama (see also the prognostic criteria on p. 184). The basic level is also effective for persons with little education, who can have a "character armor," as well as for patients with a psychosomatic syndrome, who

---

*** This abridged version is taken from a publication by W. Koch (1969).**

possibly are not in the position of giving a differentiated history of themselves. The symboldrama can gradually open them up to the unconscious world of images and the emotions connected to it. A certain proportion of hysterical structural components is favorable to treatment. It is also advantageous if the symptoms have not been present for more than 3 years. On the other hand, a broad neurotic personality deformation (character neurosis) is unfavorable.

Session Two: The Fundamental Principle

Having presented a glimpse of what symboldrama can accomplish on the basic level, I now want to explain its fundamental principle. Afterward I will describe and demonstrate methodological details.

According to what basic idea, according to which psychological principle does symboldrama work?

There is a very simple experiment that the Swiss psychotherapist and neurologist Frank performed and about which he wrote a book in 1913. It demonstrates how the psyche reveals, to some extent voluntarily, the principle prevailing here.

Historical Preliminary Experiment

In addition to Silberer's (1909) experiments, it supports the idea that the psyche apparently has the spontaneous urge to represent itself in images in its visual fantasy. If a healthy, or even better, a neurotic patient lies down on the couch in a manner as relaxed and loose as possible and closes his eyes, that is, simply surrenders passively, wanting and expecting nothing, we, with patience, allow him stay that way for from 10 to 30 minutes in our presence and something very specific will happen sooner or later. He becomes restless. His eyelids flutter a little, his arms begin to move in short, uncoordinated jerks, and perhaps his legs also. Finally, he may toss himself from one side to the other. Independent of this motoric restlessness, however, he may also report that he is perceiving strange, spontaneous visual phenomena before his eyes. He can then frequently describe them as abstract patterns, at first perhaps only very delicate shapes, such as small spheres, rods, or circles, which possibly gradually join to form geometrical figures. At the beginning, they frequently appear in black and white, later perhaps color also reported.

Advanced Level Autogenic Training

J.H. Schultz (1979) has described them in a particularly impressive and precise way in the deep relaxation of fully practiced autogenic training as the initial visual manifestations on the advanced level of this procedure. For us, it is important to know that these kinds of spontaneous visual phenomena in the sense of imagination* can emerge by themselves even without a

---

*** This requires the following clarification of concepts. By "idea" we mean, as did Jaspers, the phenomenon that man can make visual contents appear to himself. However, in their typical form they are pale, threaten to disappear, and require a deliberate effort to retain them. By imagination in our context, however, we mean the yet to be described manifestation of colorfulness, plasticity, 3-dimensionality, and internal autonomy of the visual phenomena, which emerge when the person is in a slightly absorbed state. They are autonomous and cannot be deliberately influenced; they also spontaneously stop before one's eyes or develop further. In this context one speaks of "image" or "catathymic image" as synonomous with the concept of imagination.**

systematic and long period of training, such as in autogenic training. This process can continue itself. The initial abstract forms can become complete and in further stages develop more and more to fragments of images. Colorful fade-ins of parts or entire images, which perhaps initially still appear meaningless, can gradually unite to form a scenic imaginal sequence.

Scenic Sequence

According to predisposition, these scenes ultimately appear in bright colors. They can also intensify to grotesque, dreamlike formations, and they are finally observed as vivid and alive, so that even the finest nuances can be differentiated. In other words, in the final stage completely formed visual imaginings can stand before the eyes of the patient. In its best form a kind of psychic act exists, which has the character of perception, or, as it is often called, of "inner vision." However, the patient never forgets that it is not a matter of real phenomena. In this respect the process described stands in contrast to the dream or to the hallucinations of a mentally ill person. Thus, in both of these cases the critical attitude is generally suspended and the involved persons believe that it is a matter of real occurrences. These imaginal perceptions can, on the one hand, appear like an

Ego Proximity

"internal movie," to apply a term occasionally used by patients. Without any or only slight involvement, the images can pass in

Ego Distance

front of the inner eye as something alien to the ego. However, the opposite also occurs. In the state of relaxation and submersion, which gradually sets in automatically (see later), the person in question notes an obvious emotional involvement. Moods and emotions that fit the scenic contents are aroused; for instance, cheerfulness when the patient imagines a field of flowers, contentment and tranquility at the sight of a sunset, or apprehensiveness and fear when unpleasant landscapes or fantastic figures emerge.

Imaginal Consciousness

Following Happich (1932) and Heiss (1956), we refer to the level of consciousness and experience introduced in the simple experiment previously described as "imaginal consciousness."

Previously the notion was prevalent that this category of consciousness was readily accessible to only a particular group of persons, namely, the so-called eidetic, that is, visually gifted persons. However, working with GAI for decades has shown that this imaginal consciousness can be focused upon by an extremely large percentage of persons, actually in fact by almost everyone. Spontaneously, these phenomena are also known as "slumber images," which can emerge while falling asleep and are familiar to many persons. We refer to the fully developed

Threshold of Sleep

imagination described here as "catathymic images." Their special quality lies in their colorfulness, plasticity, and emotional impact in contrast to the simple imaginings, which we have in everyday experience, when we recall a scene from the past in our imagination. As everyone can easily verify, these simple imaginal products are generally pale, colorless, and considerably easier to influence. It is an unusual feature of catathymic images that in full form they no longer obey the will. On the contrary, they

Autonomy

follow an autonomous internal course. This course can be explained by unconscious impulses, to be discussed later, that direct the imaginings. These, my phenomenological differentiations, at first clear for didactic reasons, are frequently

"See"—"Imagine"

misunderstood. In practice we often find intermediate stages, which stand between the pure idea and the fully pronounced catathymic image. However, it has become apparent that visual contents, ascribable to this intermediate stage, also become effective, that is, even those images that are still somewhat pale and quite transitory, which can only be maintained with difficulty, and in no way have the quality of a perception are referred to amateurishly as "seeing." In other words, wherever the person in question does not "see" these catathymic images in the narrower sense, he can be directed to the appearing "imaginings" and be urged to observe and to describe them very precisely. According to our most recent observations, even the much paler images, pictured when the eyes are open, are therapeutically effective as long as they are pursued with inner attention and regard.

Of course, one cannot deny that there is a particular group of persons, frequently artistically sensitive or visually gifted in other ways, who rank distinct imaginings among their everyday experience. On the other hand, more strongly rationally oriented persons, who do not tend to regress emotionally, and frequently schizoid persons as well often attain the level of imaginal

Typology?

consciousness with greater difficulty. In my opinion, however, a clear typology has not been discovered. Where one was assumed to exist, it could not be proved. The conditions under which the imaginal experience fails are diverse and frequently depend upon very individual aspects of the person. Often personal feelings toward the therapist guiding the daydream enter into this, also. Characteristically, the mental images develop best in the presence of a guide through this inner world, in other words, the attending, experienced therapist. Continuing in this line, I developed particular techniques that promote catathymic images. I shall return to this in the description of the GAI technique.

"Private Theater"

The manifestation of independent, freely rising, internal images was in principle known to psychotherapy very early. Even the first and very well-known case of Anna O., which Breuer and Freud described in the studies on hysteria (1895), provided surprising insights into the visual scenario of a woman with an hysterical neurosis. The patient had the peculiarity of reeling off long sequences of mental imagery in a spontaneously arising hypnoidal, dreamy state, which she referred to as her "private theater." At every afternoon session with Breuer, she reported on these in a trance. As an intelligent neurologist, he dealt with this scenery in great detail each time and stimulated

Freud

their further course. It was Freud himself, who for a number of years, instead of using hypnosis to gain unconscious material, evoked visual phenomena in his patients by exerting pressure on their foreheads and not only had them describe these precisely but also gathered the patient's immediate thoughts about them until the images disappeared again. However, he apparently did not recognize the great opportunity that lay in the further pursuit and research of mental imagery for psychotherapy, and later he turned predominantly to night dreams. Freud knew some important characteristics of mental imagery, however, and also described them (1895, p.285 f). I already mentioned the Swiss psychotherapist Frank, who in 1913 referred in his book to the "cathartic method" based upon the same concept of abreaction by Breuer. Kretschmer took over these ideas and gave them the name "filmstrip thinking" insofar as the autonomous filmstrip-like flow of the internal images was concerned. Subsequently, one can repeatedly find reports, scattered here and there in the literature, by authors who discovered these phenomena seemingly for the first time. They described them in their own manner and recommended that they be made accessible to psychotherapy. However, comprehensive investigations about them were not conducted. The French engineer Desoille (1945) is a single exception here. He directed mental imagery in a very pragmatic way and could thereby also produce therapeutic effects. I only learned of his work rather late. Details about these forerunners of GAI are not covered in this course. To classify them properly, it is perhaps important to stress that the catathymic images are closely associated with the so-called hypnagogic visions, using the professional psychiatric terminology, or are apparently in part identical with them. One cannot overlook the fact that man is in a slightly altered state of consciousness when scenic mental images emerge before his closed eyes. Although he remains fully oriented and can give an account of it, his active waking consciousness is nevertheless slightly lessened. It is most nearly comparable to the reduction of alertness in the state of falling asleep, during which the slumber images previously mentioned can appear. Most of you know that what is meant is the strange threshold condition between wakefulness and sleep, which some people can maintain for an especially long time. Typically, these visual phenomena can also be evoked in hypnosis and in that slight hypnoidal state that autogenic training produces. Recent investigations with GAI have shown, however, that it is in no way necessary regularly to bring about such a strongly altered state of consciousness to introduce GAI. Even the simple request, while in a comfortable sitting position, to imagine a particular motif suggested by the therapist can lead to fully distinct catathymic images. We apparently are dealing with a wide range. It extends from the spontaneous manifestation of visual imagination with the corresponding internal attention, which the evidence of poets, discussed later, speaks for, all the way to pronounced hypnosis and also to self-hypnosis in the sense of autogenic training as

Kretschmer

Desoille

"Hypnagogic Visions"

Altered State of Consciousness

Spontaneous Manifestation of GAI

deeper interventions into the state of consciousness. We previously believed that such an intervention was of basic importance for introducing GAI. Today, we know that the two conditions, lively imaginings and altered states of consciousness, correlate closely with each other. The mere instruction to imagine can gradually diminish the waking consciousness, which again deepens the imagination in a circular process. As a whole, we can draw the conclusion that the actual techniques of

Simplified Technique

symboldrama are considerably simpler than may have at first seemed the case, and distinct consciousness-altering aids are in no way an unconditional requirement.

However, I consider it much more important for us to become well-acquainted with the actual world of the catathymic images. Poetic evidence as far back as antiquity can give us

Poetic Evidence

diverse insights. In "Stress and Confusions" Goethe describes—after he had seen Frederica for the last time and was riding away from Sesenheim—"Not with the eyes of the body but of the spirit, I saw myself on horseback returning by the same path in clothing as I have never worn: it was blue as a pike with a little gold. As soon as I roused myself from this dream, the figure had disappeared completely. In those moments of parting the strange vision gave me some comfort."

Recently the French poet Micheaux described his own world of inner vision. When he closes his eyes, he can produce things that he enjoys. For example, he drives a camel into a city to frighten the inhabitants. Delightedly, he observes a shimmeringly colored frog come out of a swamp. In the essay "The House of My Childhood" the German poet Marie-Luise Kaschnitz describes the following. Contrary to her own intention to have this house become alive in her imaginal world, she constantly finds herself moving in an open landscape in which she has to take long boat trips on canals and repeatedly tries to direct the course of her excursions in this imaginary landscape. She is both astonished and disappointed that these impressive but in no way very pleasant imaginings escape her will again and again. She does not succeed in being taken to the house of her childhood in the imaginal passages, which cover a period of months. Instead, the most hideous and terrifying images soon overcome her and cause her suffering.

Imaginative Literature

At my suggestion I. Riedel (1974) made a particularly interesting survey of mental imagery in imaginative literature, which could still be expanded in many respects. It seems characteristic to me that poets and authors have always had a much more intimate relationship to the world of cathathymic images than persons who dedicate themselves exclusively to their sober everyday duties. Conversely, we have seen that the catathymic imaginal productions of our patients in therapy take on increasingly creative and surprisingly inventive forms, about which there is often something artistic, whether in the kind of bizarre contents or in the kind of linguistic representation.

Autonomy of the Imaginings

Consequently, we are interested in the literary evidence not only from the standpoint of the language, but also because we find the characteristics of the catathymic images again: the liveliness and vividness of the colors, the independent course even against the will of the person, and the frequently intense emotional involvement in harmony with the contents. Here, as well as in GAI for therapeutic purposes, the person involved is almost always able to move about as if in an actual landscape. He can perform actions, go on trips, meet people, act quasi-realistically, almost as in a second world. On the other hand, fantastic formations, which we know from fairy tales, legends, myths, and, of course, also from night dreams, can also appear. Usually, however, the fantastic elements of the catathymic experiences are not so pronounced as the uninitiated at first expect them to be. Landscapes are much preferred in the spontaneous elaboration of the mental images. We have referred to this freely developed imaginal landscape as the "catathymic panorama," which can be roamed in all directions. As I will show you in the following, this panorama is of great diagnostic value and within a short time gives the therapist a relatively broad view of the patient's predominant conflictual constellation.

Catathymic Panorama

Significance

In this connection it becomes more and more urgent to ask what significance one actually ought to attribute to these catathymic imaginal experiences. Whoever is introduced to this world of imaginal consciousness impartially frequently tends to see absurd or fantastical evidence in it at first, which has scarcely anything to do with the individual person. Thus, he is also more apt to deny seeing any relationship at all to his own psychic motives. Initially, he also often lacks that degree of inner emotional involvement that is typical of a later stage and can illustrate that the images refer to the individual's ego. This reference becomes even more pronounced and thus also much more evident when sooner or later the catathymic contents are in many ways able to decode themselves automatically. This can happen when ideas concerning the subjective meaning of an image strike the person or when an image develops in such a way that a corresponding reference is unmistakeable, for example, if a figure takes on the face of a close relative. In the early years of psychoanalysis Silberer (1912) used rather simple processes to show that the imaginings in question obey the law of "autosymbolism," as he termed it.*

Autosymbolism

The following example of a young woman physician clearly shows—and that is important for the understanding of

* Of course I am referring only to the depth psychological aspect of the imaginings here. Additional determinants are attributed to them, for example, when GAI is placed in the service of the creative process (Landau and Leuner 1976). Silberer was able to show that the autosymbolic imaginings appearing on the threshold of falling asleep are rooted in the subconscious and preconscious areas of emotional life.

symboldrama in any case—that a level of the psyche expresses itself in the images, which the person is not conscious of and which is not easily accessible to consciousness. This level can now suddenly be revealed through careful observation and penetration of its imaginal creations.

Example

The young colleague, who worked in a hospital, admitted a patient while on the night shift, who had a life-threatening circulatory collapse. Standing in front of the patient's stretcher, she had to decide how to handle this emergency. She feverishly thought about the differential diagnosis and what she had to prescribe first. To concentrate better, she closed her eyes for a few seconds. Faced with the responsibility in a state of inner tension, the image of a landscape appeared clearly before her closed eyes. The landscape was immediately flooded by a wide stream. The water rose higher and higher in an alarming manner. Its masses inundated meadows and fields, flowed into houses, and finally everything disappeared in the flood, trees, houses, and landscape. Afterward she was surprised at this imagining, passing like a flash. It seemed meaningful to her as an expression of her inner state of excitement, which she had only barely felt and believed herself to be matter-of-fact and composed in carrying out the medical routine. After the patient's condition had improved, she closed her eyes again, almost instinctively, to "look inside" herself as a cross-check. Again a similar flooded landscape appeared. However, now the floods receded and in the sunshine a landscape with large bright meadows soon appeared from under the draining waters. A spring-green birch-lined avenue wended its way through the cheerful, friendly, and calming image.

Autosymbolism

Silberer

Here autosymbolism, which Silberer described in the threshold experience of falling asleep, is impressively made clear to us in a waking state. It should be noted that the colleague was doubtlessly visually oriented to an above-average degree and had a talent for painting. The image of the flooded landscape changing parallel to the rising and ebbing of her inner excitement requires no great knowledge of symbols. As is frequently the case in imaginal experience, the image shows a clearly recognizable allegory of the flooding by water to that by the emotional excitement. At the same time we recognize that the physician's conscious internal and outward composure stands in strong contrast to her emotional state, which is far from consciousness. It has apparently been extensively repressed, however, and even as a split-second emotion or mere excitement does not step over the threshold of consciousness. Only the imaginal experience, which in this case emerges spontaneously under favorable circumstances, testifies to the strong inner uneasiness. Our neurotic patients frequently experience this kind of thing more drastically.

As I already stated, from all this it becomes clear that symboldrama picks up on completely natural capacities and

Imaginative Self-Representation of the Psyche

functions available within one's inner life. Building upon this basic principle of imaginative self-representation of the psyche, the initial task in developing GAI was to explore the diverse possibilities and dynamic background of affective imagery and to make them methodologically useful for therapy. You will understand that there is only a short step from catathymic images to dreams. Using spontaneous filmstrip thinking,

Principles of the Dream

Kretschmer (1922) in particular showed that the principles of the dream, as Freud first drew them up, also recur in visual imaginings. In the images we again find the categories of displacement and condensation. We see, for example, that an affect, which exists toward a person in reality, is displaced to the

Symbolic figures

imaginal level. We then speak of symbolic figures of GAI. In the fantastical appearances already mentioned we find human forms *condensed* with animal forms, for example, one of our patients observed how a turtle worked its way out of a hole with difficulty. Its eyes and head changed into those of a person. The facial features and hairstyle were those of her father as she had known them as a little girl. Or another image was that of a figure of a student stepping out of a forest, who at the same time, however, had the stance and gait of the patient's authoritarian father. Finally, one also sees the relationship to dreams and in general to the typical categories of the primary

Primary process

process in accordance with Freud in the fact that the concept of time is suspended. Future, present, and past fuse together, so to speak; one experiences only punctual present. The principle of contradiction is also suspended. This became clear in the example of condensation, since the turtle cannot simultaneously be the father. All phenomena are ultimately possible in symboldrama: one is able to fly, to pass through space, to disappear into thin air, and figures can fuse together.

Psychic representational processes

To understand these psychic representational processes, it is also important to know that the imaginal contents can change continuously. The most obvious example was the young colleague's imagining of the flooded landscape as she grew excited internally. After this faded away, the landscape appeared again in springlike freshness and clarity. Under the effect of autosymbolism, the catathymic images change actively in accordance with the stream of the respectively changing emotions and moods. Therefore, from a psychological point of view, symboldrama is very closely associated with the methods of projective tests. The familiar ones are sign tests, the Rorschach

Projective Mechanism

test, and Murray's (1938) Thematic Apperception Test (TAT). They all present material that undergoes a very individual transformation by way of the inner psychological structures and emotionally contingent motifs, which evoke a certain "projective pressure" (Kretschmer 1922). From these, one can draw important conclusions about the personality of the person. Consequently, symboldrama with its imaginings conveyed by fantasy can also be considered a form of projective self-representation. It has the advantage over all of the familiar test procedures in that no limits are placed on it by the type of presentation and technique and that even the slightest change of inner emotion is immediately reflected in changes of the image. I have called this active course of projections *mobile projection,* which will be discussed in detail later. The phenomenon of mobile projection naturally also applies to the night dream. However, there it is at best clear in extended series of dreams, in which the patient's therapeutic development gradually emerges.

Mobile Projection

Authorities on the subject of night dreams have repeatedly pointed out to me that the appearance and the characteristic features of the imaginal form of expression of catathymic mental imagery also exhibit considerable differences from those of the night dream. In my opinion these are almost trivial from a psychodynamic point of view. From a phenomenological standpoint, however, certain differences between the two are striking. I have dealt with this briefly elsewhere. The continuity of the mental image in GAI is often adhered to better, it remains more strongly centered on a theme, its contents are often clearer, simpler, and are frequently reminiscent of forms of expression similar to fairy tales or folksongs.

Distinction from the Night Dream

Our patients are subsequently able to vividly paint and graphically represent the imaginings, which they retain easily, so that apart from the therapeutic value of these creations, we also have an objective embodiment of the imaginings for later comparison (see Figures 1 and 2 pp.77–78).

Replies to Questions

Risks of Teaching GAI in a Course

Question: Dr. A., a colleague experienced in psychotherapy, "Aren't there certain risks involved in teaching this treatment method in a course and in encouraging your colleagues, who for the most part have had little experience in psychotherapy, to treat patients with it?"

Answer: That is an important question, which has been discussed a great deal. I must admit that for a long time I had great reservations about bringing the method into the form of an introductory course such as this. When I was first instructing small groups, I always indicated very strongly that a seminar course is in no way meant to "encourage" the participants to treat patients with GAI. That would really be a grave mistake. Imparting knowledge and knowledge about a treatment method gained from experience cannot initially be more than information. I am starting from the assumption that all of the participants view this course exclusively in that way, too. It is in no way a set of instructions, as one cannot learn any therapy from books, with the possible exception of pharmacotherapy. For example, it would never occur to anyone, after having completed his medical studies, to perform an operation on the basis of a description in a textbook.

Further Training to Become a GAI Therapist

There was a time when our experience in the instruction of GAI therapy was not as advanced as it is today. At that time, some colleagues attempted a few steps of the basic level of GAI with one of their cases after having participated in a single seminar. They based this upon their general depth psychological experience as well as instruction in autogenic training or in psychodynamically oriented psychotherapy. Due to training in empathic understanding and therapeutic experience, some of them succeeded in making progress here and there.

Risks of autodidactic use

In this connection, however, one of two things frequently occurred. One group was surprised at how easily the therapy seemed to proceed for a few sessions, but sooner or later they became perplexed about how they ought to proceed. They stopped simply because they were not sufficiently prepared. The second group, some experienced psychotherapists and also some with psychoanalytic training, introduced mental imagery at a particularly difficult time for their patients, without knowing the clear indications. They were often patients whom they believed to be particularly suited for mental imagery. Then some suggested material that was strongly emotionally laden or that produced frightening archaic contents and shifted the patients unexpectedly into a regressive state. On the basis of their previous experience, these therapists were not familiar with this possibility and did not know how they ought to deal with this situation technically. Often the patients were actually not particularly well suited for GAI (for instance, those whose egos were too weak). This kind of short, episodic experience led some of them to the opinion that the procedure is "difficult to work with" or possibly even "dangerous." The psychotherapists had met with that part of symboldrama that makes it obvious that the method is by no means neutral and demands of the therapist, above all, the ability to accept occasional emotional uneasiness or a temporary therapeutic regression of the patient and to be able to carry it through in the correct way or to direct it.

Specific Demands of the Therapist

At this point I can clarify what is particularly important to me, namely, it has become apparent that the mental imagery technique of GAI does in fact place certain demands upon the therapist and presumes that he has certain therapeutic experience, which can scarcely be gained by way of any other psychotherapeutic procedure. I am thinking of the patient's emotional involvement and along with it at times also that of the therapist, of the controlled regression, in which the treatment takes place, and the possibly necessary capacity of the therapist to make decisions quickly, in which he must be well practiced in meeting unanticipated scenes in mental imagery. Mentioning these aspects makes it obvious that only GAI itself offers the experiential platform upon which confidence in dealing with this kind of released unconscious material can be acquired.

Self-awareness, experience in the role of the therapist, and treating cases under supervision are a part of this. Naturally, some procedures are more closely associated with GAI, such as play therapy for children and psychodrama; others are more distant, such as Rogers' (1977) person centered therapy and behavior therapy, although certain elements of these forms of therapy can also be found in GAI. To complete this point, therapists trained in other procedures should not shy away from actively participating in advanced training seminars in GAI to become better acquainted with the difference between the technique that they have preferred so far and that of GAI.

Session Three: Technique I—The Methodological Steps

Fundamental Principle

The fundamental principle of GAI has become clear: man's original capacity to represent spontaneously his intrapsychic condition in autosymbolic imaginal form, that is, his preconscious and, in part, unconscious strivings, needs, and the anxieties and defense mechanisms directed against them. This capacity is present in every person, in principle, but similar to musicality, for example, it is present in varying degrees in each individual. It seems as if images that develop spontaneously are more richly manifested in patients with a schizoid structure than in those with a hysterical structure. The latter, on the other hand, are clearly more productive than compulsively structured persons (in accordance with Schultz-Hencke's structural concept, 1970). General elements of the character armor and of intellectualization as defensive behavior naturally also play a part here.

Goal of Immediate Use

To develop GAI into a "reliable" instrument that can be handled clinically and practically, I was confronted with the necessary task of developing treatment steps that are both technically clear and reconstructable for teaching. This contrasts with unsystematic methods (such as in Kretschmer's filmstrip thinking). Aided by these steps, it is possible to release the imaginal consciousness of almost every patient and to guide him through the fullness of mental imagery with an often almost experimental certainty. Therefore the patient does not need to wait until he is adequately relaxed and the mental images emerge spontaneously, rather as the first step we bring him quite suddenly and purposefully into the state of consciousness in which mental imagery appears. The second and following step is to induce the catathymic image. Here we ask the patient to imagine one of the time-tested motifs. I will go into this in even greater detail to demonstrate the more complicated steps for those patients whose readiness to imagine presents difficulties.

Step One

Alternatives:

In the following I point out three methodological possibilities starting with the formulas for most intensive submersion and proceeding to the simpler and elegant steps for attaining imaginal consciousness.

First Level of Autogenic Training

1. Practicing the first two levels of J.H. Schultz's (1979) autogenic training is methodologically the surest but also the most time-consuming way to begin. As is generally known, these are the experiences of heaviness and warmth over the entire body. In more resistant cases practice in regulating breathing can also be added. For details, I must refer the reader to Schultz's original book. First of all, we know that

not every patient is suited for practicing autogenic training, especially the more strongly neurotic and the very nonintrospective patients. Moreover, it is a known fact that 2 to 4 weeks of systematic practice are necessary for the two basic exercises, which are supervised by a therapist familiar with the procedure. With markedly neurotically disturbed patients even more time passes before these exercises are really mastered. In many cases one likes to bypass this preparatory period and the sometimes difficult to solve problems, which only a therapist very familiar with autogenic training is able to handle. Although this preparatory phase does not in principle have to signify any disadvantage for the patient, the delay in time can be very annoying in acute cases for which help is urgently needed. Also, not every therapist is prepared to delay the beginning of therapy, which can be initiated in a simpler way, for an indefinite number of weeks. The effectiveness of GAI can be reduced in these cases and the patient's motivation can be put to a severe test. As a special problem the question arises, to what extent the autonomic relaxation facilitated by autogenic training smooths over the patient's psychic pain and problems and thus initially masks the conflicts that await resolution in GAI. My concerns about this potential problem are not insignificant. This is particularly true when the patient practices autogenic training at home and works with GAI in the therapy sessions. Of course, these kinds of combinations can be productive, but they must be clearly indicated. Personally, I am not in favor of introducing GAI by way of autogenic training and of its continuation during GAI therapy.

Encouragement to Relax

2. One entrance to mental imagery, which in my opinion is much more elegant because it can be realized more quickly, is a simple, induction of the relaxed state, as unsuggestive as possible, with which the patient can also help. Formal hypnotic suggestions of even the simplest kind are unnecessary and ought to be excluded. In the examples to the induction of GAI on page 29, I present my standard formulation of the directions for self-relaxation. The therapist's influence, which enters into this, lies exclusively in his monotonous voice as he gives instructions for relaxation. The instructions are designed in such a way that the patient is requested to conduct the relaxation procedure himself.

Appropriate music can be employed as an aid to enhance relaxation. We have collected very detailed studies concerning this in the form of *musical guided affective imagery* (MGAI). It usually involves music that induces meditation or music from the classical area in the form of pastoral pieces or of intimate lute pieces. We only call upon this aid in the rarest of cases (Nerenz 1969).

Simplified Request to Imagine

3. The most straightforward and technically least extravagant introduction to the state of relaxation occurs by means of the simple request to imagine one of the typical motifs itself. The "flower test," which is mentioned again later in context, can serve as a prototype for this. It has become customary to use it regularly at the end of taking the patient's case history. It is supposed to clarify whether and to what extent the patient is capable of visualizing fully distinct mental images. Instead of instructions for relaxing, we ask the patient to direct his attention to a short, very simple test. Then we ask him to sit down in a chair as comfortably as possible, that is, in a loose and relaxed manner, as if he were taking a short, tension-relieving nap after some strenuous physical work. We wait until the patient has found a suitable position after experimenting a little. Then we ask him relatively suddenly if he

can now imagine a flower. We choose the motif of a flower because it is usually relatively pleasant and attractive, and flowers scarcely ever have decidedly negative connotations. If such a negative emphasis arises, one can assume with this test that quite considerable pathological impulses are pressing within this patient (for example, a black rose, a flower that quickly wilts, a flower made of steel, or the like). Due to the absence of preparation, this informal procedure does not arouse anticipatory tension in the patient. In fact, it is quite amazing that almost all patients (even the relatively severely disturbed ones) go along with this attempt and are able to imagine a flower. The patient is then requested to describe the flower precisely. Here, the description of the color is important to me, as well as a glance into the center of the blossom. Then I direct the imagining to a tactile stimulus by asking the patient to touch the blossom with his fingertips. This also works in the overwhelming number of cases, see also p.103.

Sitting Position

The state of relaxation in the sitting position in a simple armchair cannot be overly deep with an untrained patient. In spite of this, the test usually turns out very well due, in my opinion, to the avoidance of anticipatory tension. Apparently the aforementioned peculiar mechanism of the internal *correlation between imagination and relaxation* commences here. The request to imagine increases the relaxation, which in turn deepens the imagination in the sense of greater colorfulness and plasticity, as well as a more intensive emotional perception of the flower. In any case it is conspicuous that after completing this test and opening his eyes, the patient usually needs a little time to find his way to reality again. Often the impression arises that he is returning "from far away" and is therefore emotionally removed. The contents of the imagining have usually influenced his mood and he is attuned to this. One might also mention in passing that it is very easy to "recover from" the test. The patient is requested to inhale very deeply and to open his eyes again. Frequently, the patients are impressed and surprised by this exercise. As I will demonstrate later, this simple test serves as a bridge between the more cognitively toned interviews in the pretherapeutic phase and the imaginal phase of GAI. Discussions with experienced GAI teachers have shown agreement in the assumption that the just-mentioned circular process between stimulation of imaginings and deepening of relaxation occurs relatively regularly and that one can thoroughly depend upon this internal mechanism. More for reasons of safety, I nevertheless recommend using the technique after point 2 in the therapy with GAI, that is, the brief instructions for self-relaxation, as I demonstrate them in detail on page 36.

Correlation: Relaxation and Imagination

If one uses this relaxation technique, the first methodological-technical step in introducing symboldrama is complete. In this way, and also by introducing the imagining through a given motif, our method contrasts with the previously mentioned unspecific, older spontaneous techniques using mental imagery.

Imaginal Motif

Step Two

This step consists of suggesting the mental images in the state of absorption that has been produced. Rather than waiting until an image has appeared, GAI is immediately and directly suggested to the patient. The amazingly simple technique necessary for this has already been mentioned. It is a matter of now recommending a typical visual image to the patient. This must be vaguely formulated as a motif, which can be imagined, usually, however, without first anticipating details of this image by way of suggestion. After everything that you have heard, you will expect with good reason that this given *imaginal motif* will now no longer be a pale, blurred, gray, and colorless visual phenomenon controllable by will power, but rather that in its distinctiveness it will quickly turn into a typical catathymic image with clarity, colorfulness, plasticity, and autonomy. It thus "of its own volition" stops in the field of vision and appears projected "in front of" the closed eyes. Here it can unfold its individual existence, and the "other world" can develop, in which the patient can move as if it were a "new reality."

Intermediate Stages: "Seeing-Imagining"

As previously stated certain intermediate stages of distinctness of the images appear temporarily. In the circular process the state of absorption usually becomes gradually deeper and, with increasing practice the images of symboldrama become more colorful, more subtle, and seem to approximate reality more closely. Frequently other sensory perceptions also appear. As in reality, the patient can see every single blade of grass moving in the breeze as he lies in a meadow, can feel the wind on his face, hear the bees buzz and the leaves of trees rustle, and he looks toward the clouds that are drifting in the blue sky. Occasionally, these impressions deepen to such an extent that they seem supernatural or superreal, not only emotionally but also in sensory perception. Their significance can increase in this way, and an intense experience of often quite banal contents (of the actual reality, too) can result. There is much to indicate that, without the help of the therapist or of the patient, the hypnoidal state deepens to such an extent that a condition occurs that

"Microscope of the Soul"

Oskar Vogt (1896) has characterized as a "microscope of the soul." Underlying this is the scientific finding that consciousness is narrowed in the immersed hypnoidal condition and concentrates completely on the contents in the forefront of consciousness, so that this is more strongly emphasized emotionally than in reality. I mention this circumstance even though it in no way always determines the scenes of symboldrama. However, now you may realize the degree of emotional involvement in GAI and the significance that it has for the patient. Consequently, a high measure of sensitive and empathic guidance is required of the therapist.

Description

In the further technical procedure after the imaginings have been introduced, we ask the patient, parallel to what we would do in reality, to observe the surroundings of the given motif more precisely, for instance, of an emerging meadow. He should describe details of the landscape, and we eventually ask him what he would like to do in the imagined landscape. He can, for example, describe for us how the meadow is bordered, such as by woods, a road, or houses in a town. He can give us the dimensions of the expanse, and we finally ask him about the mood within the landscape of the meadow or of whatever he may see before his eyes. We consider it important for him to verbalize his naive feelings and moods, whether they emanate from the landscape or are determined by him internally.

Meadow Motif

As we shall see, the meadow motif has great significance for GAI as an initial motif. Other motifs are linked to it, which by nature are connected with the meadow. Thus, the patient might, for example, discover a brook flowing through the meadow. We will in turn have him describe this, too, and if he wants to, he can approach it and do whatever he likes.

Brook

He can bathe his feet in the water or moisten his forehead with it or step into the water and go swimming or catch fish, or perhaps follow the brook in one direction or the other.

At first patients rarely have the wish to lie down in the meadow, to relax in the grass and look into the sky. In

Giving Attitude

accordance with our intention to assume a giving attitude toward the client, which was rare or nonexistent in his upbringing, we not only correct early childhood experiences with the persons who brought him up, but also provide space for fulfilling his own wishes, allowing him to indulge in spontaneous impulses. We thereby achieve something else at the same time. Hidden dormant behavioral tendencies also become manifest, and in the most favorable situation (frequently with the advanced patient) the opportunity is given to shape the suggested motif creatively according to the patient's own inclinations.

The Patient's Report

However, we always expect and direct the patient to tell us about all of the emerging contents as continuously as possible during the session. In this way the therapist has constant rapport with the patient, in contrast to the night dream. In this way the therapist can experience the patient's own vision and the entire world of his imaginings, in which he moves about, for he imagines it along with the patient and can trace it visually, so to speak. We pursue this internal witnessing on principle in order to always be "in the picture," in the truest sense of the word. This tracing of the images and the attempt to understand the accompanying emotions are important requirements for understanding the patient more deeply and accompanying him empathically. Here the therapist acts as if the GAI contents reported by the patient were actual reality. His questioning interventions and suggestions formulated from the quasi-real attitude usually lead to the representation of further details of the patient's mental images, the manifestation of new contents, or existing contents can become more intensive. In an

Sketching the Scene

outstanding case the patient even becomes able to make a cartographic sketch or a picture after the session, in which the position of the parts of the catathymic panorama is represented. Mapping the symbolic "psychic landscape" can be most easily observed from a mountain that is to be climbed and then sketched afterward (see Figures 1 and 2, pp.77–78).

Therapist's Behavior

In training seminar practice sessions it frequently becomes clear that the participants have misunderstood the role of the therapist. They believe that they can best fulfill the demand formulated here of internally completing the catathymic images with the patient by also closing their eyes and forming images along with the patient. There is an important objection to this. The therapist can and also frequently will become so involved in his own imaginal world, which is controlled by unconscious impulses, that he is not at all, or only to a limited extent, able to observe and critically reflect upon his behavior as therapist. However, that is a basic requirement for guiding the patient in symboldrama. He must also be able to distance himself critically from his patient temporarily, to reflect on the catathymic productions and classify them within his store of theoretical knowledge and thus be able to continue his guidance to the patient's advantage according to clear cognitive and knowledgeable scientific conclusions. This is particularly important in critical situations within GAI, for which the therapist must be able to maintain the desired temporary distance.

I have already mentioned some of the details of the therapist's behavior during the unfolding of GAI. Therefore it is now time to demonstrate a therapeutic session. One participant in the class was kind enough to volunteer for this. He is neither trained in autogenic training nor does he have previous experience with symboldrama.

Experiment

Seating

"Please be kind enough to sit down in the armchair. Sit as comfortably as possible. You should find a position in which you can feel very relaxed. Perhaps that will be easier for you if you imagine that you are going to take a short nap here, a little catnap, as one says."

If the person is asked to lie down on a couch in therapy, which we naturally prefer, the instructions are roughly the same.

Relaxation (Teaching Model)

In the following I reproduce the kind of instructions for relaxation in illustrative fashion, as I described them under point 2. There are no direct suggestions that certain sensations will arise as, for instance, that one's arm is becoming heavy. Rather, they are requests of the person to carry out gradually the relaxation himself by directing attention to his extremities. As already stated, the intention is to leave some individual activity to the patient and to avoid everything in the way of externally imposed suggestive effects that could make him dependent upon the therapist.

"Now that you are sitting [lying] loosely, as relaxed and comfortable as possible in an armchair [on the couch], please, close your eyes. It's best if you concentrate on the fact that you would like to rest and doze a little now. Everything that was keeping you preoccupied before should become totally insignificant now. Try to give yourself fully to this peaceful, relaxed condition. Now try to relax your muscles and please start with the muscles in your shoulders. Consciously relax every muscle in your shoulders, loosen and relax every muscle in your shoulders. Then do the same with the muscles of your upper arms; relax every muscle in your upper arms so that the muscles gradually become very limp and loose. Now relax the muscles of the lower arms, too. Let every muscle of your lower arms become completely relaxed, completely loose, completely limp, all the way to your fingertips; relax and loosen every muscle. Gradually your arms will become limp, tired and perhaps later a little heavy too. Let your arms rest tired and limp.———Then go on to the thighs. Consciously relax every muscle in your thighs, let them be relaxed and loose.———Gradually go on to the calves; concentrate on them and let every muscle fiber in your calves become loose and relaxed.———Finally both your legs are resting loose and relaxed, very relaxed and loose, and then gradually they become tired and limp too. You slowly sense that your whole body is pleasantly loose and relaxed, because you are relaxing all of your muscles. Now gradually take note of your breathing; your body rises and falls as you breathe. Observe how it rises and falls, and let your breathing flow freely and loosely. Gradually, a pleasant peacefulness and ease of your body spreads. Your head is free to doze a little, too; surrender yourself to this condition, abandon yourself to it."

Nonsuggestive Requests

Voice Control

Here the voice control is natural but expressly calm, slow, somewhat monotonous, and not too loud; it should have a calming quality. If possible, each individual word is to be accentuated in a somewhat resonant voice with clear and distinct pronunciation, with pauses between sentences that make it possible for the patient to concentrate fully on the named body areas so that he can successfully put the instructions into effect by reducing the muscular innervations. Naturally the instructions can be repeated several times in particular spots and the entire process can be temporally extended in this way. However, the experienced therapist is usually confident enough and does not need to extend this relaxation period. Often this can also disturb the patient, since the first image has possibly already appeared spontaneously.

Problem of reassurance

The exercises in the intensive training seminars give the future therapist the necessary confidence in the use of this relatively simple technique. Again I point out that it is used more for reasons of reassurance in introducing imaginings and is not a basic requirement. I refer to technique 3 of the introduction on page 24.

Session Four: Technique II—Demonstration of GAI with a Volunteer Subject

Focusing on a Standard Motif

Now I will begin with the second step, engaging an imaginal motif, and attempt to focus on the standard motif of the meadow with our volunteer subject.

Protocol of a GAI Session

"Now please try to imagine a meadow. Imagining is not difficult. Simply any meadow. If something else appears before your eyes, that's all right, too. Everything that comes along is fine.———Wait calmly and patiently until something appears before your eyes, perhaps a meadow or something else, too.———And when an image appears, please talk about it.———But even if this should cause difficulties, tell me that, too, so that I can perhaps help.———You can also nod your head as a first sign that you have something in view."

The subject is sitting obviously relaxed in the armchair, his face seems relaxed and he is breathing calmly. After approximately one-half minute, he moves his lips and begins to speak slowly and softly, at first somewhat difficult to understand. Soon, however, his voice becomes stronger and clearer. He says, "Yes, I see grass in front of me, long, almost tall grass. It is moving softly in the wind, but I cannot recognize anything else."

"Please let that take its full effect on you first."

"Yes, it is pleasant, nice, soft grass, a good feeling."

Pause of one-half minute.

"Please try to look around a little further, so that you can also recognize the expanse of the meadow, its boundaries and everything else that is there."

"Yes, now I have raised my eyes; I see a lush green meadow in front of me. It is not terribly big. There are some flowers scattered here and there. Now it is getting clearer; I see the blue colors and the yellows of the small flowers. Now the grass seems shorter; the whole thing has something delightful and friendly about it. Of course, the meadow is not all that large. The sun is shining; it is almost as in spring, everything is still somewhat untouched, definitely friendly and cheerful. To the right and the left, the meadow is relatively narrow and confined by a forest with tall fir trees. The whole thing extends far to the rear and seems to become broader in back. I can look very far into the distance. Way in back there are a number of mountains, in the distance perhaps even a mountain range with snow-capped peaks."

"I would be interested to find out, whether this image is a landscape you are familiar with or whether it originated entirely in your fantasy."

"No, I have never seen a meadow like this. It is something entirely new. I would like to say, more from fantasy."

"Can you recognize anything else?"

"Yes, now to the left in front I can see something; it is—yes, it really is—a little brook, which flows through the meadow. It is not especially wide, but has very clear, clean water. I would almost like to drink from it."

Protocol

"Then do so!"

"Yes, now I'm already down on my knees and brace myself with my left hand on the other bank. The brook is not more than 50 centimeters wide, and I scoop the water out with my right hand. It is nice and cool, pleasant. I drink from my cupped hand; I also rub water over my face; it is pleasantly cool. I do it again, really refreshing! Now I have enough, the sun is shining very warmly. I am tired and would like to lie down."

"Please do!"

"Now I'm lying in the meadow with my eyes closed. The sun is burning my face. The grass is rustling in the wind, and I hear the bees buzzing around me. Now the brook is babbling a little, too. Everything is breathing calm and peace, and I wish I would never have to leave here again. It is a splendid feeling of inner calm and cheerfulness. It is very wonderful, what you are doing with me here. I am also totally indifferent to the fact that colleagues are sitting here listening to me. In the meantime I had already completely forgotten them."———

"Please look around once more, after you have enjoyed this calmness, and see if there aren't some animals there too."

"Yes, I'm looking around, now I see that the meadow had gotten wider in the meantime. Where the border of the forest was before, there is now a pasture for cattle fenced in with barbed wire. A lot of cows are grazing leisurely. I also see a horse in the background. It is restless, first pawing up and down and then running around with its tail to the wind."

"At this point we want to stop for the time being. Now you return from the relaxed state in the same manner as in autogenic training. Please clench both your fists and now bend and stretch your arms vigorously three times———and please breathe in deeply and open your eyes. Now you are completely here again, returned from the inner imaginal world to reality. Your head is clear. You are wide awake and fresh again."

Follow-up Discussion

The colleague is now asked to tell something about his experience

"Yes, it was very strange. I was in a state of deep relaxation quickly. That didn't cause me any problems at all. I feel that way too in the evening when I fall asleep, that is, when I plan to go to sleep. The green grass, that I was supposed to imagine, spontaneously appeared in front of my eyes. Of course I had some trouble stretching it out into a meadow afterward. At that point the vision hesitated a little; I also had a certain reluctance, perhaps I would have much rather imagined something else.*

---

* Here resistance to the guidance becomes clear after the fact. We

However, then I followed your words. I have already described the rest. The clarity of the images particularly amazed me. Everything became increasingly clearer and more flexible, once the meadow had appeared. The colors were very clear before my eyes. After some time, everything around me was forgotten, and I really lived within this landscape. I clearly felt the cool water and heard the bees buzzing. The whole thing was an extremely pleasant impression, and I was completely filled by it. I feel calm even now. I saw the cows very clearly too, how they lay there lazily chewing their cuds. The entire thing was a peaceful image extending far out into the countryside."

"Didn't it surprise you that the meadow was wider after the drink of water and the initial boundary created by the forest disappeared?"

"Yes, that's true. After what you had told us, however, I was prepared for such surprises. I even have to say that at first I had expected something much more fantastic. If it had not all been so distinct and lively, I might perhaps have been a little disappointed that I experienced to some degree an everyday situation so similar to reality. I was more prepared for symbolic figures or something dreamlike."

Commentary

It seems important that the patient also learns to perceive the emotional aspect and the mood that the landscape radiates. In the present case the image of the meadow was peaceful, radiated calmness, and an untouched springtime. At the same time, however, an initial restriction of the landscape was obvious. The colleague could naturally yield to this mood relatively easily and in this respect also give us a good report about the basic motif of the meadow. This is what we can expect of a healthy person or even of a neurotic person who has developed very strong defense mechanisms. Then, however, something characteristic happened. After he had refreshed himself with the water, the landscape became broader. He also experienced this process in quite lively fashion, and we have learned to pay close attention to such changes. We should always be aware that even the most banal everyday contents of GAI, even though they seem quite real, always simultaneously have symbolic characteristics for the person, that is, significance for his inner life. Although the person can communicate well with the therapist, we must not forget that he is ultimately in a dreamlike state, thus on the level of imaginal consciousness, which I spoke about previously. Seen from the psychoanalytic point of view, the so-called primary process is prevailing at this time. It is characterized by the laws of the dream and not of waking consciousness. Therefore when our volunteer subject refreshed himself at the brook, not only is a deeply felt experience

---

encourage our patients to verbalize their own intentions during the session and allow them the possibility of imagining other pressing contents, too.

connected with this for him, but a very particular theme of drive dynamics has been addressed. The topic is refreshing oneself by drinking and, thus, the satisfaction of the oral drive. The assumption is suggested that as a result of this oral satisfaction, the colleague was actually thirsty, as emerged in the interview afterward, his inner emotional state changed insofar as the landscape almost seemed to become even more positive. It stretches out; the original restriction (negative emphasis) thus disappears (*phenomenon of change*).

Phenomenon of Change

For the present I would like to call this connection, as described from the two observations, only a supposition. At another time I dealt with the observation of the peculiar phenomena of change and showed that therapeutic interventions of whatever kind, for instance, by GAI, by an interpretation, or by verbalization and clarification of conflictual contents, even by spontaneous current experiences between two treatment sessions, can effect this kind of phenomenon of change. It is a result of the previously mentioned *mobile projection.* Since as a projective phenomenon GAI needs no material foundation, the imaginal contents can change very easily according to changes in the emotional constellation and give us clues to these intrapsychic processes. Therefore these stand out clearly and frequently rather precisely each time in the change of the image. Someone experienced in this learns to register changes in nuances. For the time being, we usually do not tell the patient anything about this. Either he perceives this change himself or it is still too small, so that one waits until it appears obvious to him, and further discussion about it is unnecessary. These phenomena of change do not always only turn in a positive direction, in which they can announce a small step in therapeutic development. They can also change to the reverse and show negative character, for instance, when a conflict is brought up or arises spontaneously in the course of symboldrama. As already mentioned, we can also trace the development of the therapeutic process in GAI by these changes, when they are repeated.

Mobile Projection

Motif of the Cow

Again I return to what the colleague described. One can assume it was scarcely a coincidence that, of all things, cows showed up in the meadow and were included in the peaceful mood. Cows are important to us for, among other things, the milk that they give. Thus, the stated oral motif also appears again here. On the other hand, another stylistic aspect seems to emerge only sketchily for the moment in the restlessly pawing horse in the background. Perhaps a dynamic is announced in this, which, however, is not represented further yet.

Accompanying Emotions

I would like to make another subtle point clear. I indicated that we deliberately observed the accompanying emotions during GAI and also have them described to us. In the present case, the closeness of emotion and of mood was particularly striking or, expressed in different terms, there was "unity" of the mood of the landscape and of the colleague's experience. The colleague's mood seemed particularly elevated and was also stressed accordingly by him when he said, "What you are doing with me here is really very wonderful." (This kind of verbatim quote is often more characteristic and reflects more than a sober report.)

This statement is interesting, because apparently the colleague experiences his own mental imagery and the uplifting feeling he described, as if I "am doing it to him" rather than, as it is in reality, an independent production, as an expression of a creative accomplishment of his ego. He is perhaps indicating that at the moment he is longing for calmness and relaxation; thus, the contents of the mental imagery correspond at least in part to satisfying a wish. The fact that he attributes "it" to my doing gives a clear indication of his present relationship to me. He experiences me as the giver and thereby also characterizes his subjective experience of our dyadic relationship as it exists at the moment. I appear to him as someone, who is giving him something "wonderful," something that he did not expect at all.

Transference

He is thereby expressing a *transference relationship* toward me, which can be translated as a transference between the infant and the giving mother, with which we will become acquainted later as the anaclitic transference. It plays an important part in GAI over longer periods of time.

I also believe that the technique of communication between patient and therapist in GAI has become clear to you through this example. It is relatively informal, and my therapeutic interventions did not disturb the colleague, as was obvious.

Style of guidance

You will have also noticed something else if you observed my style of guidance attentively. I allowed the colleague a lot of time to develop his imaginings gradually. In my opinion I never actually pressed him but rather allowed pauses and also accepted the occasionally somewhat longer pauses without becoming impatient. I did that entirely consciously. This patience and the giving style of guidance are very important. This type of guidance is based upon the following consideration. One must not make the mistake of thinking that the essentials to therapy during treatment, thus, what is effective, lie predominantly in the mental images. In fact, the imaginal contents often end relatively quickly, and the person can also adapt from one image to the next relatively easily.

However, I must again point out the importance of the accompanying emotions. Namely, these come about much more slowly and sluggishly than the cognitive imaginings. Moods arise slowly and expand. Emotions originate only after suitable mental preparation and run their course according to their own rules and laws. The same holds true in analogous fashion for the affects. Thus, if we really want to become effective in GAI treatment, we must follow the rules according to which moods and emotions are manifested, that is to leave space for the emotions to develop freely, in other words, to allow time and to intervene occasionally only a little or not at all. The therapeutic process can be interrupted by the therapist's obvious need to find out details of the catathymic scenery with a greater number of specific questions and to inform himself as precisely as possible. In the early period of GAI we adhered much more strongly to the imaginal phenomena. Only later did we have to become convinced that there is a large difference between the cognitively oriented active-diagnostic technique in GAI and the wait-and-see therapeutic attitude in the sense just stated. One should not confuse the two or use them interchangeably. The further development of GAI made it obvious that in a refined guidance style, the therapist cannot be confined to the patient's continuous report and questions about details in the narrow fashion previously described. Namely, if the patient is more strongly involved emotionally, questions about details of the contents and about emotional nuances can be disturbing. Rather, the therapist must try to find out using empathy, also of a nonverbal kind, whether appropriate questions can have a disturbing or a facilitative effect. If the first is the case, the experienced therapist will be prepared to leave gaps for the time being, while the patient "traces" the catathymic contents, rather than being constantly directed toward a cognitive "exploration" of the patient's catathymic experiential world. If there are still unclear passages, he can inquire about the missing details after the mental imagery phase has ended.

Empathy

In this connection I would like to emphasize that the technique of guidance in GAI always prefers open questions, for instance, "What do you think of that?" "Can you describe that a little more precisely?" rather than questions that are only elicit "yes" or "no" answers as, for example, "Is the tree big?" "Is the house light or dark?" The development of the standard motifs is broadened through open questions and the subsequent imaginings entwined around them become wider and go into more detail, and the contents also manifest themselves more clearly for the patients.

Tactics of Questioning

At the end of each GAI exercise, I use the method of "retraction" following J.H. Schultz's instructions for autogenic training in the form described by him. The patient is urged to clench his fists, to bend and stretch his arms vigorously three times, requiring a good deal of muscular tension. Then he is supposed to breathe in deeply and open his eyes. This strange ritual is not an end in itself. On the contrary, we know that after 10 minutes of a GAI exercise a relatively deep hypnoidal state emerges, which frequently leads to a pronounced feeling of heaviness in the extremities and to an altered state of consciousness. Both can potentially be more pronounced than what occurs in autogenic training alone. This exercise of "retraction" has physiological importance: namely, it reactivates the cerebral cortex, which is deactivated during GAI, and leads back to the full waking state relatively quickly. That is ultimately important because the patient always needs some time

Retraction

before he becomes fully awake and clearly oriented in his real surroundings. In his own training sessions the person interested in GAI will have the experience that after a GAI session he is little prepared to produce knowledge cognitively, that is, in a waking conscious state, or to perceive the surroundings with greater watchfulness. For that reason follow-up discussions

Follow-up Discussions

usually do not lead very far. On the contrary, the patient is still strongly occupied with the world of inner images and with the emotions holding him captive. Therefore one should not send him into the street and into traffic immediately afterward, and

Return to Reality

even less so, if he drives a car. We have him remain in the waiting room for 10 to 15 minutes and "come completely back to his senses" again.

With this I conclude the demonstration of a GAI session with a healthy subject, who is neither neurotically nor psychosomatically disturbed. The counterpart is planned for the next hour, to reproduce the session of a person with many problems, to show you the difference.

Replies to Questions

Question: Dr. B., a colleague interested in psychology, "Can one actually distinguish so clearly between visualizations and catathymic images, as you described them? I mean, are they really so different?"

Phenomenon of Imagination

Answer: The descriptive categories, which I gave you, represented developments of an ideal type. The differences between visualizations and catathymic images are correct as far as that goes. However, one cannot deny that they overlap in practice. We see patients who initially have only vague visualizations over longer periods of time. Sooner or later the images gradually become more dense, and they get closer and closer to the catathymic image. This can also at one time become quickly available and then also fade again. The phenomena can even occasionally oscillate between the two poles of mere visualization and of the autonomous, colorful, and flexible catathymic image. However, we also come across persons whose imaginative faculty is so intensive from the start that they already have a fully distinct catathymic image before their eyes while concentrating on the flower. This is potentially very distinctly the case with artists, who when glancing at a white surface can creatively picture a form and then only need to paint it.

Tactics

For symboldrama, we would, of course, like to have the completely developed catathymic image, the vivid imagination sustained by fantasy. To stimulate it, we also have the patient give us information about the colorfulness of the contents, for example, during the first session with the flower test, we casually ask him if it is a "genuine" product of his fantasy. Incidentally, we, of course, do not say to him that images from memory or mere visualizations are "not wanted." That would either discourage the patient or stimulate him too much to achieve actively, so that he then becomes inhibited and accomplishes the opposite. Thus, the term "see" should be avoided. Rather, I find it important repeatedly to emphasize imagining concepts when I intentionally say to the patient, "Imagine," or "describe to me what is before your eyes now." Incidentally, it has been shown in practical therapy that the degree of distinctness, that is, the plasticity and colorfulness of the images, does not have the decisive importance that we formerly assumed. Therapeutic steps also succeed when the image at first remains pale and vague or blurred. As a rule one is, of course, confident that the patient will develop more and more intensive imaginings in the course of the individual session and from session to session. However, even if that fails to take place, there is nothing that contraindicates the continuation of treatment. In the meantime we even go a step further. We recommend that patients who are afraid, for instance, of being flooded by excessively powerful images, open their eyes and continue their "visualizations" with their eyes open; paler imaginings are meant here. Usually they can also report that they can differentiate these, and they describe changes and developments that indicate the progress of the therapeutic process.

Value of Pale Visualizations

To answer your question in summary, the ideal differentiation between visualization and catathymic image is ultimately of more academic significance and marks the two ends of a continuum.

Verbalization of GAI

Question: Dr. C., "When should the patient describe his imaginal experiences?"
Answer: I ask the patient, at the beginning of treatment sometimes repeatedly, to keep me informed through his verbal report of the emergence of the individual imaginal experiences as they occur. If it seems necessary to me, I even interrupt to ask, for if extremely long nonverbal passages occur, then one does not know what is really happening inside the patient. Interposed questions can, but do not necessarily, disturb imaginal experience, but they are kept discreet and do not run counter to the moods and the emotional tone prevailing at the time. Moreover, one must distinguish between two separate phases in the guidance technique. The first sessions still represent a learning process for most patients. Through the questions, the patient learns what parts of the mental imagery or of the emerging emotions are important to communicate to the therapist and thus what degree of exactness is appropriate. During this period, I also accept that at first the patient occasionally feels disturbed. In the course of subsequent, more strongly therapeutically oriented sessions, the therapist should, of course, learn to accept longer pauses from the patient and also

situations in which he is not completely informed concerning every cognitive detail.

Disturbed by Questions?

Question: Dr. C., "Isn't the patient distracted by the questions? Perhaps something else occurs to him due to the question than if he had been left on his own?"

Answer: That is certainly possible. However, the questions can be beneficial and deepen the contents by stimulating the patient to look around for what has been asked. In this way details of what is imagined often become more clearly clustered. This is important right at the beginning within the framework of the learning process already mentioned and is often perceived by the patient as help. Patients, who tend to imagine or to express things very globally at first (hysterically structured), can be encouraged to greater precision in their imaginal observations in this way. Entire imaginal elements can arise that were previously neglected. However, the reverse also applies. The therapist can initiate certain things by his questions. The questions can more or less strongly structure the imaginal field. This initiation possibly may not be very desirable. If the patient continues to develop his imagery on his own, his fantasy follows its own path, perhaps deviative from the given motif. I consider that to be an expression of his creative fantasy at work and am of the opinion that then one should intervene as little as possible. However, the patient should try, if possible, to report continuously about the fantasy development. In this way important circles of conflict can also arise spontaneously. Conversely, the patient may also unconsciously try occasionally to circumvent passages that indicate unpleasant conflicts and negative emotions or even to fool the therapist using certain maneuvers. Here the defense mechanism of avoidance becomes obvious. That cannot be prevented and being extremely strict about returning the patient to problematic contents can also easily be perceived by him as overcontrol. On the other hand, it is naturally a part of the procedural technique to now and then, when the opportunity spontaneously arises, cautiously and in a somewhat more elegant form lead the patient up to the fixed images and thus to the conflict-laden structures of mental imagery. That will need to be discussed in more detail within the scope of the course of therapy. A suggestive, controlling aspect cannot be avoided in the basic level. On the one hand, the patient is directed to roughly adhere to the fundamental motifs and to solve the tasks connected with them more or less successfully. On the other hand, on the basic level he is supposed to be protected from extremely disturbing or frightening contents, which occasionally can likewise make it necessary for the therapist to increase the structuring. I will describe the training procedure and the therapist's behavior in detail later. Structuring is also a necessity for many patients because they lack spontaneous fantasy productions of their own.

Guidance on the Basic Level

Basically, however, the therapist should always strive to

keep the suggestive aspect as slight as possible, for example, by asking questions in rather vague and open style and always making only circumspect suggestions when directing the patient or perhaps explaining something to him. A discussion can also precede difficult situations in which a problem is to be solved, and the next step can be negotiated together with the patient rather than having the therapist decide alone what the next step will be.

Session Five: Technique III—Demonstration of GAI with a Patient

Unforeseeable Developments in GAI

After having showed you the relatively simple technique of GAI with a healthy person, today I would like the first session with a female patient to serve as a demonstration of symboldrama. My concern is that you recognize the difference and the greater demands upon the technique of guidance. In problem-laden GAI the therapist must be prepared for unforeseeable developments and reactions and must know when to intervene within the framework of the context according to depth psychological therapeutic practice. These are in any case completely different categories from those familiar to us from scientifically oriented studies in medicine and psychology.

Taped Transcript

I am reproducing the tape-recorded transcript of a session with a 38-year-old married woman. One cannot say that the person has a manifest neurosis. However, she is in a crisis situation at the time of this session, and she is clearly experiencing the possible loss of her mother, which she is apparently anticipating in her thoughts, as a threat at least emotionally. It is to be noted in passing that GAI normally always registers currently prevailing psychic problems. However, from the contents of the imagery, it is difficult to decide whether it is a matter of one of the typical crises that all of us go through at some time in life or if it is the manifestation of neurotic development. Only a careful case history can supply the decisive factor for the differential diagnosis. I mention this circumstance, because we ourselves needed a long time, for instance with participants in seminars, to distinguish one condition from the other, which is naturally very important.

Tape: "Try again to imagine a meadow, any meadow or whatever else comes before your eyes."

"I see a field of stubble with burnt off stubs, the ground is black, burned; here and there a stub is still sticking out of the ground. It is very desolate, very abandoned, and very run down."

"And what is the weather like?"

"Gray, the sky is gray and overcast."

"Please look around to see how the whole area is bordered."

"There is a forest on one side of the stubble field, and the other sides are enclosed by a fence, by a hunter's fence."

"And what kind of an effect does it have on you in terms of mood?"

"Yes, I'm standing in the field, and I would like to walk in the woods because the woods are green. The field depresses me, the fence depresses me, it confines me somehow;—it's coming—it's coming closer and closer to me, making the field smaller, and I would like to run up to the woods. I can't, I am rooted by my feet in the burned earth, I would like to tear my feet out of the ground, but that can only be done with difficulty. The ground is tough, and it pulls my feet back again and again, and the fence is slowly coming closer and closer, and I'm becoming afraid that it will completely surround me."

"Yes, perhaps you would walk over to the woods, walk along the edge of the woods and somewhere over there you'll find a little brook."

"Yes, I see a trickle rather than a brook, for the time being a trickle. It meanders through the grass at the edge of the woods."

"And please try to follow the trickle."

"Yes, where the woods come to an end, the trickle widens and becomes a stream, a large stream with rapids."

"What kind of effect does this stream have on you, your mood, your feelings?"

"Raging and devastating, dragging down, engulfing, even sweeping away."

"Would you have the courage to walk along this stream and to pursue it further?"

"I would like to jump into it and let myself be swept away by the water."

"Don't you think that would be dangerous?"

"No, no, it feels almost like a compulsion to me, to go into the water and let myself be carried away, even over some rocks, I'm not afraid."

"Good, but in any event you should first be careful, and please walk along the stream, keep pursuing the stream to see where it leads."

"I'm coming to a waterfall, it drops very steeply down a wall, a wall of rock, the water drops down but it doesn't reach the bottom. It stops in the middle of this wall of rock, it turns to icicles. It freezes, the water freezes, in the middle . . . . Yes, above, it is still flowing downward, and in the middle of the wall of rock it turns into ice, and only single drops continue to fall down further from the icicles."

"And how does that affect you?"

"At first I'm surprised, and I don't know what I should make of it, I'm somewhat perplexed."

"What emotional tone does this part of the landscape have?"

"Something unreal, everything bizarre, these icicles are bizarre, and when I look around, I see tree stumps, which also rise into the sky in really bizarre shapes, it is a very dead landscape and surroundings, . . . desolate, very desolate, very hopeless."

Interpretation of the GAI Contents

At this point I will stop the playback of the taped protocol. Now you will want to know details about the meaning of the contents. That is an obvious and also a legitimate concern. However, before I go into that, I have to make a few comments about the interpretation of mental imagery, even if they are unsystematic for the present. The onlooker, who is not very familiar with psychoanalysis, usually knows that the interpretation of dreams plays a large part in that discipline, but he is apt to believe that the therapist should tell the patient directly the meaning of the individual parts or images of the dream or attribute them to certain figures of his past or present, among other things. This kind of attempt to interpret directly is occasionally made, but then always in the form of a proposal. However, neither in psychoanalysis nor in GAI are interpretations of contents of prime importance in the technique of therapy. I cannot go into detail at this moment. I would only like to point out the danger that occurs all too easily when attempts at direct interpretation are made, which questions the effect of the therapy in the long run. When the therapist more or less directly tells or proposes to the patient that a particular content in GAI represents something specific in his behavior or in his relationship to others in the present or the past, he establishes a connection, as is familiar and customary in the area of language by means of concepts. There are purely cognitive attributions, which stand, so-to-speak, in a one-to-one relationship. The depth psychological symbolism, on the other hand, obeys entirely different rules and laws. Freud studied them very precisely in the so-called primary process. According to this, for example, all of the symbolic contents of night dreams and of mental imagery, thus also of GAI, have multiple meanings, which the therapist must take into consideration. If that does not occur and these kinds of one-to-one attributions are made, the patient is directed away from the therapeutically important emotional level of experience in GAI to the cognitive-rational level. After such an interpretation, the patient may leave the therapy session with the notion: "Aha, now I know, the big tree in the meadow, that is my father." Such attributions are, of course, not wrong in principle, but are absolutely one-sided as a suggestion for the patient and are frequently too much is read into the interpretation by the therapist. Such direct interpretations are avoided in psychoanalysis, too.

Multiple Determination

Temptation to Clarify Rationally

Although it is not completely incorrect to say that contents of GAI also refer to important referential persons from the patient's childhood, such global interpretive attempts do not lead any further, but instead stifle the free emotional oscillations that are extremely important for the advancement of the therapeutic process in GAI and that must be preserved. The conclusion from this is that the therapist, still inexperienced in this area, does not as a matter of principle make any interpretations of contents at all on the basic level and also avoids proposing interpretations as far as possible. Elsewhere I have described the whole problem of depth psychological symbolism clearly and also the approaches, the explanatory and interpretive work, as we conduct them anew

Symbolism

in an individual manner with every patient. I refer the interested reader to this study (Leuner, 1978).

If therefore we avoid directly clarifying the meaning of the contents to the patient on the basic level of GAI and systematically do not perform this at all, still an approach presents itself spontaneously, which for the patient lies to some degree between interpretation and recognition. Here I am refering to the slow and gradual, yet still clear, self-interpretation of the symbolic contents of symboldrama, as the American

Self-Interpretation of the Symbols

psychiatrist Kosbab (1974) has termed it. I would like to explain this further. The contents of every image and the development of every scene or story (even if it is only made up of a stringing together of scenic fragments) regularly convey elements of moods and emotions and always make a certain statement. Seen from the visual standpoint, this message does not absolutely have to be expressed in words and concepts. In therapy it is frequently much more productive to simply leave them as "image puzzles," in a manner of speaking, as an *expression of the language of*

"Language of the Images"

images with its wide, diverse meanings, with its "suggestiveness." This vivid language is frequently very well understood by parts of the psyche, thus by the preconscious and by a regressive, that is, more childlike, way of comprehending. Owing to this preconscious capacity of the still strongly experiential perception, the imaginings in GAI have an effect so that for the time being we can simply leave them as they are. Naturally, there are additional levels of recognition, on which the contents become increasingly precise and also directly refer to facts and persons so that the self-interpretation of the symbol in the course of a series of psychotherapeutic sessions with GAI, what the psyche means with the image at that particular moment, can also become increasingly clear cognitively.

Analogy to the Image of Language

If we apply this naive perceptual language of the imaginal world, for instance, to the previous example of the physician faced with an emergency situation who visualized the growing inundation of the landscape, we realize the following. The allegory "flooding of the landscape" and "emotional flooding" at the moment when the emergency situation needed to be handled was so evident that it really would not have required any interpretive talent to see an extremely meaningful connection here. In our last example, a number of allegories are also evident, which refer to how the threatening loss appears allegorically in the subconscious of the person concerned and how radically it is experienced in the emotional core. The *theme*

Theme of the Mental Imagery

of the mental imagery is undoubtedly clear to the patient in detail, in part preconsciously, in part consciously, without a direct and rational attribution of the meaning having to be conveyed to her. It already starts when a field of stubble appears instead of a pleasant friendly meadow. Here a situation becomes apparent in which the value of a ripe harvest, in which the periods of autumn and winter can be expected, thus becomes a somewhat dreary scene in nature marked by death. Incidentally, everything has been cut off, even burned over. If one lets one's own associations play (which is productive for the therapist in silently tracing the catathymic scene with the patient), the concept of "scorched earth" may involuntarily occur, thus the obliteration of all life and of all human evidence. Moods, such as hopelessness, sadness, and depression are signified here. In forming a working hypothesis for the joint understanding of the scenery, the therapist must also be able to bring in his knowledge about the current situation of the person involved and the case history. In the case at hand one can probably justifiably presume that the present inner situation of the patient is reflected in this initial image: the threatening loss of her mother, which is perhaps internally already anticipated and experienced as certain, to whom she is still very attached. Her father had died in the war, and mother and daughter grew very close in sharing a stressful refugee fate.

On the other hand, this scene as a whole is not totally hopeless; rather a shimmer of hope comes from a portion of the catathymic panorama, namely, from the world of trees, from the forest. In connection with this the person concerned remembers that her father, who was always very friendly and gave her a lot of attention, had taught her to appreciate nature by taking many walks with her, sometimes in the woods. Her mother, on the other hand, was very concerned about her "good upbringing," and as a child the patient experienced her mother more as cool, matter-of-fact, rationalizing, and at times also as rejecting.

Brook

Usually the brook expresses something of the aspect of flowing psychic development, of inner continuity, and the water is something like a bestowing fertile element. In the present case, however, very little of this is left. The organic flow of the brook's course is broken by the drop of masses of water in the waterfall. The bestowing, fertile element of the water has actually been almost nullified and turned into the opposite, when the water expresses a great deal of coldness, having frozen into icicles. We can presume that the patient must have experienced personal coldness in her childhood and perhaps also adapted some of it unconsciously, from which the emotional flow of her own psyche is suffering. Measured by the conditions of real nature surrounding us, this image is already relatively crass. Perhaps one can also assume that the patient is experiencing her present situation with the threatening abandonment as such a natural event of icy coldness, in which "the flow of her warm emotional development" has frozen.

Waterfall

Compulsive Structure

The confining fence, which approaches her, has a plainly alarming effect, as does the situation, which is well-known from dreams, that someone is unable to move away, as if rooted in the earth. The aspect of confinement can be related to anxiety and to a compulsive structural component in the personality. In actuality, the patient had had a phobia for a long period before this catathymic panorama. The confinement by the fence indicates that she is inclined to confine herself, probably based upon a tendency from her family upbringing. This can relate to many things, including motoric expansion, the free unfolding of emotions, and to confinement through the formation of certain ideals and confinement of flexibility in thought. It is of great value to the therapist in forming hypotheses to know the case history thoroughly.

Maternal Image

Being rooted to the earth ("Mother Earth") may in some way be connected to the strong tie to her mother and her principles of upbringing and ideals, which are the basis for the obstruction of her actual flexibility and independence.

Forming Hypotheses

However, you already see from my cautious formulations that we are dependent upon hypotheses as long as an extensive case history is not at hand. These can be confirmed or can be proved to be wrong or be in need of correction according to new material that is gathered from additional sessions and the augmentation of the case history. Upon this basis patients then gradually also gain more and more semiconscious or fully conscious insights or even punctual "aha experiences." To have

Spontaneous Insights

found the insights himself is much more productive for the patient than if they are precipitately expressed by the therapist and then become for the patient, at best, rationally comprehensible. Thus, the admonition is again emphasized that on the basic level of GAI we do not give any direct or indirect interpretations. At another point, I explained in great detail the much greater importance for therapy of the continual

Perceptions

clarification of the contents of the mental images through detailed observations and through perceiving the images, including their nuances, the scenic lapses, the patient's own behavior in this imaginal world, as well as, above all, the accompanying moods and emotions. The therapeutic guidance should concentrate primarily on these things, as I will explain in context later.

Replies to Questions

Knowledge and Contraindication

Question: Dr. D., "Is a knowledge of the method a contraindication to its use?"

Answer: In my opinion that is usually not the case. Indeed that would mean that the participants of this course are already prejudiced by the knowledge gained here to such an extent that they would not profit from the procedure themselves if it were to be used with them. That can be the case extremely rarely in a few initial sessions. Usually, however, the fully mature mental image develops autonomously in a state of relaxation. Then something completely different happens in the imaginings than the person involved expected beforehand on the basis of his

Autonomy of GAI

knowledge. This discrepancy already can occur when I conduct the flower test in a seminar. Many participants are surprised when a different flower from the one they had initially made up their minds to imagine appears before their eyes."

Demand for Fantasy Images

Question: Dr. E., "You have emphasized that it is important for the images not to refer to memories, rather they ought to be products of fantasy. Should one and can one make that demand at all, and how is that to take place technically?"

Alternative

Answer: This question does in fact occasionally arise in therapy in practice. As already stated, we do not let the patient notice at first that we do not totally approve when he occasionally offers us products from his memory. In principle, however, one can assume that an internal reason must exist, that there is an unconscious motive for the appearance of the specific memory that is offered from the wealth of all available memories at precisely this moment. Frequently one can have the experience of asking a question and having a pressing problem emerge after all. I recall, for example, a young girl, who in one of her first GAI sessions described a mountain climb from her vacation 3 months previously, after I had asked her if she could climb a mountain. She eventually described a panoramic view from the summit in splendid summer weather. It all seemed too smooth and nice to me, and I chose a very simple tactic to penetrate a little deeper. I asked her how she had felt up there on top of this mountain at that time. The decisive thing here is asking for the emotion, not for cognitive contents. After just a few seconds, she suddenly broke out into tears and sobbingly reported that she felt rather alone on the mountain and kept thinking that actually her engagement had already practically broken up. This example demonstrates how the problem can lurk under the surface of the first repression and is in a manner of speaking "supplied" along with the memory image.

Actual Contents as Resistance

With intellectuals and professionals, however, one can occasionally observe their "clinging" to material from memory for a number of sessions, perhaps remarking that the method apparently does not work with them, because they were not able to drop their memories for fantasies. This can actually be the defense mechanism of intellectualization. There are two ways to overcome this.

Techniques

First, one can tell the patient it would be nice if he would try just once more to imagine a motif that is really foreign to him (born of fantasy) and that he does not take out of his store of memories. However, if the resistance is as obstinate as just described the following technical trick has proved to be successful. First, I patiently have the person describe the landscape of his last vacation to me and then have him follow a path, a street, or the course of a brook or of a stream. Here I lead him increasingly further along this dividing line away from the starting point. Ultimately the remembrance leaves him at some point, and he begins to add to the landscape using his fantasy.

Session Six: The Standard Motifs of the Basic Level

From the technique discussed to this point of inducing mental imagery as the second step after reaching a relaxed state, it emerges that the "entry into the imaginal world" occurs as the patient is offered a motif to imagine. This introduction of a motif seemed to be a technical necessity in GAI to create stable and reproducible conditions. However, it soon became clear that along with suggesting a motif, a *thematic focus of the experiential field* of the imagination, or rather of the thereby aroused projection of unconscious contents, *is induced*. Thus, whether one wants to or not, along with every imaginal motif a theme is also introduced. It is determined by its respective symbolic value. At one point it can be of more universal nature and apply to many persons thematically, another time it can bring up a specific theme in the individual, which gains in significance for him due to his individual motivational system. This *process of thematic focusing* is not only reserved for mental imagery, rather thematic connections are regularly touched upon in everyday situations and in cognitive-rational dealings. For GAI, I very soon found a possibility for thematically focusing the projectional field by directly structuring the imagination with the help of a standard motif. This provided an incomparable opportunity in view of the numerous coincidences and the occasionally infinitely great possibilities of visual fantasy. With this help, one is able to structure the projections into a meaningful organizational structure relatively informally. It is comparable to a map, which the visitor to a foreign country likes to have at hand to be able to orient himself there geographically. According to Kosbab (1974) and Singer (1978) the thematic structuring of mental imagery is specific to GAI when compared with other mental imaging techniques. I see one of its particular strengths in this, which does not mean, however, that the procedure is absolutely and always bound to this structuring. This is demonstrated by the advanced technique of the associative procedure on the intermediate level. Suggesting the motifs greatly facilitates the teachability of the procedure. Moreover, it makes the scientific examination of the depth psychological positions possible. The respective motifs or the individual projective sets can be repeatedly examined quite precisely, also in terms of changes, as they emerge in the mental imagery. This was recently demonstrated again in a very interesting work by Stamm (1980).

Thematic Focus of the Experiential Field

Teachability of GAI

Selection of the Standard Motifs

I have often been asked how I justify the selection of the standard motifs for GAI. Their choice is essentially based upon clinically empirical observations. During the long period of diverse experiments with the mental imagining technique, which I started in 1948 and published for the first time in 1954, a number of motifs crystallized out, which repeatedly appeared automatically and apparently spoke for an inner readiness on the part of the patients to manifest mental imagery precisely at these mostly scenic motifs. I then additionally brought a small portion of the motifs, primarily within the intermediate level, from the knowledge of the depth psychological readiness for conflict and symbolism and studied them for their usefullness for projection in the specific drive areas. Eventually it became apparent that not only the symbolic meanings of the individual motifs complement each other well, but also that a number of the motifs are made very broad, so-to-speak as a stage on which symboldrama can take place and through which all possible pressing conflicts can be depicted. Other motifs are more restricted and some are very narrowly defined thematically, so that only a limited problem area can be reflected in them. In subdividing the procedure into three levels it was natural to choose only those motifs for the basic level whose symbolic value leaves more space for the spontaneous development of individual projections. Thus they are not all too narrowly focused upon specific conflictural areas. Moreover, it seemed appropriate to introduce the unconscious psychodynamics more from the surface with the help of these motifs and therefore not to encourage more strongly regressive tendencies and thus not to provoke more deeply repressed, highly stressful conflicting material. In this way we prevent the still inexperienced therapist from penetrating important, protective defenses in the patient, from using the affectively laden material incorrectly, arousing anxieties and bringing himself into situations that he cannot control. In this respect it is practically a distinctive feature of the basic level motifs that they are easy on the patient and are in part organized rather protectively without losing therapeutic effectiveness on that account.

3 levels

Symbolic Value of the Motifs

Motifs of the Basic Level

The following are the *standard motifs of the basic level,* which we gradually offer the patient during the training procedure.

1. *The motif of the meadow,* which usually can be used as the start of the mental imagery and as a stage for current conflictual projections
2. *The motif of the brook,* with the request to follow it either upstream to the source or downstream to the mouth, depending upon the wish of the patient
3. *The motif of the mountain,* which is to be viewed from the distance and then to be climbed to gain a panorama from there
4. *The motif of a house,* which is observed from the outside and then inspected in all its details from cellar to attic
5. *The motif of the edge of the woods,* with a view from the meadow into the darkness of the woods to let symbolic figures emerge from it

Fixed Images

Conflict-free Motifs

As has repeatedly been demonstrated and as I will present in greater detail, we notice in the manifestation of these standard motifs, above all, the conflict-laden scenery in the form of the so-called *fixed images*. It corresponds to the conception of psychoanalysis that these areas are to be sought out again and again and dealt with using the respective technique of mental imagery. In the decades of therapeutic work with symboldrama it has been repeatedly seen that conflict-free contents can also be depicted in a broader form using some of the motifs listed. When the patients dwell longer on these points, they tend especially to satisfy regressive or even archaic drive needs. These are predominantly of an oral, more rarely of a narcissistic nature. They most frequently arise at the following places in the five standard mental sets of the basic level:

1. Resting and enjoying of *scenic views*, for instance, while looking at a sunny summer meadow from a mountain or wherever else the patient happens to be
2. *drinking water* from a spring or brook
3. *bathing*, for instance, in the brook, in a banked up spring, in a lake, or in the ocean
4. *swimming* in an imagined lake or particularly in the ocean, which has a clearly more active component in the same connection

All of the remaining standard motifs of GAI—the list of 12 motifs appears in appendix I—have been deliberately excluded from the basic level. They are important for the intermediate and advanced levels and have been described in detail in the text about the entire procedure (Leuner, 1984).

Therapeutic Significance of the Basic Level Motifs

In connection with the examples of case studies about the accomplishments of the basic level, I indicated that, surprisingly, focusing on the five standard motifs and going through the scenes and achievements connected with them can suffice to unfold the psychotherapeutic effect, which will be described in more detail later. The studies mentioned involving treatment with the basic level of larger numbers of patients have shown that the motifs cited here, which even the beginner can control well, are, by far, enough to conduct a successful therapy with symboldrama. I emphasize this particularly because some beginning therapists believe that the advanced levels would permit a better and more effective therapy than the basic level. However, that is not the case. Rather, the basic level is the foundation of the entire procedure and can be construed as a therapeutic method complete in itself. For this reason, I urge all future therapists to restrict themselves in their subsequent work at first to the limited number of motifs presented here. The patient, who is gradually developing in his fantasy life, usually

Creative Development

takes care of the natural unfolding based upon the suggested motifs himself, as long as he is given the necessary creative freedom by the therapist. I will come back to this again in the section about the technical procedure in the basic level.

For the moment, however, the question arises, how we guide our patients to imagine the individual motifs and how the therapist seeks to comprehend for himself (without expressing it) the depth psychological meaning of these motifs in general and occasionally also individually.

Quasi-real World of Mental Imagery

As I made clear earlier, we always assume that the patient moves in the imaginings of symboldrama almost as in a real world. We also formulate all interventions relating to guidance through the mental images accordingly. We speak to him just as if we were leading the patient through a real landscape or into a real house, and we adapt ourselves in the choice of words when intervening according to the conditions prevailing there.

First Standard Motif: The Meadow

The first motif is the *meadow,* already mentioned. It can be used as an introduction in general and also as a starting point for each individual session with mental imagery. Of course, that is not a requirement. With the advanced patient one can begin mental imagery with the other motifs, too. The motif is only very vaguely proposed to the patient, formulated as follows, for instance, "Please try to imagine a meadow," possibly with the addition "imagining is not difficult, this will not be an effort for you."

Current Mood

The scenario of the meadow that can usually be imagined, and thus also perceived in fine details of the surroundings and the nearby distance, frequently reflects the patient's more or less *current* conscious *mood.* Accordingly, details of the meadow image can also vary from one session to another. The patient is at first often not even conscious of the change of inner mood expressed in the meadow. I recollect, for example, the change in the imaginal landscape of the physician in the hospital faced with an emergency situation who did not really perceive that she was excited internally, as the flooding of the landscape emerged before her inner eye. The therapist tells the patient his supposition in this situation, that the mood of the meadow motif could perhaps be reflecting his inner condition. Most patients agree more or less hesitantly. Sometimes they are also astonished when behind the fascade of cheerful behavior a "darkening" of the meadow motif appears, for instance, when the weather becomes dismal and rainy. It potentially also arouses astonishment and insight into the background of his own mood for the first time, which now becomes obvious through the meadow motif. At the same time, one can also gradually make clear to the patient his unconscious readiness to repress.

Elements of Mood

The aspect of mood can appear in this motif in the most diverse areas; naturally, the easiest and the most frequently is in the weather. The sun can shine, the sky can be gray and overcast, the entire scenery, gloomy, or it can rain and ultimately be stormy. However, the prevailing season gives indications of probably still deeper and more firmly structured basic mood tendencies. An autumnal situation points rather to a sad mood, spring to an optimistic expectation, and summer to satisfying fulfillment, just to name the principal ones.* The symbolic content of the meadow motif is very broad, as becomes apparent from the variations in weather and season stated here. Basically, in the so-called ideal and healthy person we naturally expect a friendly, rather delightful sunny meadow in summer, which portrays its fertility in succulent grass, its friendliness in flowers, and the entire atmosphere in pleasant surroundings. Under this sign, the meadow motif could primarily be related symbolically or allegorically to paradise, to the Garden of Eden, and put into human terms as an expression of a peaceful, harmonizing, relatively free of conflicts and rivals, inviting a maternal world representing fertility. This can be accentuated even more when cows are grazing in it.

Broad Symbolic Content of the Meadow Motif

However, not only in the healthy person, but also and by no means rarely in our patients, who consult us because of a neurosis, can such a harmonious green meadow image emerge in the sunshine to begin with, possibly animated by flowers or animals, similar to the way it was presented earlier by our colleague. In other words, we can occasionally recognize a paradox and must be prepared for the possibility that the appearing mental image does not always fundamentally reflect the internal disorder. In the last-mentioned case, where a meadow image free of disorders becomes visible in a person with a neurosis, we must look for the explanation in the particular psychodynamics of the person. They are characterized by the following, which is frequently also demonstrated in other manifest ways. The person in question has developed a talent for masking conflicts and intrapsychic problems, and for strongly repressing or rather for developing general defense mechanisms in the sense of psychoanalysis. In this way he is usually trying to protect himself against pressing anxieties, depressive moods, or other conflicts. This is relatively rarely the case, but it does occur and must be respected for the time being. This paradox has in rare cases given us much to think about and has led to insights that I will come back to again later. These particularly "charming" picture-book meadows, as participants in a seminar once called them, have an especially specific characteristic.

Paradoxes

---

* In an interesting statistical study Prindull (1964) demonstrated the typical features of the catathymic panorama in depressive neurotic patients in comparison to healthy persons.

Projection of the Individual's Conflicts

Of greater interest in our context are the projections of the individual's conflicts onto the meadow motif, that is, forms of disturbances through which the previously mentioned ideal meadow of the Garden of Eden with its fertilely bestowing and refreshing character is encroached upon. The last-named example of the woman, who was struggling with the possible loss of her mother, gave very pronounced indications of possibilities of such disorders. In other cases they appear approximately as follows. The meadow has been chewed bare, scorched by the sun, is particularly small or is confined by a barbed-wire fence or rigorously divided up, or a forest surrounds it in a rigid, geometric rectangle. In rare cases the patient himself has been, in a manner of speaking, caught in the meadow in a closely confined area, which can be regarded as a particularly severe neurosis. The scenario of the meadow motif is naturally in general even broader. A typical image was described to me by a young man, who was displaced in the postwar period and suffered because of the loss of his homeland. Instead of a green meadow, he saw a broad square site, which was surrounded by woods on three sides, as if one had artificially cut down a clearing. The grass was dry, burned, and trodden, its color a brownish-gray. The sky was also gray, the season indeterminable but dismal. In the middle of this site there stood a watchtower made of wood, as is familiar from the Russian prisoner-of-war camps. After I had urged the patient to let the image take effect on him for a while and to observe more closely, his glance finally wandered from the slightly sloping clearing into the distance. There he saw far in the distance a white city lighting up, almost as in a fairy tale, illuminated by the late afternoon sun. The contrast between the desolate, dismal, and trodden camp meadow and the distant, promising city impressed him a great deal. He looked for an explanation for the dismal image on his own, which, however, seemed to signify an alternative through the distant, white city. Even if viewed relatively superficially at first, it was still reassuring for him to interpret the meadow as his, at that time, seemingly hopeless situation in which he existed as if deserted in a disbanded prisoner-of-war camp. In the distant city he saw that glimmer of hope for the fulfillment of wishes and anticipation of a future life, which was at least promised him there. It is obvious to the expert that illusory expectations are probably also reflected in this. For the time being, I avoided any reference to this supposition. It is often astonishing that the encounter with such a motif, that is, with oneself, for instance with the insight, "Yes, it apparently really looks that way inside me" or "Yes, that's the way my inner situation is," the insight connected with this, the increased cognitive clarity, and the higher degree of certainty have a relieving effect, even if the image possibly has a negative, or in any case not particularly encouraging, character. Naturally that has its limits. Very intensely negatively tinged contents, above

Breadth of the Meadow Motif

Depressive Contents

all, those that radiate depressive moods, can intensify a depression and thus be disturbing.

Lacking Indication for the Basic Level

The last-described example of the meadow motif shows no flagrant signs of severe or decompensated neurosis. Treatment on the basic level would be readily possible and even recommended. As a contrast, I will follow with an example, which particularly blatantly indicates the stated depressive general attitude and carries with it the risk of further intensifying the depressive mood or rather of the patient moving passively and helplessly further in this direction. A 25-year-old woman, after focusing on the meadow motif, immediately describes a relatively small meadow at the edge of a woods. It is rainy and patches of fog drift across the meadow. The patient is standing in the middle of it and does not dare to move from the spot, as the meadow is wet and swampy. However, even if she wanted to, she would not be able to leave the meadow, because a strong fence surrounds it. There is no gate to be found, through which she could pass. All around it there are tall trees, which give her the feeling that they could overwhelm her. The weather as a "barometer of mood" and the meadow, barren in the form of mire, express deep hopelessness and abandonment. This requires no skill in interpretation. One also scarcely needs to tell this to the patient. The strong enclosure and the immobility, which the patient senses and from which she cannot free herself, point to the degree of internal confinement and to her passive helplessness. Thus, she "internally" feels, that is, emotionally but unconsciously, her current life situation in this same way. Only with a knowledge of the external circumstances and of the patient's history can one judge whether this image expresses a momentary crisis situation or whether it is a representation of a neurotic-depressive basic mood in a severe, decompensated neurosis. In fact, the patient, who had been neurotically ill for years, was in a hopeless and isolated, increasingly critical stage of this condition.

Neurotic depression

As I have already said, in the case of a pronounced depression such as this, the procedure is perhaps more apt to be dangerous, since the depressive mood intensifies through the confrontation with depressive contents. When equivalent scenery appears, the question arises whether the therapist cannot perhaps intervene in a meaningful way by calling upon the patient to concentrate on another, geographically distantly situated landscape motif, which is, however, radiating a positive mood. I am thinking, for example, of the scenery of a section of beach on the Mediterranean with sunshine and blue sky. Usually the therapist is disappointed here, as the patient cannot free himself in this way from the depressive mood completely filling him. Rather, if such a change of the image is possible at all, the depressive mood tone will intrude there too. The weather is then also gloomy, the sky overcast, the sea leaden, sluggish, and gray. Another way out, for instance, would be to invite the patient, in view of the confining fence, to climb over it or to undertake other active measures. That can occasionally work. However, frequently there are insurmountable difficulties in this (as in this example with the basic mood of hopelessness covering everything). Through the therapist's active intervention, resistances can be even more easily provoked. I will go into more detail about this in connection with the treatment of the so-called obstructive motifs (p.63).

Typical signs of disturbance

In this example I would therefore like to stress that even when the meadow motif is focused upon for the first time, very specific and distinct signs of disturbance can appear, which need attention in depressed and neurotically disturbed persons. For example, a field of stubble, a swamp, a site covered with asphalt, or even a desert can appear in place of the meadow. That can be a temporary situation as a starting motif; it can, however, question the possibility of treatment on the basic level or with GAI at all in consideration of the general mood, the symptoms of the patient and his current situation, and neurotic disorder with other similar contents. I mention this problem at this point precisely because characteristics of mood can be particularly clearly and forcefully manifested in the meadow motif. However, I do not want to go into more detail about the question of treatment prognosis and the indications for GAI here. In principle, depressive neuroses have a relatively good prognosis, if the personality of the patient has already stood the test of time in life and is socially integrated to some extent.

Particularly pretty, charming meadow images potentially signify a hidden defense (reaction formation), behind which the actual problem is obscured. I at one time treated, for example, an older preclimacteric woman. She had established a platonic relationship with an old, confirmed bachelor and came into most difficult conflicts when they wanted to become engaged and to marry soon. This defense against sexuality, usually expressed in other motifs, was additionally expressed in the patient's sweetish, infantile-teenagelike world of illusions. She saw a bright green meadow. A square was marked out by small flowers, whose petals had the form of a heart. A white bench stood under two delightfully blooming trees. Everything radiated in the bright spring sun in a cloudless, clear blue sky. Of course, no one sat down on the white garden bench, and the patient also avoided taking this seat. I can save myself a commentary. In any case you recognize in the tendency to make things cute and in the unnatural formations, which in such cases can often have a somewhat "corny" or toylike quality, the childlike-narcissistic compensatory world as part of a reaction formation.

Freedom of movement

Our dealings with the meadow motif are, of course, not exhausted in the diagnostic aspect presented here. Seen from the therapeutic standpoint, we offer the patient for the time being, provided the meadow is to some extent acceptable to him, the complete freedom to do what he wants. We ask, for instance,

"What would you like to do now?" Then wishes can appear, such as go for a walk, lie down in the grass, look for flowers, explore the surroundings. In other words we can assume a giving attitude to a large extent and leave a part of the guidance through the mental imagery up to the patient himself. Frequently, however, we make the patient somewhat perplexed by this, and nothing suitable to do occurs to him. In this, as in every kind of behavior of the patient in GAI, behavioral tendencies show up that the person usually also has in reality without always being totally conscious of them. The person who cannot think of anything to do apparently does not really know what makes him happy. He is not accustomed to pursuing his own wishes and impulses and tends rather to a passive attitude. He is generally used to receiving advice and directions from other people, thus externally. In this respect giving the patient great freedom cannot only trigger off embarrassment and perplexity, but also confront him with an inner dilemma, which should not be approached until an advanced stage of therapy.

Guiding Suggestions

What then are the *guiding suggestions* that the therapist can provide within the scope of the meadow motif, which is the one first focused upon? Basically, the *structuring interventions of the therapist* are quite similar in all of the motifs. They are concentrated, above all, on hints toward increasingly subtle perception of the imagined scene and are to be directed, on the one hand, (1) to what is *near,* thus to the *observation of details,* and on the other hand, (2) to the dimension of *distance,* thus to the *further surroundings* of the individual's position; added to this are (3) questions about the *individual's mood* (apart from questions about his intentions as already stated); (4) questions about the *mood of the meadow* or of the entire landscape image; and, finally, (5) also somewhat more pointed questions about the *typical attributes* of the respective motif. With the meadow, the latter can be about flowers, the weather, the season, the boundaries of the distant view (as already mentioned), about animals found in the grass or grazing in the meadow, among other possibilities. The *basic idea* is to *exhaust in terms of perception* such a motif, if possible, into all the nuances and details and its mood. In this it has already become obvious that the *perception* goes in two directions: on the one hand, in the

Perception

cognitive direction *with an attention to facts* and, on the other hand, in the direction of *moods and feelings,* thus of the broad spectrum of *emotional* animation to its *refinements* of mood. With the two aspects, a more *contemplative perseverence,* taking effect upon the individual of scene and mood, can be combined for a longer period of time. Of course, here it is necessary that markedly negative, for instance, depressive or anxiety-laden contents not be in the foreground. I cannot go into further details of the technique of guidance here. However, no fast rules can be given, either. The interventions are different for each individual case and are connected with the total context and the therapist's empathic understanding of the patient's situation. Many patients also develop a degree of their own activity and unfold the scenery creatively so that the development of the respective motif can be left up to them for a long time.

Clarifying questions

The meadow motif can take up the first or even later sessions completely with everything that is centered around it. However, it can also be only a short episode, from which the other motifs are approached. The question concerning in what way and how often the therapist should ask clarifying questions often causes the beginner particular difficulties. As I previously emphasized, these questions can contribute a great deal to making the imagery clearer, more colorful, and more precise so that new details appear and the image as a whole is enriched. On the other hand, too many questions or awkward ones, which do not conform to moods and scenery, have a disturbing or depressing effect. Without saying more, it may be obvious to you that the *style of guidance* can really only be learned and *practiced* with the help of *intensive seminars,* as we regularly conduct them in appropriate study groups about GAI. In them, the participant switches his role, at one time being the patient, another time being the therapist and thus receives continuing feedback about his style of guidance or he can correct that of his therapist.

Session Seven: Second Standard Motif: The Brook

In the same or the following session we ask the patient, starting out from the meadow motif, to look around for a *brook*. Frequently the path of a brook spontaneously presents itself in the meadow. Otherwise, we suggest to the patient that we would expect there to be a brook nearby. This is an offer of structure through a mild suggestion, which, however, remains very vague. Usually it is enough of a nudge for the patient to find a brook, perhaps after another few words of encouragement. Naturally, the reverse can also occur and the brook motif fails to appear. This implies the existence of a defense or of resistance. If the brook appears, we first ask the patient to give an account of his impressions instead of asking for specific details. In this connection I recall the two examples, the report of the colleague and of the young woman, the latter in connection with the critical conflictual problems and the frozen brook.

Offer of Structure

The brook can be a small trickle or wider, possibly already very large, even a river can appear. We have the patient observe such characteristics as swiftness of the current, the purity of the water, the kind of shore and its vegetation. Again we can ask what he would like to do. Whereas some do not take the initiative, others would like to put their feet in the water, wade in the brook, look for fish, or follow the brook. In reality brooks also have a strange power of attraction for man, just as has water frequently in general. The fuller the involvement with the brook motif is, the more therapeutically productive it becomes—apart from the previously stated accomplishments of pursuing it in the one or the other direction. Here we also do not forget to have the patient perceive the mood by asking a suitable question.

Distinctness

What symbolic meaning can we attribute to the brook motif, which in our geographical latitudes is closely connected with the motif of the meadow and the countryside?

Symbolic Meaning

The brook is *flowing water,* which extends from its source through various currents and finally all the way to the ocean into which it empties. Its basic motif is that of the continually flowing current, in which a *development* is revealed at the same time. In this respect the motif of the brook, which, of course, has various facets, can also be interpreted as the expression of the flowing psychic development, of the unobstructed *unfolding of psychic energy.* At the same time one must not forget that water in general as an "element" has within it something akin to *vital force.* It refreshes, stimulates, and without water life is not thinkable at all. As far as this is concerned, water belongs to the area of the concept of *fertility.* Water must also always be present where one finds a meadow or a fertile landscape: a trickle, a brook, a river, a lake.

A larger brook or a stream can also represent *a boundary,* which can be overcome by bridges or ferryboats or also by a fording.

Spring, Stream, Ocean

The pure, refreshing and cool *spring* arises from the womb of the maternal earth. The end of the stream, the *ocean,* is a special case of the motif "water" in general and is commonly regarded as a *symbol of the unconscious.* One can rely upon this in certain images in GAI. However, that is not the point here. The well-known German-American psychoanalyst Niederland (1956) devoted an extensive, very interesting study to the symbolism of the river.

If we have the ideal healthy patient pursue the course of the brook downstream, he will not have any great difficulties and will report how the brook becomes wider and wider. It flows through various landscapes, whose scenery changes; towns and cities appear and perhaps it flows into a river. Pursuing it further eventually leads to the mouth and to the sea. The sea then becomes a motif of its own. Dealing with it goes beyond the realm of the basic level.

Brook as Guideline

After the patient has observed the brook in the manner just stated, we give him the choice in therapy of pursuing the brook upstream to the source or downstream as far as he can go. Sometimes patients have difficulty deciding which path they prefer. Apparently the path upstream to the source is easier than the path downstream. In fact, certain motifs of obstruction (general term, "fixed images") appear almost regularly while following the brook along its course, even in the not decidedly neurotic person. They signify problems and can be regarded as signs of disturbance. For this reason the *path to the source* usually has priority in the *first phase* of therapy. Among the obstructions that may be encountered are a path that is strongly impeded or even disturbed by undergrowth, or a steep ascent of

Signs of Disturbance

a mountain slope. Only in very rare cases is the patient unable to locate the source at all, which in my opinion can be regarded as a sign of a severe disorder. At the source, the water can emerge from the earth, from a rock or from a pipe placed there by man. Sometimes there are also complex devices, for instance, a reservoir or a container with a cover, beneath which the source has been contained. Signs of disorder indicating conflicts are situations in which the water trickles out of the sand very inconspicuously and thinly, or the spring barely flows or wells up from several small individual rills in a meadow. If the flow of the spring is broad and plentiful in the imagery of a person who is otherwise neurotically disturbed, one can speak, it seems to me, of unbroken vitality and emotional intensity.

Having reached the source, we suggest that the patient taste the water. It is certainly important whether he senses the "cool wetness" at all or is, on the other hand, completely insensitive to whether he feels refreshed by it or not, to what extent he perceives and can describe the scenery of the surroundings, and what feeling tone and mood exudes from it.

Symbolism of the source

First another word concerning the symbolism of the source. The relationship to the giving maternal world, here at the source, is very clear: "out of Mother Earth," the symbolism of oral maternal care and thus also the maternal breast. If a serious disorder exists in the area of the source, as already stated and as I will describe it here, then one can conclude with high probability that frustrations existed for the patient in the earliest mother-child relationship and therefore in the area of oral drives. Denials and emotional gaps seem to have emerged ("oral deficit").

Signs of disorder

Not only the absence of the development of the source, but also difficulties in using the water from the source are regarded as signs of disorder. For that reason, we encourage the patient to try to drink from the source, to rub parts of his body that ache or have other disorders with the water, or even to try to dam up the water at the source so that he can bathe in it. Here, signs of disorder can appear insofar as the patient refuses to taste the water because he thinks that it is dirty, has bacteria, or could poison him. When he drinks it, the water can taste bad, unpleasant, or sour; it can be hot or extremely cold. We can see diagnostic aspects in these observations. Gradually coming to like the water, advancing in larger steps, can also possibly have therapeutic significance.

If the patient perceives water as pleasant—no matter whether at the source, a brook, a stream, a spa, or the ocean—these kinds of application can have a frequently surprising effect. Some colleagues have jokingly talked about "catathymic hydrotherapy" (Pszywyi, 1980). I myself used to smile about that. In the meantime, however, we have a larger collection of case histories in which bathing in the water or putting it on parts of the body that ache or are otherwise

Effect of bathing

afflicted has had an amazing therapeutic effect, above all, for those with psychosomatic symptoms. Observations described independently of one another about the effect of the imaginal use of water have in fact something incredible about them, and one is inclined to place such a method in the realm of magic. For us, the theoretical understanding can result from a knowledge of the previously mentioned primary process according to Freud. Here, it is not only the typical conversion symptoms of more strongly hysterically structured patients that respond to this, but very plainly psychosomatic symptoms as well, which have remained resistant to other treatments. I would like to cite a few examples in brief to illustrate this.

Case 1 (5)

Disappearance of a wart

I have G. Krapf to thank for this example.

An approximately 8-year-old girl with a large, very ugly and unpleasantly appearing wart on her thumb came to the office accompanied by her grandmother. After the usual preliminaries, the colleague begins GAI with the child and has her concentrate on a brook. She is able to do this with no difficulty. He then asks her to, in her imagination, hold the thumb with the wart in the brook for a while and to wait. He does not make any further comments and lets patient and grandmother go home. When the girl comes to the office 3 days later as prearranged, she reports that the wart dried up and dropped off, which corresponds to the outward appearance. Here, one must bear in mind that warts are, as is generally known, due to a virus, but also apparently have a psychosomatic component, for warts also disappear by "putting a spell" on them.

Case 2 (6)

I owe this case example to a colleague who took part in one of my seminars for physicians years ago and whose name I no longer remember. The physician is a specialist in internal medicine and treats his patients in a clinically oriented sanatorium. Frequently among them are cases of hyperthyroidism, thus an overactivity of the thyroid gland.

Help with a Case of Hyperthyroidism

He reports as follows: "The patient was a 30-year-old woman with hyperthyroidism, about whom the treatment with us was said to be the last attempt; otherwise we would have to transfer her to a psychiatric clinic. She cried a lot, had cardiac sensations, and could not sit up in bed. She had no organic pathological findings relating to the heart; it was all clearly psychogenic. These symptoms had existed for 5 months and the patient was unable to work. Chlorpromazine had not helped either. She had not responded at all to thyrostatic treatment. As with most of my patients, I first had her practice autogenic training. However, nothing was achieved this way either. Then I began with symboldrama. I mainly had her "picture" the source and the sea. She was always ready to go into the ocean. In reality she liked to swim a great deal too, and now in her imagination she splashed around in it spiritedly. After 20 minutes, I had to break it off, because I had the impression that otherwise she would not want to get out again. Afterward, she in any case had the feeling that she had bathed. In a manner of speaking that was a hydrotherapeutic measure. When it would not work with the ocean, I tried to dam up the spring. She experienced merely putting her legs and arms in the water as intensely refreshing, whereas this did not happen when she rested in the countryside. Water was always the most impressive thing for her. I never discussed it with her later, but simply let her experience it. Afterward I had trouble each day because she wanted to go "to the movies" again and again, as the patients called it. They definitely like to do it without further questioning. They do not find it in any way absurd and take even the funniest situations totally seriously. After six sessions, this patient had improved appreciably. After 8 days when her husband visited her, she now went for a walk with him, whereas previously she had not been able to get up out of bed. She soon drove to the mountains with him and recovered superbly. Also she now seemed to respond to the medication, which previously had had no effect. At first, of course, she apparently did not want to feel better. Whenever I used her weight gain to prove that she was recovering she would not talk about it. At the end, she thankfully accepted that she was feeling better. The surgeon, who had been called in, no longer needed to operate on her, and I was able to discontinue the thyrostatic treatment."

Commentary: If we knew to what level the basal metabolism has been increased, we could say something more definite about the dimensions of the organic disorder. With the amazing improvement and the symptoms described, a very severe psychogenic overlay must have existed.

The cases described by Pszywyj (1980) will be mentioned only briefly. The female patients were observed for several years afterward.

Case 1 (7)

Help with hyperhidrosis

1 was a woman over 70 years of age, who had a severe general hyperhidrosis and for whom all therapeutic procedures, even of a dermatological kind, had had no results. The extreme tendency to perspire made it necessary for the patient to change her underclothes several times a day. She was very annoyed by the symptom in general. Just a few sessions in GAI with bathing scenes, which in reality had taken place with her fiance during the period of her engagement, freed her from the torturing symptom almost from one moment to the next.

Case 2 (8)

Drug abuse

The second case was a depressive female student with a severe work inhibition, who misused medications and other drugs. In addition to focusing on corresponding swimming scenes in GAI, a few therapeutic dialogues were held. The outcome was that the patient did not take drugs any more, her work inhibition disappeared to a large extent, and she passed her examinations and was able to start a suitable profession.

Case 3 (9)

With Hives

The third case concerned a 9-year-old girl with recurrent hives. The symptom had existed for more than a year. Her mother had the condition also. In a few GAI sessions swimming scenes were focused upon with the two of them together, and the conflictual problems, which were brought up, were then discussed with them. After brief recurrences, the skin disorder disappeared completely (3 years post observation).

Pszywyj investigates the possible theoretical connections of these kinds of therapeutic effects, which have a physiological and for us, above all, also a psychodynamic aspect.

Pursuing the course of a brook

I now return to the *second exercise* of the *motif of the course of a brook.* As previously stated, in the ideal case the "healthy" or well- and successfully treated patient reaches the goal by traversing the brook from the source to the river and finally all the way to the mouth and the ocean. Our particular interest in this long stretch applies to the conflictual obstructive motifs, which the patient almost regularly comes across. They are of a diverse nature, to be sure, but recur in a similar manner for many patients. After following a section of the brook, it is frequently dammed up, either by a cement wall or a wall of boards or it flows into a larger pool, which has a concrete dam and prevents the outlet from being found. In this connection I recall that in his early writings Freud (1895) spoke about the "damming up of affect" in neurotic patients. The conception of the "flowing off of affects" was frequently discussed in early psychoanalysis in connection with catharsis or abreaction. Measures to make this possible were discussed and have recently also been stressed by Greenson (1967) as psychotherapeutically significant.

Obstructive motifs

Other obstructive motifs are apparent when, for instance, the water gradually seeps into the sand and the empty bed of a brook remains. Another typical situation occurs when the water in a broad stream suddenly disappears into a big hole in the ground and apparently continues flowing underground. If one then has the patient search further, the underground current possibly emerges again some distance away. I interpret this as a strong sign of a disorder in the current dynamics, when the patient finds an empty and dry bed instead of a brook, thus that water cannot be found from the start. A more subtle version of resistance in pursuing the brook's course occasionally lies in an involuntary deceptive maneuver. True to our assignment, the patient pursues the course of the brook. After a while he notices somewhat surprised that strangely enough the landscape always remains the same. The development, which we justly awaited, apparently does not proceed. Another deceptive maneuver, with which the patient naturally deceives himself, too, lies in discovering that after following the brook's course for some time he arrives at the same spot at which he had been a while ago. The brook flows in a circle, just as the patient in a way moves in a circle in his development. In both cases no long commentary need be made to the patient. He is frequently surprised himself and is prompted to think it over, when he encounters one of these contradictions. Another unnatural situation arises when the brook flows not only downward but also upward surmounting

Deceptive Maneuvers

heights; thus, the natural law of gravity is overcome in fantasy. Such a scene, which is mainly found in somewhat naive patients or those who seem childish, points to tendencies to deny reality, which these people also practice as a specific defense mechanism, usually without noticing it. In this respect the kind of obstructive motifs appearing along with the brook motif can also give us information about unusual tendencies, attitudes, and illusory expectations of a patient. On the basic level of GAI, we will not, of course, deal with this at first, but will rely upon the stated gradual spontaneous insights of the patient.

Denial of Reality

Motif of the Waterfall

We have already encountered the motif of the waterfall in one of the examples. Depending upon the extent of the neurotic disorder, this can take on extreme forms, for instance, on the way down the water can freeze into an icicle (as in the example described previously) or does not land at the bottom, because it evaporates over the long distance that it drops. Both cases seem to be signs of considerable disorders.

Aids

In the session in which we have the patient pursue the brook's course to the ocean, a long period of time usually passes even when no obstructive motifs appear. We can bypass these by staying within the general sense of the motif and at some point offering the patient a rowboat, thus enabling him to move down the river or stream faster. Finally, having arrived at the mouth to the sea, a seaport can realistically be located at the shore and bustling industrial life unfold or, on the other hand, the stream flows into a landscape extending into a broad plain. Both are realistic, although each scene has a totally different value of its own.

Motif of the Sea

At the ocean there is the possibility of offering the patient the chance to swim or to bathe. We are already familiar with the significance of this from the example of the 30-year-old patient with a thyroid disorder.

The now appearing *motif of the sea* already exceeds the competency of the basic level, as I mentioned earlier. Despite this, I would like to deal with it once more in context. Seen from the standpoint of significance, the sea is an endless reservoir of water with unfathomable depths. Its closest symbolic relationship is just as unfathomable as the sea in its expanse and its depths, *the unconscious* in general. Its size is naturally very indistinctly defined. But the dimension addressed here lies, above all, exactly in this approximation and immeasurability and unfathomableness. The sea can have a friendly quality insofar as one can swim in it. One can also dive into the depths and can come across the miracle of the sea or fairy-tale-like underworlds with the palace of a sea god, with nymphs, and much more. However, the sea can have a hostile quality, just as do all symbols, and reality as well. It can be stormy and can devour ships, which are in it, as well as persons. Its depths can also hide monsters and monstrous animals, such as huge octopuses or large hostile fish, such as the whale or the shark, which could devour him. In suited cases of neuroses the sea monsters can rise up out of the sea even *at a glance from the beach across the ocean.* The same is true of a gigantic crocodile-like creature or some type of huge fossil reptiles or monstrous fabled creatures, for instance, dragons and others, which send people into panic.

Avoid Diving

The dimensions of the unfathomable and the fear of exposing oneself to incalculable dangers prompt me emphatically to warn the therapist not to let his patient dive into the ocean until he has reached the advanced level techniques in his training. The opposite recommendation is made by the French engineer Desoille (1945) and was partly adopted by Thomas (1967) as an extension of the advanced level of autogenic training. Actually there are three reasons why I strongly advise against having the patient dive into the ocean at all, as Desoille (1945) likes to do, and especially not within the scope of the basic level techniques. Most important is the danger that the patient will meet the monstrous, archaic symbolic figures, and the therapist is neither experienced enough nor sufficiently trained to make dealing with them therapeutically productive through appropriate management models. In most cases the therapist exposes himself to greater anxieties than the patient and loses the necessary degree of confidence and advantage to guide the mental imagery. Secondly, diving, as all techniques used to forcibly penetrate to greater depths in mental imagery, contradicts the proved basic principle that the organic

Justification

development of the therapeutic process is accorded only when the material reaches the stage of being dealt with step by step, in other words the material that the psyche (the unconscious) releases from the surface automatically and without arousing any anxieties. Techniques that distinctly "probe" the depths run the risk, however, of activating not only anxieties but diverse defense mechanisms and repressive tendencies in general, from which the patient must first protect himself. In a pronounced case this can lead to prolonged transference resistances that undermine the patient's trust in the therapist or force him into a dependent position because he feels manipulated by the therapist. For this reason, these kinds of forced techniques, which cut into deep layers of the unconscious, run counter to the relaxed and cooperative style of guidance especially cultivated in GAI. Finally, the therapeutic results of the techniques in question here are if not negative then rarely more productive or more far-reaching than the mental imagery work with the unfolding material in the range of the spontaneously appearing "surface" of the imaginal scenery. The fact that patients themselves occasionally express the wish or even insist upon diving does not contradict these arguments. The way patients treat themselves is frequently determined by neurotic impatience, forced actions, even pronounced self-destruction and masochistic submission. In this respect the patient himself is therefore by no means always his best advisor in connection with managing mental imagery.

Spontaneous Behavioral Tendencies

Elsewhere (Leuner, 1983) I dealt with this problem on a larger scale and tried to show that the therapist must also reflect upon and control the patient's spontaneous behavioral tendencies and actions.

With this, I naturally do not want to exclude the possibility that in certain cases and under certain circumstances, a diving excursion by the patient can be productive and that the stated dangers do not always have to be connected with it. *However, the therapy with the basic level technique is definitely directed toward security and protection* in the interest not only of the patient but also of the therapist. Moreover, these kinds of "depth research" always have something terrifying or severely confrontational about them, if the whole area is not repressed by the patient from the start and the corresponding encounters of an archaic kind do not take place at all. Discovering wrecks and investigating them is likewise problematical.

Reply to a Question

Genetic Metaphors

Seminar participant: "Do you also attach biographical importance to the path along the brook, upstream or downstream?"

Answer: One could naturally consider that. However, I have hardly gained evident illustrative material, for instance, that detailed conflictual material from the past is released on the path upstream to the source. Only in the area of the source motif does conflictual material seem to appear embedded in strong symbolism, which belongs to the oral realm of the relationship to the mother. I mentioned that previously when I spoke about the various negative qualities of the water at the source, which the patient lists and for that reason perhaps also refuses to taste the water. Incidentally, it has always impressed me that the path upstream is usually followed in a more carefree fashion than it is downstream. If one looks for material indicating early childhood conflicts, one usually has more success with the house motif, especially if one has the patient find and empty out trunks and crates in the cellar of the house, still to be discussed. Children's old toys or family albums can be found, and various memories can be reawakened by this. However, biographical material appears even more frequently and more immediately spontaneously or when guided, if at important conflictual points of symboldrama the image suddenly skips and the same theme is almost realistically faded-in in the form of a childhood experience (age regression). This recourse to the genesis of important conflicts is taught and practiced within the scope of the intermediate level.

Session Eight: Third Standard Motif: The Mountain

Focusing on the Motif

Today I come to the *third training motif* of the basic level, the *mountain.* Seen from the technical aspect, the mountain motif can be focused upon in two different ways. The first and shorter method mainly concerns observing and exactly describing the mountain from a distance; the second is climbing the mountain. The latter begins directly in the meadow starting out from a path that will lead to the summit. Oddly enough, the mountain frequently appears differently during these sightings. The reason for this can scarcely be determined. I will begin with the first approach, *viewing the mountain from the distance.* The technical instructions to the patient can begin directly with the following announcement, "Please, try to imagine a mountain (which you are looking at from the distance)." Usually difficulties scarcely arise here for the patient who is somewhat familiar with GAI. Perhaps various forms of mountains appear at first. The patient is urged to talk about this and to wait until a decision is spontaneously made when one of the mountains comes to the fore. However, the other mountain forms should be registered and briefly sketched on a piece of paper, perhaps directly after the session.

Description

I have the patient describe the mountain that finally took form, as usual very precisely regarding the form, its height (with estimated specifications in meters), whether it is forested, of what material it is made, whether it is covered with snow, all in categories that the patient usually describes spontaneously. If he leaves gaps, the therapist asks about them. The especially important question at the end refers to the possibility of climbing the mountain or rather, whether the patient himself would dare to undertake the climb.

Examples

The ideal healthy person or the patient who has been in successful therapy usually describes a mountain of average height up to 1000 meters, forested, perhaps with a rock peak, which he believes he will be able to reach, although perhaps with some difficulty and effort and have a panorama from there. Examples of shapes of mountains, which we find with neurotic patients and which thus represent more or less pronounced forms of disturbance are as follows. The mountain is only a hill, perhaps only a mass of sand or a heap of snow, or, the contrary, the mountain is extremely tall and covered with snow and glaciers. I will come back to this point again. The mountain is made of paper-maché, out of sheer rock, possibly smooth and shiny or polished marble so that it cannot be climbed. It has the configuration of a triangle. Due to its steep walls and because there is no path (zigzag) it is likewise impossible to climb (we frequently find these kinds of mountain formations in adolescents or immature persons).

Gestalt qualities of the mountain

As elsewhere in the description of the natural scenes in GAI, we encourage the patient to describe the kind of atmosphere that emanates from the mountain, that is, how the mountain "immediately and naively impresses him." The patient who has some practice is usually capable of formulating this in terms of the gestalt qualities (technical term from Gestalt psychology). He says, for instance, it impresses him as being "sharp and jagged, but unapproachable," or "lying there broad, massive, and inert like an enormous immovable mass" or, for instance, "lofty, projecting, dominating (because it is situated on a wide plain), but at the same time unapproachable, massive, and awe-inspiring."

Why do I place such great value upon the description of these qualities and of its form and other characteristics of the mountain? I cannot go into detail about the important theoretical positions in this practice-oriented seminar, so must remain brief. If we take the qualities of a mountain described in the last three examples, especially in the last case, one can easily apply these characteristics to a person, or, stated the other way round, the patient describes the mountains with adjectives that one commonly applies to people. That has a good result, of course, because the most diverse parts of natural scenery can, in fact, be unconscious representations of early referential figures. Focusing on the landscape motifs in GAI makes possible their strongly cryptic, symbolic disguise. At another point (Leuner, 1983) I examined these scenic representations critically and in detail. The relationship mentioned here will become immediately obvious to you, when I tell you that the description of the mountain cited last stems from a manager in industry, whom I asked, on the basis of these qualities, if he could also possibly apply them to a person whom he had already encountered in his life. After thinking about this briefly, he associated Adenauer with them. For him Adenauer's personality embodied an outstanding, quasi-rigid, unbending, but enormously successful leading figure. Further associations to persons with analogous characteristics then led to male models further back in his life, who had apparently played a decisive part in his formation of ideals (superego), although from the standpoint of his natural disposition he himself was a rather soft, more emotional, and intellectually contemplative type, who believed he had to gain the stated qualities for himself to do justice to his position of leadership.

Symbolic representation

Mountain as object representation

The mountain motif in the form appearing here is a particularly good model, through which the object representations can easily be made evident, that is, the reflection of the closest referential figures from early childhood, in the form of scenic configurations. The same also applies analogously to the brook motif, frequently to the motif of the house, to the source, and also to a single tree or to a cluster of trees as an association of people (family). Naturally, however, it would be too unilinear and would not correspond to the true relationships in depth psychological symbolism, if one started from the assumption that all mountains always related to the male-paternal world and all springs to the female-maternal world. The relationships are far more complex, and I can only repeatedly warn against this kind of simple, one-to-one correlation. Mountains, trees, streams, and many other formations can also belong to the female-maternal world without regularly having a connection to the patient's own mother. I refer again to the chapter already mentioned in the major textbook about GAI (Leuner, 1983).

Nevertheless, from this example of the mountain motif, it becomes very clear what answer we must give to the occasionally asked question, where are the referential figures and the encounters with them, so important to the person's maladjustment, actually represented in the basic level of GAI. Here we deliberately avoid stepping away from the level of symbolic disguise and having the persons appear in their actual form on the stage of symboldrama within the scope of the basic level techniques. They are not lost in spite of this, but are manifested in the landscape motifs, and the patient's actions within the scenery depict confrontations with them in the stated cryptic form. The same is true for the encounters with animals or other symbolic figures. This will be discussed within the framework of the edge of the woods motif. What is remarkable here, however, is that the patient's mere actions in the scenery contain precisely such confrontations with referential persons of early childhood and have astounding therapeutic effectiveness. Finally, I must emphasize that considering the landscape motifs as expressing representations of referential persons is naturally only one interpretation, and conforming to the nature of depth psychological symbols in general, they are multiply determined and therefore have more than one meaning.

Metaphors of the landscape

Female-maternal representation

With this short digression into the theory of depth psychological symbols, I wanted at the same time to illustrate to you an important meaning of the mountain motif. If we look at the form of the mountains, there are naturally also some that are characterized by a rounded summit or whose profile reminds one of, for instance, a seated or a reclining girl, from which one can plainly guess the object representation of the female-maternal world. An extraordinary situation is ultimately signified when, instead of a mountain, an entire massif appears and is possibly constructed in the form of a ring around a deep circular valley in the middle of which the patient is standing. From this, one will conclude that the person involved feels virtually crushed or encircled by the paternal-masculine world, which he can scarcely penetrate.

Climbing the Mountain

Now I come to the second technical aspect of the mountain motif, *climbing the mountain,* and will again take up the problem of representations in this context.

We give the patient instructions, after the meadow has been focused upon, for example, "Please, look around (in the meadow). Perhaps you can find a trail somewhere or just a little path." That usually works quickly. After the patient answers in the positive, we ask him to follow the trail. We tell him in advance that it will lead him through a forest and then up to the mountain, from whose summit he will have a panoramic view. Usually the patient can also follow this trail in his imaginings, which then actually leads him to the summit of a mountain in the predicted manner. This simple instruction at the beginning of the path and the prediction connected with it thus constitute an entire scenic development, which is then, of course, individually arranged in its details by the patient in projective fashion. This refers to the path itself, its surroundings, and the scenery of the ascent in all its phases, the position on the summit and finally also the panorama with all of its details, which are created by his unconscious dynamics. That is, of course, true not only for the neurotically ill, but also for healthy persons. The ideal so-called healthy person or successfully treated patient can generally follow the path without difficulty. He actually wanders through a forest and across moderate inclines, gradually reaching a moderately high mountain. On its summit, he will find a spot from which he has a panoramic view in all directions. In this by no means rare, ideal case even the weather is nice; he has a full view and the customary landscape stretches out in front of him with ordered fields and villages, country roads, and people at work. In the distance he may recognize a city with factories and will make out a river or a lake, perhaps catch sight of the ocean or see a mountain range on the horizon. If the panorama turns out in this way without being restricted in any direction, for instance, and if the climb proceeds without overly great difficulties in the manner described, one can conclude that the person in question has no serious difficulties in the complex of problems raised by this motif.

Panorama

Meaning

We first turn to the *meaning of this motif.* If we analyze it more precisely, it quickly becomes obvious that it is divided into three components, each of which has a different quality of meaning. The *first component* concerns the *ascent* itself. The patient is thus given a task, which he can refuse to carry out. That only happens in the rarest of cases, however. If we simply start from the linguistic expression, which is always to be recommended when searching for the meaning, then we speak of "ascent." The word has several meanings. First of all, one is reminded that ascending can be connected with the idea of a career in the sense of proof of success in the professional field, for example, mastery of the tasks of professional training, the tasks, which people are faced with in life in general, especially if it is a matter of a still relatively young to middle-aged patient. He sees a part of his current task in proving himself in life and in mastering everyday life as well as in the long path through the

Mastery of a Task

stations of professional development. One is familiar with the saying in reference to everyday life, "Today stands before me like a tall mountain." In this respect the ascent of the mountain can signify the equivalent of mastering a task. We often set these tasks for ourselves. Many people set high or extremely high tasks for themselves; others are content with an intermediate level and consequently also have fewer problems in this area. In a very thorough study made by the psychologist Kornadt (1958), a highly significant correlation resulted between the height of the mountain and the level of aspiration of the person imagining. People who make exacting demands upon themselves, thus often especially ambitious people, imagine a tall mountain that is troublesome and difficult to climb. However, even the path or the peculiar features of the climb in the first place, the steepness of the individual sections, the necessity of climbing perhaps with full climbing gear, is worth noting. In addition, whether the patient locates an easy path, such as for strolling, or is soon worn out and must rest frequently are all contents indicating the way in which the patient is accustomed to solving tasks and attaining his goals. For example, I am thinking of the group of particularly zealous people ready for action at all times, who do not need to be invited to climb the mountain; when they catch sight of a nearby mountain in GAI, they start to climb it without being asked. It is an entirely different situation, if on the way to the mountain someone repeatedly spots a bench every few hundred meters, where he has to sit down exhausted and take a rest. In contrast, people who are very achievement oriented and ready for action, often imagine climbing conditions for which they have to rope themselves up, climb through chimneys, and put themselves through a lot of strain in order finally to reach a rocky summit cliff. It is, of course, particularly unfortunate and depressing at the same time, if after a strenuous climb like that, someone "loses his way in the mountains," can go neither frontward nor backward and requires the therapist's help to get back on the right path or to get down.

Level of aspiration

Obstructive motifs

Other disturbances of the ascent can lie in the following situations. The path is muddy and the patient repeatedly slips, or the path does not lead up a mountain at all, but, as I experienced with a depressed patient, corresponding to his mood of resignation, led deeper and deeper into a dark forest, from which he scarcely found his way out. Another distinctive feature can be the avoidance of the ascent altogether. Particularly hysterically structured patients have enough imagination to skip over the toilsome, step by step ascent to surprise the therapist with "already having reached the top." I also experienced such a denial of reality in a patient, who from her panoramic view of the landscape all around saw only solid clouds enshrouding the earth. In reality, she also seemed to live literally in "cloudland." Other obstructive motifs during the ascent are, for instance, trees blocking the way, deep ditches cutting through the path, or the

Avoidance

patient suddenly becomes afraid in the dark forest and asks permission to turn around.

Ascent = Identification

At this point I would again like to return to the *meaning of the mountain* as a representation of an important referential figure, frequently from the paternal world. Seen from this standpoint climbing the mountain is the equivalent of *identification with* an important *father figure* in the life of the person. In reaching the summit of the mountain the patient places himself to a certain extent in the position awarded to the father. This interpretation can be clearly derived from the psychodynamic experience of psychoanalysis. Accordingly, the son has in principle the need to put his own masculine role to the test and to occupy it by identifying with a father figure. We know very well how difficult it is, for example, for sons of prominent men "to make something of themselves," to "hold a candle" to their father for once, that is, to occupy an analogous position through identification. In the early period in which I was still experimenting a great deal with GAI, I experienced a particularly vivid example of a mountain taking on the paternal-masculine representation, with the *ascent of this mountain* bringing along with it the *confrontation with the father image.* Here the identification was also apparently successful, as I was able to conclude from the fast therapeutic response of the patient. I am citing the example in abbreviated form and have described it in detail elsewhere (Leuner, 1983) because it has a key to understanding this problem of identification.

Case 1 (10)

Example

Using hypnosis, I had treated an 18-year-old adolescent due to severe stuttering, which had existed for 4 years. At that time I was still a young assistant and a little proud that I had succeeded in considerably improving the generally very persistent speech disorder in this manner. A trace of the speech disorder had, however, remained. Characteristically, it always emerged when the patient wanted to speak at the dinner table in the presence of his father or at his position as an apprentice in the presence of the master craftsman. It required no great psychodynamic interpretive skill to conclude that a residue of his problems with authority figures, which he had not yet come to terms with, still remained. The patient felt he could not assert himself in comparison to the father figures, whom he perceived to be outstanding. Based upon my knowledge of the possible meaning of the mountain, I gave the patient the motif of climbing a mountain in GAI. He imagined the type of "triangular mountain" already mentioned and was able to climb it, expending some effort on a zigzag path. While viewing the panorama from the summit, he caught sight of a higher and considerably more massive, broadly situated mountain on the other side of the valley, on whose summit stood a huge observation tower. Nothing was more obvious than the assumption that the mountain he climbed corresponded to the level of accomplishment that he himself had to perform, particularly since this one, when measured by substance, was considerably inferior to the mountain across the way. It seemed to be equally obvious that the massive mountain with the strong tower on the summit, that typical Freudian symbol for masculinity, represented for him the paternal-authoritarian world. From this I formed the following hypothesis. If I succeeded in having the patient climb the fatherly mountain with its tower, a change in his relationship to the paternal authorities should come about. I directed him accordingly. Wandering through the valley and climbing the massive, great, and tall mountain succeeded, although with difficulties, as did climbing the tower. At the last moment, a threatening thunderstorm also came up, which made him anxious and due to which he certainly would not have climbed the tower without my encouragement. He seemed proud of his accomplishment, which I commented on somewhat positively. Of course, I had not undertaken any interpretations whatsoever, and the patient could not consciously know (but perhaps suspect) that he had come to terms with the paternal-authoritarian representation. When the patient came to my office again 3 days later, he spontaneously reported that the trace of his speech disorder no longer existed and that he could speak clearly and freely both in the presence of his father and his master teacher and was also able to assert himself courageously in a confrontation. From this I drew the conclusion that my previously made hypothesis was correct. The successful ascent of the mountain representing the paternal world, the occupation of the paternal position in the sense of identification with the father, had been with my help a symbolic confrontation with the powerfully appearing father. This strengthened his ego and eliminated the rest of his aggressive inhibition.

Example Demonstrating the Contrary

I had a contrasting experience with opposite portents with the manager previously mentioned who ascribed the attributes of a prominent personality "like Adenauer" to the mighty, solitary mountain. He considered this mountain to be absolutely unsurmountable in spite of small aids that I offered him. Then I made the following test. I made him the offer of flying to the summit by helicopter, to which he hesitantly gave his consent. Having finally arrived up there, a raw wind was blowing. He felt extremely uneasy and could not perceive the panorama properly, not to mention enjoy it. All of these were clear signs that my transference offer could not be taken up by the patient.

Proof of Correlation with Level of Aspiration

In order to make the psychological problem prevailing here even clearer to you, I would like to cite a brief supplemental example. I once treated a quite gifted physics student, who had a severe obsessive-compulsive neurosis with desperate depressive moods and anxiety states as well. While focusing on the mountain motif, he turned down the climb from the start. He had suddenly flown to the summit of an, as he said, 10,000 meter high mountain and hovered some meters above its peak. During the attempt to view the panorama he recognized a lone wanderer in a valley. I had him study the man's features more carefully by using an imagined pair of binoculars. To his own astonishment, he spontaneously said that the man looked like Albert Einstein. It becomes clear to a very convincing degree that the young man was expressing his elevated level of aspiration and his extremely ambitious attitude with the extremely and supernaturally high mountain. His professional ideal in his fantasies, which he also admitted later, consisted in someday becoming a "second Einstein."

Ego-ideal

We thus see in brief that in the last two examples the mountain motif does not portray the representation of real father images, with whom identification is nevertheless possible, but of masculine-paternal ideal figures of unattainable prominence, such as Albert Einstein and Konrad Adenauer. The abysmal problems with self-esteem that these people have can only be guessed at from the formation of an excessively high ideal. In psychotherapy in practice, dealing with the ideal conceptions and the excessive demands put on the person by himself (superego) plays an important part in the analysis of the character disorder in such cases as these. However, that can only be the task of a fully trained therapist, who can work through the character structures with advanced techniques.

To conclude this section about the mountain motif, I must also mention that in the course of a longer therapy with GAI, one must naturally consider what additional possibilities the persons concerned have with their mountain motifs, that perhaps have more realistic elements. For example, one patient demonstrated the discrepancy regarding her standard of accomplishment in the following different portrayals of the mountain. She first "saw" a very tall, steep, and rocky mountain, which she was only able to climb with the greatest effort. Subsequent to this, a small, 30 meter high, grass-covered hill appeared, which she was able to climb very easily but from which she could not have a panoramic view.

Session Nine: Continuation of the Third Motif: The Mountain

Panorama

I now come to the *second component of the mountain motif,* the *panorama.* After climbing the mountain, the panorama is in a manner of speaking the reward for the pains and effort expended. We now glimpse the world from an entirely different perspective than usual. Although we are standing up there precariously, possibly alone, we are at the same time more intensely exposed to the inclemencies of weather, such as wind, storms, and cold. However, the panorama gives us the dimensions of the broad view of the landscape, in our case of the catathymic panorama, which one could also term a "psychic landscape" in technical professional jargon.* Although we are removed from the earth and the details have become smaller, the dimension of distance and expanse, of the spacious overview of the structures of this landscape as far as the horizon, can literally be taken in at a glance. Besides the current use of an airplane or the transformation into a flying bird in GAI, these dimensions can only be grasped by means of the panoramic view from the summit of the mountain. The various experiments that have been made with GAI in the course of decades have made us familiar with some normally frequent occurrences in the panorama. Our first interest applies to the question, whether the patient in this position actually has a view on all four sides. It is significant among the signs of a disorder whether the view is obstructed on one or more sides at once, such as by rocks, trees, or whatever. We therefore have the patient describe these possibilities to us and at the same time observe what the patient can recognize when he looks back (opposite to the point from which he climbed the summit), as well as to the front and to the right and left. Here the view to the back usually stands for the past, to the front, for the expectations of the future, to the right as understood in right-left symbolism accentuates the direction of cognitive, rational, and also masculine attitude, and to the left, accentuates the emotional and also feminine attitude. However, I have become cautious about drawing precise conclusions from this.

Catathymic panorama

Signs of Disorder

Synchronic Transformation in the Therapeutic Process

Another particularly noticeable regular occurrence is the transformation of the landscape in the course of the therapeutic process (synchronic transformation). The panorama in the early phase of a therapy frequently shows scenic images, which correspond to early spring, thus, for instance, a landscape as it appears in March or April. If we repeat the mountain climb at greater intervals in the course of therapy lasting 20 to 30 hours, the landscape gradually changes from spring through summer into the harvest season with fields of yellow grain. An

---

* See Leuner (1959).

enrichment of the scenic images almost regularly takes place parallel to this. It increasingly shows more evidence of human activity and of a structuring of nature. The first becomes obvious as people increasingly work in the fields and villages and cities become visible, even a large city in the distance. Streets, superhighways, and high-voltage utility lines stretch across the countryside, and initially desolate parts of nature are cultivated more and more. The second becomes obvious when the countryside becomes more fertile, above all, more rivers or lakes emerge, perhaps there is a glimpse of the ocean, extremely high mountains or mountain chains become lower and the eye can roam farther into the distance. This development of the catathymic panorama seems to indicate that the psyche registers in the *change of the seasons* an *unconscious* self-assessment in experiencing the advancing therapeutic process and reflects it in this way. The greater development and enrichment of the ego apparently appears in the increasing animation, with a reduction of rigid defensive structures. The expanding creative unfolding of the ego is connected with this. It lies parallel to the expansion of the radius of action of the patient's actual behavior as he gradually overcomes his neurosis. It goes without saying that there are limits to this and far longer treatment periods must be envisaged until this process is complete in cases of pronounced personality disorders. However, the synchronism between the transformation of the catathymic panorama when looking down from the mountain and the advancing therapeutic process is unmistakable and could also be subjected to precise, quantifiable investigation, as we have already done in another connection (Prindull, 1964; Stamm, 1983).

Quantitative Record

Cartographic Sketches

Another way to compare objectively the catathymic panorama with respect to the view from the mountain is to have the patient make quasicartographic sketches (after the GAI session), as a patient did in Figure 1. After the patient undergoes an an intensive psychotherapy, he is instructed as follows. "Imagine the Mediterranean landscape again, which we saw the last time from a dome-shaped cliff." The result is shown in Figure 2.

Symbolism of the Panorama

To illustrate this further, I would like to reproduce the example of a panorama, which comes from a 42-year-old single woman who came into treatment with me because of tension headaches. After I had given her the mountain motif, having started from the meadow, she had to climb up a steep zigzag path through a dark forest to the mountain summit. She sensed anxiety temporarily with the feeling that the forest might never end. Here I encouraged her a little, reassuring her that she should go on and that the woods would finally come to an end, which she was relieved to find happened. Having reached the summit, she had a panoramic view. Mountain chains stretched out in front of her, which shifted the view onto the distant landscape. Behind them the evening sun was setting, creating a

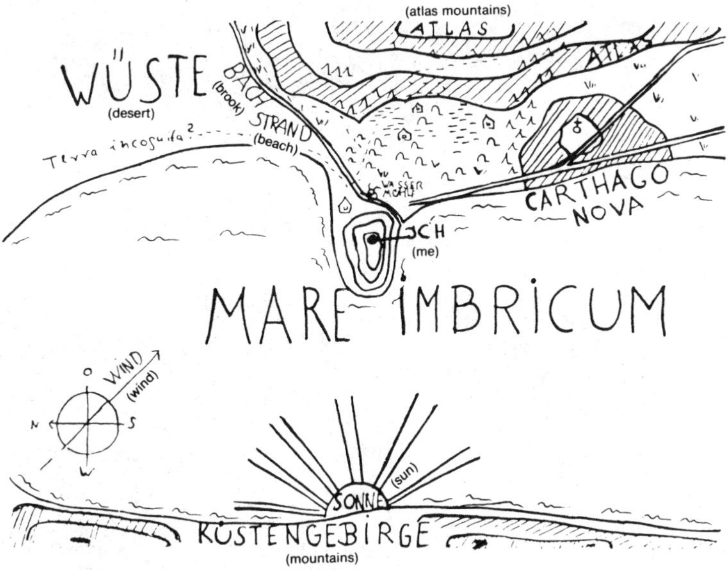

Fig. 1. A patient's cartographic sketch of the landscape he viewed from the summit of the mountain he had climbed in his imagination. He is standing on a hot, dome-shaped cliff, with Mediterranean vegetation, which juts far out into the sea. To the front he looks to the lowlands, which are carefully cultivated, irrigated, and divided into lots. To the left, the ocean breaks in shallow waves, and he sees the white spray. An unexplored broad sand desert without vegetation stretches out to the left. To the right, on the other hand, a larger city with square, white houses, cypresses, and a mosque with minarets lies along the ocean. On the horizon in front of him there is a dark, tall mountain range, possibly the Atlas. Behind it, a rocky area with a volcano filled with water drops off sharply. In the haze in the distance is the ocean, which he cannot quite see and behind which he suspects a high coastal range.
(From H. Leuner: The landscape image as a metaphor of dynamic structires. In: Stolze H., (ed): Physician in the Realm of Experience, Publication in Honor of Ernst Speer. Lehmann, Munich, 1959.)

flaming red sky. Looking to the rear, she saw a city far away and tree-covered valleys with small villages to both sides. I interpreted the rarely occurring sunset in this patient, who was nearing menopause and had fallen in love with a man late in her life, as an indication of her fear of the approaching decline of her feminine capacity to love. The shift of the view to the front through the mountain chains indicates that aspects of the future seem incalculable, whereas the view to the back to the city (as "center of life") can be judged more positively. The city can also be a symbol belonging to the maternal realm (the patient lived with her mother and was very attached to her, she gave her "support").

The described example of a panoramic view shows the signs of various individual problems of the patient. However, I would

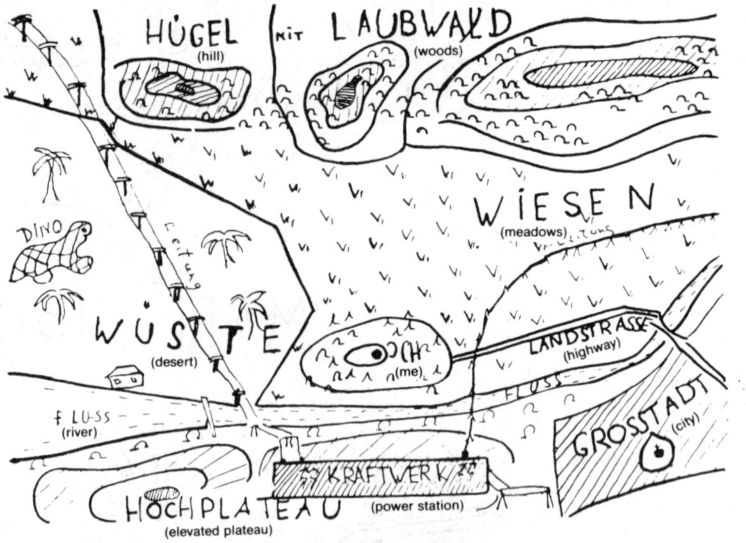

Fig. 2. Transformation of the landscape image (panorama from the mountain) in comparison to Figure 1 after intensive psychotherapy. "The mountain, on which I am now standing, has shrunk in comparison to the one in the previous drawing. The volcano has disappeared, and the ocean behind it is now only a brook flowing quickly and clearly behind me. A park landscape covering the slopes of the hill separates me from the brook. The sand desert stretches out to the left, where the water becomes wider. On an expedition there, I discover the house of a military guard and a power line, which comes from a power station situated to the south. I catch sight of a dinosaur and a few palm trees. Now there are hills covered with trees, through which footpaths cut, where the Atlas was before. To the right of where I am standing, there is again a large city, which now, however, has a more European quality. The river can be crossed by bridges, and also to the right there is a power line coming from the power station. With the help of a telescope, attached to my stand, I can bring the details in closer." (From H. Leuner: The Landscape Image as a Metaphor of dynamic structures. In: Stolze H, (ed): Physician in the Realm of Experience, Pubication in Honor of Ernst Speer. Lehmann, Munich, 1959).

Comments: The extraordinary change in the cartographically recorded landscape cannot be overlooked when the two illustrations are compared. The ocean has shrunk to a brook, the Atlas reduced to hills, and a more European landscape has arisen. The city has been Europeanized, the streets, a power plant, and people indicate the development of the appropriate life in the landscape. The desert also shows the first signs of life, even if in a somewhat peculiar manner. It seems to be better defined, no longer "terra incognita." The power lines are noteworthy as an indication of experiencing energy and strength. Altogether there appears a change from the oriental-romantic, in many respects unclearly explored genre with strong extremes between sea and desolate mountains, to the central European image familiar to us, of activities of man, who makes the land his own, just to very roughly work out a few characteristics of synchronic transformation (see p.113) of this patient's panorama.

not assess them as all too serious and would make the prognosis that treatment with the basic level is definitely possible. (However, as far as the symptom of chronic headaches is concerned, the experienced therapist knows that it is quite resistant to psychotherapy. Therefore the goal of treatment in such a case will lie more in dealing with existing psychic problems than in the expectation of being able decisively to influence the psychosomatic symptom. This comment in passing seems important to me so that no misunderstanding arises.

Signs of Disorder in the Panorama

How do distinctly pathological, that is, severely neurotic, signs of conflict and disorder look in the arrangement of the panoramic view from the mountain? The situation is particularly serious, if a view is not possible in any direction, for instance, due to forested areas on all sides or because of rocky cliffs on the summit. Perhaps the view only opens up on one side, which also represents a considerable limitation. In assessing the signs of disturbance we must additionally consider the landscapes that the concerned persons describe. The situation rarely arises in which the patients only look down on clouds or the scene is too hazy to be able to perceive any details. In judging the manifesting landscapes we start from the expectation that patients from our latitudes usually picture a landscape as described previously. Exotic landscapes, for instance of an endlessly wide savanna or desert stretching out or other uncultivated land, also signify problems, such as the situation in which the mountain summit, which has been reached, lies in the middle of other prominent peaks. With regard to the desert motif, I refer the reader to Figure 1. Moreover from his relatively low mountain, the patient catches sight of the massive Atlas mountains as an adversary. The scene has fundamentally changed in Figure 2. The desert shows the first signs of plant and animal life, is divided up by a power line (energy), the high Atlas mountains have become a hill, and finally the ocean has shrunk to a river. In other words, the first image shows far more pathological structures than the second. From this it becomes clear in what form the landscape seen from the mountain can change in the course of therapy.

For a neurotic situation in general, it is also characteristic that a patient sees forests stretching out in all directions without the least hint of settlements, streets, or other evidence of human activity. If one starts with the hypothesis that forests are symbolically concerned, among other things, with the unconscious, thus unclarified and at first also cognitively inaccessible areas, this scene can be freely compared with the inner situation of a patient at the beginning of psychotherapy.

However, the therapist will direct his attention not only to these marked deviations but will take note of all of the finer details described by the patient and will perhaps be able to gather ideas relating to them. I am thinking, for instance, of a young female patient, who stood on the dome of a mountain in front of a large, mighty tower made of stone, which took all of her energy to climb but without which she could not have a panoramic view. At the same time, however, a little booth was located at the end of the tower with a woman selling souvenirs, who made, on the one hand, a very friendly and kind impression, but on the other hand, seemed to radiate the untiring joy in working that her own mother had, which until then she had perceived as more oppressive than helpful.

Descent

I now come to the *third part of the mountain motif, the descent.* At first one may think that the descent from the mountain is relatively unproblematical, merely a return to the fields from which the patient originally came. Actually, that is true in the predominant number of cases. When we have the impression that the patient has stopped at the summit long enough, enjoyed and described the panorama or perhaps when he himself feels compelled to climb down, because the weather is unfriendly, we leave the choice up to him whether he wants to use the same path or a different one. In any case I consider it important not to end the session before the patient has again arrived on the ground at the bottom in his imaginal world. We can ask him to return to the starting point. Usually he does this of his own accord.

Signs of Disorder

For many patients, however, *the descent* is problematical. We already know from reality that walking or climbing down is often more difficult and more laborious than climbing up. Some patients, in my opinion, especially those already mentioned with a high level of aspiration, do not like to climb down, encounter various difficulties in so doing, and find this exercise strenuous. The simplest explanation for this probably lies in the frequent use of the word "descent" in figurative speech, for instance, as social decline, giving up a higher position, and rarely, even as moral decline. For some patients, leaving the mountain peak is even the equivalent of returning to the harder side of daily life, with its banalities, to a world in which there is often friction. For them, the view from the summit can be experienced as relieving and especially liberating, the return being the opposite. On the summit another group of patients feels exposed, unwell, and separated from the world of people and finds it pleasant to return to the world of human dwellings, their warmth and their togetherness. The therapist will register all of these impulses, perhaps also ask the patient about his respective feelings before beginning the descent, if he senses that the patient is hesitating or beginning the descent noticeably hastily. If possible, we have the patient describe details of the landscape through which the path leads and pay attention to whether the patient perhaps ignores the descent by skipping over the actual situation (as hysterically structured patients like to do) and suddenly announces, "I am already at the bottom."

Return

No matter where the patient ultimately arrives (frequently it is the meadow from where he started out), we have him describe

Signs of Change

the surroundings for us if possible. Then we often encounter the previously described phenomenon of *synchronic transformation.* The original meadow (which can best be compared to the meadow motif before the ascent was started), or another landscape has very frequently changed in smaller details or in larger characteristics. Typical descriptions are, for example, the following. The grass in the meadow is taller now, and more new flowers are discovered, the weather has improved, the countryside has become more expansive and spacious, or many other characteristics become obvious, from which one gets the impression that they have a more positive accent compared with the initial position. From this we believe we can conclude that completing the climb and viewing the panorama have had an influence upon the patient's unconscious experiential structures, so-to-speak, as a minimal step in the desired direction of therapeutic development. Formulated in depth psychological terms, the successful ascent is equivalent to a strengthening of the ego, a degree of self-confirmation, as long as the climb has ultimately been experienced as positive. If the reverse is true, this will also show up as synchronic transformation in the initial motif with signs of the reverse. However, that is relatively rare and can be regarded as a sign of serious disorder in the area of the need for expansion and accomplishment correlating with the mountain motif, or of problems with competition.

Strengthening of the Ego

In the practical work with symboldrama, the therapist comes across *synchronic transformation* in the most diverse places. It can be useful to him to confirm that the therapeutic process is advancing at this point. You should not overestimate its significance, however, since it only indicates the smallest initial steps.

Therapeutic Meaning of the Mountain Motif

I have deliberately presented the mountain motif in full breadth, because it is extremely important and the climb up the mountain should be focused upon every now and then at longer intervals. If this does not happen, we give the patient the option of excluding the problem of competition and achievement to be dealt with, for example, due to inner resignation, depressive passivity, or a problem with the masculine-paternal world that has not been resolved. On the other hand, the motif of the mountain climb also cannot be forced upon this group of patients, and we must give positive feedback even for small successes. It will have become clear that this motif potentially demands a lot of time and takes up an entire session.

Session Ten: The Final Two Standard Motifs of the Basic Level: House, Edge of the Woods

Fourth motif: the house.

Conflictual Material

The house is a very diverse motif, which also requires much time to deal with, sometimes even two sessions, and frequently involves varied and serious conflictual material. For this reason, the house motif should not be used until the patient has become familiar with symboldrama and the therapist has the impression that he can be expected to handle a certain amount of strain. At the same time, one can also say that, with the exception of very severely disturbed patients, the persons have enough ego strength and defensive possibilities to protect themselves from the penetration of conflictual material to an extent that they can also cope with it. Occasionally, the house motif initially remains relatively uncharacteristic and uninformative due to increased defenses and must be repeated now and then.

Metaphor for the Individual Person

To understand the house motif, it is important, as for all the standard motifs, to be acquainted with its meaning, at least in a general, more collective respect. It is certainly broad and diverse, as are all symbols. According to our previous experience, however, the house is rather predominantly experienced by the patients as a *representation of their own person* or one of its parts. What is meant is that structures are expressed in the house motif in which the patient perceives himself emotionally, as well as his wishes, preferences, defensiveness, and anxieties in various areas. As in all mental imagery and night dreams, *realistically founded "truths"* are *not* reflected in their contents, but rather the fact of how the person *experiences* and assesses this symbolized psychic part *emotionally in the present moment.* Particularly with the house motif, the specific current mood can be a contributing factor in determining its prominence, which is analogous to the meadow motif. Another symbolic element is the fact that we ask the patient to enter the house, which on another level can also be experienced from the male perspective as a motif of introitus, thus of sexual penetration into the female body. To me this version seems to apply rarely and has not convinced me much, as this motif usually reflects various aspects of the *patient's own behavioral tendencies.*

Introjects

Generally, it is amazing how rarely persons are found in the house. If that is the case, however, and if the same ones are always there when the motif is repeatedly focused upon, it indicates a strong attachment to the persons in the sense of the psychoanalytic theory of introjects, that is, that he has not yet separated from an important referential person "included" in his ego and superego or he has not fully assimilated him yet. I also recall a dramatic scene described elsewhere (Leuner, 1980). In the treatment of an adult woman, who as the mother of three children had to come to terms with life on her own, the grandmother was for a long period stereotypically found in one room of her house. In the patient's childhood she had played an important part, decisive to the fate of the entire family. My attempt during one mental imagery session, together with the patient, to turn her out of the house, led to an unexpected dramatic reaction in the patient. For me it was not only a striking indication of the level of involvement in the catathymic images, but also clearly showed that the house is grasped as the patient's own ego and persons in it as introjected portions of the ego. To give them up, to separate from them, and to become independent requires a longer personality-structure-changing therapy, such as is familiar to us from psychoanalysis, too.

Technique of Focusing on the Motif

Technically, we proceed by directly asking the patient to imagine a house. We avoid any specifications and wait to see what kind of house appears. The technique of using an opportunity in which the patient encounters a house on his own while walking from the meadow or somewhere else is more polished. Then the systematic directions again begin with the request to describe the house from the outside, not forgetting to have him also portray the surroundings in which the house is located. For instance, a garden is examined with regard to its condition and also the mood radiating from the scene in accordance with our professional bent for detail. (However, let me repeat that not all patients are prepared to do this without further ado and perceive too many questions about details as disturbing, so that the desired descriptions of details only become possible in the course of further development of the GAI therapy and under the influence of the learning process that the patient goes through during it.)

It is also advantageous to ask the patient to look at the house from the back. Here, one can come across surprises. For instance, the front can conform to an attractive (ideal) one-family house; the back, however, gives the picture of an old, dilapidated barn. Inspecting the house is most productive of all.

Entry

We therefore ask the patient whether he feels like entering the house to have a closer look. Usually, that works without difficulty. The behavior of individual patients is characteristic, if they say, for instance, that the house belongs to somebody else and one cannot just walk in, one cannot disturb or trespass. In such cases it is completely recommendable to discuss the question with the patient in order to talk over the reasons for his restraint, which he perhaps shows elsewhere in life, too. One rarely finds the door locked.

After the patient has entered, we again ask him to describe everything he sees there exactly, so that we can follow him and picture for ourselves the interior of the house and its furnishings. We leave the description of the entryway and the first rooms he wants to enter up to the patient. The therapist takes precise note, however, of which rooms the patient avoids. These are signs for repressed problems.

Kitchen

The *kitchen,* for example, is of particular importance as the place where foods are stored and prepared. There is doubtlessly a large difference between an impeccably orderly, gleamingly clean, modern kitchen with furniture made of synthetic materials, of which one has to ask oneself if it is used at all or not, and a kitchen with a friendly, quite active young woman who is preparing a meal and visibly enjoys cooking, with pots steaming on the stove and food in various stages of preparation. The scene is again different if the kitchen is deserted with everything left standing or lying just as it had been after being used; dirty plates, garbage, leftovers, flies landing on the foodscraps, to juxtapose two extreme examples. Ultimately, we will ask the patient also to inspect the supplies. Contrasts appear, for instance, if in one case a large pantry is present, in which country ham, good sausage, onions, preserves, numerous canned foods, bread, cake, and much more are available, or if there is no pantry at all or if only a very few groceries are lying around in it, which will just about suffice for the next day. The smaller version of the pantry is ultimately the refrigerator. Conclusions about the patient's attitude toward the world of oral enjoyment are perfectly permissible from the availability of provisions and the condition of the kitchen. In this respect oral attitudes far removed from pleasure are signified, or perhaps the opposite in which an overemphasis on the oral world is indicated when especially tasty foods are served in excess. However, the latter is usually not the case with our patients.

Cellar

In addition to the kitchen motif one might consider the *storage of supplies in the cellar.* The cellar is inspected at a later point. Perhaps provisions are stored there in excess, expressing an ascetic attitude with strong oral needs for security, for instance, with the fear that one might starve someday if one is not economical and keeps supplies on hand. We also find age-specific differences in the regard held for this area of oral significance, which is not surprising.

Living Space

The *living room* should not be forgotten. As with all the rooms, including the kitchen, we have the patient describe the prevailing *atmosphere of the room* for us. If need be, we offer suitable attributes, such as "cozy, modern, attractive and bright, or gloomy, uncomfortable, repulsive, old-fashioned." Would one like to live there oneself, or does the house seems to be "lacking in style, cheerless, functionally cold," among many other things? Experienced patients can even look at pictures hanging on the walls of the rooms, from which additional material can come.

Cleanliness, which one should ask about, as the adversary of a comfortable living atmosphere ("warm scent"), can indicate an antianal and thus compulsive attitude.

Particular importance is attached to the bedroom as an

intimate area, in which various details about the patient's relationship to his partner, all the way to erotic-sexual attachment, are expressed. Of particular interest is the question of whether there are two beds and how they stand in relation to each other or whether there is a double bed. We can examine the scene in more detail to find out whether the beds are used. Examining the contents of the closets, the night tables, or other furniture also promotes interesting indications. Adolescent patients, who find old-fashioned clothing in the closets, which at best their parents would wear, are indicating their repression of sexual relationships or those similar to marriage and their attribution of such relationships to their parents. As the oedipal problem has frequently not been resolved in neurotic persons, that is, the son's attachment to his mother and that of the daughter to her father, we also find in these cases clothes or shoes belonging to a female patient next to those of an older man, who could be her father, and conversely those of a young man beside the clothes of an older woman, who could be his mother. We pay particular attention to the shoes, whose erotic-sexual aspect is expressed if, for example, they are fashionable and elegant or, conversely, the repression of this interest if they are coarse, shabby, and unattractive.

The hints that we gain through such a careful inspection may at first have more diagnostic significance and are initially recognized by the patient very sibliminally or not at all. I recall a 21-year-old female patient, who found a coat in a closet, which she had worn at the age of 14. There was a pair of pants belonging to her grandfather hanging next to it. From this and from much other information (apart from the case history), it became quite clear that her oedipal relationship had not been directed toward her father but toward her grandfather. To her great sorrow, her father had in fact disappeared from her view after her parents divorced when she was 7 years old. According to the case history, her grandfather had played only a rather incidental part in her upbringing. However, after these indications, it became evident that he had occupied an important place for her erotic development during puberty and that she had also loved and admired him a great deal. The whole complex could only be discussed with her in light of this image.

All kinds of personal utensils are often found in the drawers of the night table, from which the patient can obtain hints about the person or the attitudes of the owner of the respective bed.

Stronger repressive tendencies become evident when clothing, shoes, and other objects seem to belong to totally unknown persons, whereas in textbook style we can always assume that persons appearing in the house or their traces are related to introjects (thus, incorporated early referential figures). I am reminded of the case of a 36-year-old widow, in whose house there was a bedroom with an old rustic alcove. Her grandmother, who had died long ago, lay suffering in it. She had played a central part in the patient's family because she had owned a farm. The inheritance would have considerably improved the family's social situation, for example, making it possible for the patient to go to an advanced level high school. The grandmother had become an introjected referential figure, although the inheritance had not materialized.

Attic

The last to be inspected are the attic and the cellar. The therapist can predict the presence of old chests, boxes, and closets in both and have the patient look for them. Things from the past are kept in them, such as old toys, old clothes, family albums, picture books, and other keepsakes. We can ask the patient to look at these things and then occasionally encounter important reminiscences.

Sometimes the inspection of the house cannot be completed in one GAI session. Then it is perfectly possible to continue the investigation in the following one.

Examples

For purposes of illustration, I would like to present a few brief examples of the practice of focusing on the house motif. With unproblematical persons, we can usually expect a residential house, which in most cases is suited for only one family. A business, a restaurant, or something similar lets one know that the patient's private sphere is apparently neglected, particularly if living space is scant or not present at all. A small hut raises the question as to how self-confident the person concerned is. From the absence of windows, one can infer strong withdrawnness and distrust of the environment. A castle, in which there is possibly even a throne room and chair, indicates the patient's grandiose expectations and a narcissistic overestimation of himself. The same is true, for instance, of a multistory building or a skyscraper.

Changing House Motifs

As with the mountain motif, the therapist should also ascertain whether completely different house motifs can possibly be sighted by the same patient at different times. I remember a very hysterically structured, immature 19-year-old female patient. Once she saw a Baroque castle made of red sandstone, another time a bourgeois house, which was, however, made completely of glass, so that one could observe everything that was happening in it. The third time it was a golden shrine in Gothic style, which was locked up tight, whose contents therefore remained concealed. If we start from the symbolic significance of the house motif explained earlier, then in this case of extremely contrasting houses one can most likely say that the person concerned can live out of different ego-nuclei or roles but has not yet developed or only inadequately developed a consolidated identity. If the contrasts are less extreme but the house motifs are nevertheless different, one can probably recognize a greater degree of flexibility and versatility of the person. It, of course, remains open, where the line lies between the one and the other. However, it is certain that the more neurotically fixated the person is, the more rigid the structures are and the more stereotyped particular structures reappear in repeated house motif sessions.

Pathological House Motifs

Other, particularly pathological house motifs may appear, for instance, when instead of a house a 16-year-old patient pictures a concrete bunker in the meadow without doors or windows, or a young working woman enters a "spook house," through which she must grope in the dark as if through a chamber of horrors. The house motif can also reveal certain distortions, when a serious problem pushes to the fore. For example, one patient with a cardiac neurosis imagined a stately house, which was totally filled on the inside by a large royal staircase. It led him through the roof into the sky and came to a dead end there. The image fit his one-sided ambitions and his attitude toward accomplishment with a total neglect of striving for pleasure and love, and of his private sphere and his family.

Two detailed examples of original forms of the house motif follow.

Case 1 (11)

Fortress

A 19-year-old patient, who has severe difficulty in in making social contacts and has obsessional thinking with a pronounced personality disorder, imagines a conspicuously square and massive house. It is whitewashed, has a flat roof, as is common in Arabic houses, and very few small windows. It has a large defense tower with small barred windows, rising high above the roof with a cross on its peak. Upon entering, an enormous vestibule strikes the eye and impresses one as being cold. Some rooms are completely empty, others are locked, and the defense tower is also empty inside. The cellar is dirty and untidy with cobwebs hanging on the walls. A picture of the patient's mother is hanging on one wall. Finally, using an axe, the patient forcibly gains a view into the locked bedroom. The double room has been rummaged through and the bed linen is dirty. Here the patient thinks of scenes between his mother and her friend, with whom she lived after the war but did not marry to avoid forgoing her pension. A crucifix dominates the unpleasant living room.

Case 2 (12)

Multistory Building

A house motif is shaped with additional creative development. In focusing on the house motif a 19-year-old female high school student, who had a pronounced personality disorder, pictures a multistory building. It rises beyond the clouds, and work is still being done on the top of it. Several construction workers and the patient herself are working on it because it is supposed to rise even higher. It tapers off to a point and sways back and forth in a strong wind. The three workers fall from the one meter square platform on the top "screaming terribly" to the depths. The patient is able to hold on. The view to the bottom is partly concealed by clouds; she sees snow-covered mountains to the sides, which are much smaller than the building. In another direction she recognizes the sea and ships. She continues building to get even higher. Finally, it is so high that she comes to the entrance to heaven. She enters heaven through a strange modern glass door, which opens automatically. A guard forbids her to go further. She pleads with him "terribly" so that he phones around, probably to God. Then a woman comes along, a saint in white clothing, barefoot with a garland of roses on her head, black hair, blue eyes, and pure white skin. She scrutinizes the patient a little and leads her through long pathways; everything is cold, bare, and plain, as in a science fiction film. The woman, on the other hand, is nice, friendly, and kind. Emaciated prisoners with shaved heads are pulling a wagon in which the devil is sitting. He is more like an animal, a wolf, with horns, a horse's tail, and hoofs. The saintly woman falls to her knees upon seeing him. The devil is arrogant, has the wagon stopped, climbs down to turn to the patient. He is gigantic, threatening, and terrifying. He would like to force her to kneel down, too. She refuses, whereupon the devil orders his men to beat her about the face and in the stomach, leaving her lying on the path bleeding terribly as the devil drives on. The companion bandages the patient, who can only continue on crutches now. War chariots come racing down the pathway, so that one has to press against the walls. They are driven by Romans with the characteristic profile "terribly proud and wild" (the patient gets dizzy and must stop). She reports that she was afraid of getting run over by these chariots; the Romans had impressed her despite their arrogance.

Elaboration

Metaphors

Commentary: Some hypotheses about the meaning of the multistory building can be deduced from a knowledge of the patient's case history. Its mammoth height symbolizes her extreme level of aspiration, her extremely high demands of a sadistic superego, which was shaped by her father very early. The house is also a phallic component; the patient would like to identify with her father, and the entrance into heaven speaks in favor of the patient's wish to get closer to God the Father. Her own father was the director of a hospital, in which the patient lived from early childhood until recently. Her father's pedagogic aphorisms and his behavior reinforced the patient in her narcissistic idealization of the father image in reality, too. The figure of the young saint is difficult to decipher, but rather corresponds to a form of her sisters, who in part had a better relationship with their father than she herself did. The masculine aggressive militant world also apparently obtains her esteem, first as represented by the devil, then by the imposing figures of the Roman warriors. The patient's father always glorified military tradition and made no secret of his pride that his only son became a soldier. In contrast to what was previously the case, the patient recently has fantasies more often indicating aggressive impulses. For instance, the wind catapults the workers from the multistory building; she defends herself against the humiliation by the (father-) devil and glorifies the Roman warriors. However, the aggressions are still partially directed against herself, which is the clearest when the devil appears, who has her beaten up. She provoked this herself and in a masochistic manner also accepted being overpowered. One could see the image of the "bad father" in the devil (who also had experience in drastic punishments). As a whole, the scene described could be interpreted as expressing a confrontation with the phallic (masculine) world (with which she identifies in part), as well as with the images of the good and bad father. I do not want to go into further detail here.

Sometimes it is meaningful to ask the patient, even when viewing the house from the outside, what it reminds him of. Occasionally there are similarities to the house of his own parents, grandparents, or other important referential figures, which also holds true for parts of the interior. Dependencies or the problem of incomplete separation are reflected in this. I point out again that the house motif, that is, the mere inspection of a house, can make a deep impression on a patient, if he guesses or it becomes clear to him preconsciously that it "looks like that" inside of him or that the imaginal house absolutely deviates from what he has previously envisaged as "his house," which he would have liked to build in his secret dreams. Therefore caution is in order with the house motif. It should not be focused upon too early in the therapeutic process. At first the therapist must refrain from giving clues to the contents. What I emphasized during the motif of the panorama from the mountain naturally also holds true for the house motif, namely, in the course of the advancing therapeutic process or when influenced by strong experiences, such as falling in love, the motif gradually changes. As a therapist, one is also often amazed or concerned at the extreme distinctness of this motif the first time it is visualized. However, one can usually assume that the image will become more harmonious and refined with advancing treatment.

Confrontation

Change

Finally, I come to the last of the five standard motifs of the basic level, which are the starting points of the training procedure. It is the edge of the woods mentioned previously.

Fifth Standard Motif: The Edge of the Woods

Focusing

We sometimes make use of a spontaneously arising opportunity in which a seedling forest appears from the meadow or while on a walk in the countryside. Secondly, we can also engage the meadow motif directly and ask the patient to check whether he can see a forest. He should walk closer to it. We then ask him to face the forest in such a way that he stops at a distance of approximately 10 to 20 meters in front of it and looks into the darkness of the forest interior. We predict that in all probability a figure, whether an animal or a person, will come out of the darkness of the woods. He should wait patiently; perhaps at first he will only see something vague or blurred. If he is afraid, there will be a bush or something similar nearby that he can hide behind.

It is certainly clear to you that this exercise serves an entirely different purpose than the standard motifs listed previously. Here it is not a matter of achieving something specific or of developing activities on one's own in the catathymic panorama. Something entirely different is at issue. For the first time within the scope of the basic level, the patient is given the opportunity of stimulating unconscious material in relatively pointed fashion, which develops into the form of

Symbolic Figures

symbolic figures arising from his unconscious. Here we must first bear in mind the *symbolic value of the woods.* It is generally regarded as a symbol of the unconscious, which I mentioned during the description of the panorama from the mountain. It is a dark region on earth that one cannot look through, in which everything or nothing can be hidden. Wild animals live free and undisturbed in the forest, and from fairy tales we know that evil or friendly figures, such as robbers, giants, dwarfs, fairies, or even a bad witch, can be active in the woods. Something is at work there, which first remains completely indefinite and can only be located with difficulty. Incidently, adult patients, mostly women, frequently shrink from approaching the woods too closely, to say nothing of entering it, because it fills them with an undefinable anxiety.

Entering the Woods

That is the one side of the forest motif. On the other hand, there are also patients who like to walk in the woods very much. We find this most frequently with children, who feel safe and secure in the woods or would like to hide in them. Then the forest does not have a dark and threatening effect; rather the trees stand a clear distance apart from each other. The sunlight plays through the leaves, and the path into the woods seems to be attractive, comforting, or even inviting, with a feeling of anxiety and thrill at the same time. No other motif of the basic level can be experienced so diversely, even in diametrically opposed fashion, as the forest. Very ambivalent experiences can be projected onto it. That is the main reason why we avoid on principle letting the patient enter the forest in the techniques of the basic level of GAI. The therapist, who has not had all that much experience yet and the patient as well should be protected from surprises, from unexpected impressions and scenes, for whose mastery the therapist is not yet sufficiently prepared. That also applies to the case of the patient who would like to walk into the woods on his own accord or even insists on doing this. As I have already said previously, the patient is in no way always his own best advisor within the framework of mental imagery. One of the therapist's most important tasks on the basic level is to avoid dangerous situations for the time being and rather to take a cautious, protective attitude.

Dangers

To illustrate the "dangers" that can await the patient and the therapist during a walk in the woods, I would like to cite one example.

Case 1 (13)

A research subject (not a patient) walked courageously and self-confidently into the woods. There she found an old log cabin. She looked in the window and saw a few figures indistinctly. She opened the door of the cabin with some effort and saw several figures facing her, which upon looking more closely proved to be skeletons. One was lying down, another was running around in the room, and a third was sitting at a table and playing with a skull. You can imagine how surprised and at the same time how terrified the person was, and all the more so when, after leaving the eerie house, she saw individual bones and human skulls lying on the ground in the vicinity. She left the woods in a hurry. An image like this is unusual, to be sure, and the reference to the subject's biography became clear in a discussion that followed. In spite of that I would like to draw the mandatory conclusion that entering the forest can be equivalent to entering the unconscious, strongly conflict-laden spheres.

Instead of doing this, we follow an old psychotherapeutic recommendation not to liberate more unconscious material than the psyche is prepared to reveal spontaneously of its own accord.

In this respect focusing on the motif of the edge of the woods or rather on the darkness of the woods signifies precisely the realization of this possibility. It also represents a protection for the patient. If one compares the forest motif with other

Protection

motifs symbolizing the unconscious, such as the ocean or even better the cave and the swamp (introduced on the advanced level), the edge of the woods is distinguished by the fact that here one does not go to the depths. Areas are not touched upon that lie below the surface; rather an unconscious realm is reached that already lies level with the surface (the earth), that is, closer to consciousness. In this way we give the patient the chance to manifest symbols directly, but to remain near the

Border area

border area and avoid triggering anxiety and resistances, which usually appear when intrusion is forced. Our further goal is to bring the symbolic forms emerging from the woods onto the meadow, in a manner of speaking, out of the unconscious into the light of consciousness. Occasionally, the attempt can turn out to be seemingly insignificant. Completely ordinary animals, such

Symbolic figures

as a hare, a fox, a little mouse, or even a mole, come out of the woods. Nevertheless, you can be certain that the emergence of of these animals has symbolic import and its own individual reason.

For example, a female patient, who each time pictured a mouse coming out of the woods, also had in reality the attitude of a "little gray mouse" and was called "mousy" by her mother even into adulthood. However, larger animals can emerge, too, such as the shy deer frequently seen by young girls, a magnificent stag in pose seen by a man, and unusual animals, such a a big brown bear or a snake, which raises its head and darts its tongue in and out. In addition, human forms naturally also appear: a hunter with a large shotgun, a ragged tramp or even several of them, an old woman picking berries, a witch, a young rebellious man as a "gunman" with a number of pistols in his belt, and many other figures.

Symbolic Meaning

What is this all about? From our knowledge of depth psychology regarding symbols, we know that these forms can be interpreted according to the rules of dream symbolism. Although we do not make these interpretations on the basic level and at most can make cautious offers in this direction with advanced patients, the therapist should account for this as soon as possible, or rather try to form a hypothesis about what is reflected in the respective catathymic images.

Subject Level

There are two complementary aspects to be considered in regard to these *symbolic figures.* On the *first interpretive level,* the emerging figure can be explained on the *subject level,* that is, the figures can personify *unconscious tendencies* of the *behavior* and the attitude, or rather affective and instinctual wishes, of the patient. They are usually behavioral tendencies, which he represses unconsciously or has split off from his behavior patterns. Thus, a piece of "unlived life" is frequently embodied here. An example of this follows. A long time ago I treated a very upright, extremely diligent, and ambitious craftsman. He had had a cardiac neurosis for a year, which had been overlaid by depression and psychosomatic dystonia. Therapy proceeded well with this relatively unpretentious man, but returning to everyday life seemed difficult for him with the psychic pain of his symptoms. Among other symbolic figures, a bear appeared when he focused on the edge of the woods. It came out into the meadow walking upright and staggering a little. Then it lay down, stayed there, and evidently fell asleep. I had no doubt that for this so markedly diligent and ambitious man the sluggish and lazy bear embodied exactly that part of his ego that he could not admit existed, but that indicated one of his inner needs, namely, to not always have to be so extremely diligent, active, and markedly efficient.

Still another example is the emergence of an imposing stag with magnificent antlers, which appeared in favorable sunlight in the meadow. This was imagined by a patient who came into treatment because of impotence. He was a somewhat shy, reserved man, and to me the stag seemed to embody his exaggerated, to a certain degree exhibitionistic, ideal of masculinity, which he would like to have emulated and which, of course, inhibited him all the more from developing his naturally given masculine traits.

Therapeutic goal

Therefore the therapeutic goal lies in bringing these repressed tendencies or rather symbolic forms, which are split off from the person, into consciousness through their emergence into the light. They are adopted and accepted by dealing with them, approaching them, touching and stroking them, as one usually does with animals. Frequently, the patients are not prepared to do this at first. For example, the craftsman was quite annoyed at the lazy bear and would have liked to scare him in an unfriendly and rough manner instead of using the friendly principle of reconciliation and approach, which will be explained later.

C.G. Jung speaks of the "shadow" of the person in the connection discussed here, a vivid concept, which from the standpoint of ego psychology of psychoanalysis we would formulate as *split off, suppressed parts of the ego that are pressing for gratification and integration.*

Object Level

The *second interpretive level* of the figures is that of the so-called *object level.* We can consider the same figures to be the *embodiment of the* patient's *referential figures,* who appear distorted and not to be recognized under the conditions of the neurosis, that is, as he experienced them emotionally based upon the affective experience of his early childhood with analogous persons within the dimensions of infantile experience. The interpretation on this level is particularly obvious, if actual figures emerge from the forest, such as the patient's own father, a teacher, or other referential figures.

We can make these spontaneous experiences useful for directive therapy by predicting to the patient that a referential figure, chosen by us, who is connected with a current problem will emerge from the woods. However, this technique belongs to the intermediate level and demands more experience of the therapist.

The aim of dealing with the symbolic figures is, above all, to bring them out into the meadow, possibly to satiate them there, and, as already mentioned, to establish reconciliatory contact with them. Not much more can happen for the time being on the basic level. However, the therapist should carefully observe what characteristics the patient uses to describe these symbolic figures spontaneously, how he feels about them emotionally, and how the figures act toward him, after they have seen him.

Behavioral Tendencies

Information about neurotic behavioral tendencies can be gained in this way and be shown to the patient, tendencies that more or less consciously enter into his everyday life and are an expression of his neurotic character.

Frequency

In reference to technique it must still be noted that the therapist cannot overtax the motif of the edge of the forest excessively. He will have at most 2 or 3 figures develop from it in one session. Resistances can also emerge here, when perhaps no figure at all appears initially, a lot of time passes until it is manifested and perhaps it appears at first only very inconspicuously and is thus uninformative. Therefore we do not press the patient if performing the exercise fails. At best, we support his readiness to wait patiently, or we postpone the exercise to a later time. Within this framework, one can ultimately succeed in having a whole menagerie of figures in the meadow. The therapist can occasionally have the patient call on them again to observe and support the patient's attempts to approach them, to become reconciled with them, and to make friends with them.

Session Eleven: The Management Models of the Basic Level

Characteristic Features

In connection with the appearance of symbolic figures it is important to discuss the two management models of the basic level. By the concept "management models," we mean technical instructions in symboldrama, which refer to the guidance of the symbolic figures or rather to the dealings with them. In my numerous experiments with mental imagery, which I completed in the period between the end of the 1940s and the end of the 1950s, just a few management models crystalized out of the multiplicity of such possibilities for managing symbolic figures. They are characterized especially by the following:

1. Therapeutically they have proved themselves to be surprisingly effective.
2. With an amazing internal consistency, they invariably run an analogous course, no matter which patient or which therapist is using them.

The two management models reserved for the basic level were selected, among other reasons, because they are relatively easy to handle and produce practically no resistances or anxious reactions in the patients, which conforms to the technical rules of the basic level principle. When employed purposefully, they can nevertheless open up a clearly definable therapeutic effect.

Two Forms for the Basic Level

It concerns the *principle of nourishing and satiating* and that of *reconciliation and affectionate embrace* (see Table 1). The starting point at that time was the observation that the symbolic figures that were released occasionally appeared hostile, for example, during the edge of the woods motif or under other conditions. Accordingly, they frighten the patient, threaten to attack him, and arouse his anxiety proportionately. The therapist thereby is in a difficult situation. Even today, he still has few alternatives. In such a situation he can look for a way to intervene or, at worst, urge the patient to flee. From the therapeutic point of view, the latter advice is certainly not the best, if one bears in mind that these figures emerge as split-off drive and wishful tendencies of the patient and that the goal of therapy should be to integrate them gradually. Looking at these cases in practice, a lion, for example, can emerge from the woods and tear open the patient's throat, or the snake mentioned previously can move toward the patient darting his tongue in and out. Grim-looking, hostile human figures can also dominate the scene, such as the witch, the hunter, or others. The two management models make it possible for the therapist when confronted with such situations to show the patient how to deal

Hostile Symbolic Figures

Split-off Images

with aggressive or at least unfriendly symbolic figures, especially when they appear at any time, even unexpectedly.

With regard to the question concerning the way to proceed here, one can remember how, for example, an animal trainer calms down his wild animals. Aggressive resistance, such as attacking or hiting the animals, scarcely leads to their becoming tame, as is generally known. Although patients are occasionally inclined to attack a hostile symbolic figure, to hastily and to possibly kill it, there is naturally also aggression directed against the self or rather against the concerned portion of the individual's own ego included in this. The patient has already practiced this action, that is, the suppression of the individual's own pressing impulse, long enough within the scope of his neurotic behaviors. The steps to the therapeutically productive integration of the impulse, that is, of the symbolic figures, come about in a way parallel to the procedure of the trainer who attempts to put the animals in a friendly mood and make them affectionate, first of all, by feeding them. However, I deliberately did not call *the principle* "feeding," but instead *"nourish and satiate,"* because the point is that the success of the action actually lies in satisfying the respective symbolic figure in the sense of orality. Whether that succeeds or not, naturally depends upon the kind of nourishment offered. For example, in fantasy one can put a saucer of milk in front of a snake, but one will have to provide a great many pieces of meat for a lion.

Meaningful Association

Technique of nourishing

The therapist proceeds technically in the following manner. He actively offers the patient the nourishment intended for the specific purpose, saying, for instance, "For very specific reasons I would not advise you to approach the animal aggressively now, even if it has made you angry. I have the distinct impression that the animal is hungry and needs something substantial to eat. In my experience that would be the best way to calm a vicious animal and then to gain its favor." Then the therapist either names the food that is to be given or discusses it with the patient beforehand. Awkward situations can arise, and the therapist may be unclear, for example, concerning what to give an evil witch to eat, who is emerging from the forest. At first, he can talk with the patient about it to come to a decision. Then the therapist might continue as follows, "Please, imagine (for example, in the case of the lion) that I have gotten a big pile of pieces of fresh meat for you, which are now lying next to you. You throw them to the lion one after another and observe carefully whether it eats them and how it reacts to this subsequently. The only important thing is to feed him a lot, for the time being more than you think is necessary for him to be totally satiated. Always offer him another piece, there is plenty available."

Usually the symbolic figures now begin to accept the nourishment with more or less interest, often even greedily. The instructions must therefore take into consideration that the goal is not simply to "feed" but that an excessive amount of food is

Table 1. Overview of the Instruments of Guided Affective Imagery

	Standard Motifs	Structure	Therapeutic Techniques	Management Models (Operation on the Symbol)
Basic level	1. Meadow	Broad		
	2. Brook	Medium	I. Training procedure	a) Reconciliation
	3. Mountain	Broad	II. Developing creative imaginings	b) Nourishing
	4. House	Medium		
	5. Edge of woods	Broad		
Intermediate level	6. Referential figures	Narrow	III. Associative procedure	
	7. Sexuality (rosebush)	Narrow	IV. Night dream	
			V. Bringing acute conflicts into focus	c) Inner guide
	8. Aggressiveness (lion)	Narrow	VI. Inspection of body organs	d) Confrontation with the symbol
			VII. Working through	
	9. Ego ideal	Narrow	VIII. Analysis of transference	
Advanced level	10a. Cave	Broad		
				e) Exhausting and killing
			IX. Combination with conventional psychoanalysis	
	10b. Swamp	Narrow		f) Magical fluids
	11. Volcano			
	12. Folio			
Musical GAI (MGAI)	(1.–8. Focusing) possible		III. Associative procedure	—
GAI in Groups (GGAI)	(1.–8. Focusing) possible		Individual fantasies	—
			Group fantasies	Feedback techniques

to be offered. It must be much more than a neurotic patient can imagine with his own oral inhibitions. The element of "overfeeding" apparently has great significance.

This procedure may seem strange at first, perhaps even grotesque. But, please do not forget that we are operating on the level of mental imagery in the realm of magical occurrences, psychoanalytically speaking in the realm of the primary process. GAI has this in common with fairy tales and myths. When applied with some decisiveness, possibly with a certain suggestive impact on the patient, this method has an almost absolutely certain effect, which is always in the same direction.

Consequences

What happens after we have fed the respective hostile symbolic figure in excess with the appropriate nourishment? Actually that is easy to imagine. The symbolic figure becomes full, tired, and usually soon lies down to sleep, as the creature also does in real life. Thus, its behavior changes decisively and the figure loses its dangerous character. It is peaceful even before it falls asleep. Now the patient can approach it and even stroke it. That would be the aforementioned action of the *management model of reconciliation.* Perhaps the patient will have to overcome the rest of his anxiety at this point with the therapist's help. However, I am of the opinion that the practice of reconciliation following this is equally as important. Haronian (1967) and Stierlin (1968) conducted some interesting experiments on this technique of becoming reconciled with conflictual figures, which previously received little notice in psychotherapy.

Reconciliation

These two management models do more than merely serve as a safeguard in emergencies to reduce anxiety. Indeed, they represent an eminent therapeutic action, whose effect cannot be overestimated. To illustrate this, I am including an especially characteristic example.

Case 1 (14)

Example of Crisis Intervention

Crisis intervention can be aided by the management models of nourishing and satiating and of reconciliation:

A 21-year-old chemistry student consulted me after having failed an intermediate examination with the professor (full professorship) in his first semester due to an insurmountable test stupor. A few hours before the examination he had known the test material while talking with the assistant of the institute. He was given the chance to repeat the test on the next day. That was the reason that he was looking for help from me late that afternoon. Acquainted with the family from previous consultations, I knew of the young man's severe authority problem. His father had held an upper level officer's position in the Austrian army before World War I and had used a strict authoritarian hand with the family. Seen from the psychodynamic perspective, it seemed impossible decisively to influence the overriding father image of this patient with a brief therapeutic intervention. Failing the examination was apparently based upon a transference of the patient's fearful child-father relationship onto the professor. After an introductory discussion about his former chemistry teacher, an esteemed but strict older gentleman and his current professor, I had him focus upon the following image in GAI. He is in the meadow near the edge of the woods. A figure will emerge, either his chemistry teacher or the chemistry professor, when he looks into the dark woods. Only after hesitating for a long time and after some words of encouragement from me (which I construed as resistance reactions) did the patient's old chemistry teacher finally appear. His face was sullen and rejecting, and he went on his way without paying any attention to the patient at all. Initially the patient refused (resistance) to walk toward and greet him, in GAI. With some effort he was finally able to start an imaginary conversation with the old gentleman. Reluctantly, the patient accompanied him and in so doing slight emotional reactions occurred repeatedly. To give the principle of nourishing a chance, I finally asked the patient to imagine that he had everything necessary for a nice picnic in his pockets. He should unpack the food, including two chickens and a bottle of red wine, and spread it out on a napkin on the ground and then invite the old gentleman. As a sign of the resistance, the teacher at first refused indignantly. But finally the plan to stage a common meal worked after all. Soon the old gentleman was enjoyably eating the food that was offered and drank red wine from the bottle together with the patient. Subsequently, he became visibly friendly and jovially patted the patient on the shoulder, which the patient returned, so that they met each other man to man, in a manner of speaking, as equals and in this way also became friends through physical contact. Then I advised the patient to concentrate on the same scene again before going to sleep and told him that what matters is to entertain the old gentleman as amply as possible.

The following day the young man came to see me in the afternoon again and was able to report that he had been emotionally steady and relatively calm during the examination by his professor. Now he had the knowledge at his disposal, which had been blocked emotionally on the previous day, and had passed the examination.

The First Session

Initial Contact

In this hour we have time enough to concentrate on the topics of the subsequent sessions. They deal primarily with the practical questions of treatment with GAI. Without intending to get ahead of things, I would like to inform you about the structure of the preparatory sessions for GAI and about the first steps in initiating the patient. In so doing I touch on a few technical steps that are basically valid for every kind of psychotherapy. Some of you are certainly already familiar with them; others, whom I would particularly like to address, need precisely these technical hints, which are usually only rarely described.

To state it explicitly, we conduct an *initial interview* with the patient, who has consulted us for psychotherapeutic treatment. The external setting is such that the therapist does not sit at a desk, but rather patient and therapist talk with each other from lounge chairs, if possible in one corner of the room. They do not sit opposite each other but at an angle of 90 degrees or less so that neither one is forced to look into the other's face. I structure the first contact according to the criteria for a first interview. I give the patient considerable leeway to present his complaints and problems with a minimum of intervention on my part. I do not ask direct supplementary questions until the second part of this discussion, lasting approximately 50 minutes, in order to elicit information in the direction of a depth psychological case history. Here I deliberately stay within the current scope to as great an extent as possible. I have him describe the symptoms, for which he is consulting me, as well as the full breadth of the current conflictual situation in the patient's present social surroundings. Thus, it may be the situation of his marriage or relationship with his partner, of the family in the broadest sense, as far as he is still rooted in it, of his occupational world, and of whatever else may be playing a part in terms of social influences. It is particularly important to have him describe a connection between the first appearance of the symptoms or their later aggravation and the emotional situations that especially affected the patient at that time or before these phenomena appeared. For the time being, I deliberately refrain from extending the case history into the patient's childhood and family of origin, that is the genetic scene of his neurosis.

Triggering situation

Accentuating the *triggering situation* is a key to the psychodynamics of the origin of the symptoms and of the patient's problems in general. However, detecting the very important triggering situation within the first exploratory session occurs in only approximately 70 percent of the cases. I deliberately dispense with all interpretive hints or corrective interventions, which one might give with the intention of conveying certain insights to the patient.

Behavior of the Therapist

It is especially important to convey two things to the patient in the first contact, either verbally or nonverbally:

1. that he and his existing symptoms are taken seriously by the therapist and
2. that the therapist is interested in exploring his problems and is capable of leading the patient to the important points related to this and drawing conclusions from them.

It only very rarely makes sense to offer the patient treatment immediately after the first exploratory session of approximately 50 minutes. This is generally reserved for very experienced therapists. The understanding of a number of factors is necessary for this, which I will deal with in detail later. To stay free of biases, it is advisable to talk with the patient at least a second time (50 minutes) to expand the history and to record a number of data, enabling one to make a prognosis for psychotherapy, in particular for GAI. Here I refer to p.114–116.

I am concluding the hour here. The subject matter will be

continued in the next class session, in which I intend to present as clearly and in as much detail as possible to you the technical steps for introducing GAI.

Session Twelve: Introducing the GAI-Treatment—The Flower Test

The question concerning how psychotherapy with GAI is to be introduced is of much practical significance, since the therapist has to guide the patient in the transition to the nonverbal level of imaginings through the techniques of mental imagery after having recorded a depth psychological history of several hours duration. This occasionally causes problems for the inexperienced therapist and sometimes for the patient as well.

Transition to Mental Imagery

The use of a quite simple but effective test has proved successful as a transition from the verbal technique used exclusively at first to that of mental imagery. It gives the therapist a first and at the same time casual glimpse of the patient's ability to realize symboldrama. Yet precisely this casualness and spontaneity of the test facilitate the transition from the one level to the other and form the first point of contact for the subsequent introduction of the techniques of mental imagery at the regular therapeutic sessions.

Flower Test

What kind of a test is this? At the end of the second or third hour of recording the history, I tell the patient that I would like him to take a short, harmless test. I ask him to stretch out in a relaxed and comfortable way in the easy chair he is sitting in, approximately in the way he would try to take a short nap. Here I make sure that he stretches out his legs, that his arms are lying loosely on the armrests, and, if possible, that his head is resting on the back rest. I wait until he is properly settled and ask him to close his eyes. Usually the patient has already become confident enough in the therapist that he follows this request, even if he is surprised or hesitates. If bright sunlight is shining into the room, I close the curtains to dim any harsh light. Then I ask the patient directly with the following words, "Can you imagine a flower?" After a short pause I add, "And now tell me, what you have imagined?" Here I am assuming that with his eyes closed the patient will begin to describe what is appearing before his eyes as soon as possible. If a longer pause arises, I ask him if he is having difficulty following my request. Usually it works quickly, and the patient tells about a flower that he has imagined. Of course, it is unimportant here that the patient name the flower. Frequently, they are imaginary flowers, or he does not know the name. I ask him to describe the details of the flower to me, such as the color or the center of the blossom,

Formulation

I would like to stress that in all of these exercises I never use the word "see." I only speak about "imagining," even in the introduction to the mental imagery itself. Some patients believe they have to "see" something and are consequently disappointed if, as a phenomenon, what is imagined does not compare with seeing but perhaps is pale, without good contours, and also varies in clarity at first. If the patient uses the word "see," I correct him, and if he claims not to have "seen" anything, I have him tell me, all the more, what else appeared before his eyes that was less clear. Then it usually becomes evident that due to his excessive striving to perform, he is dissatisfied with the not so prominent initial image, does not want to have it count, and thus claims that he cannot complete the task.

Casual Imagining

Altogether, it is highly astonishing how easily most persons succeed in imagining a flower ad hoc in this informal situation, in which no demands to achieve are being made, and then faced with what is imagined to report directly about it in detail. Now I go one step further and ask the patient to try in *his imagination* to touch the petals of the flower with the tip of his finger to find out what the flower feels like. Here I have him describe the sensations to me. Some patients experience this scene so realistically that they actually raise their index finger to touch the imaginary flower in the air. Usually they can describe the quality of touch very well, too.

Examples

The persons can imagine a red or yellow tulip, a red rose, a gerbera (expecially popular with women), a sunflower, and many a daisy. Only in the rarest of cases do the neurotic problems show through to such an extent that an extreme or abnormal form appears in the flower motif. I consider it a pronounced sign of disorder if, for example, someone imagines a black rose or a flower of steel or if the flower wilts after a short time and the leaves droop or even dry up. Imaginary flowers, which do not exist in reality, speak for an extreme gift for fantasy, or the merging of two different flower motifs into one, which I always have the patient describe very precisely for me.

Types of Disorder

In my experience it is very rare that imagining the flower does not work out at all. Then one must first ask oneself whether the patient is not perhaps too anxious and has hidden fears. That can become apparent by the fluttering of the closed eyelids or if one sees how little he can relax and sit loosely. Then one probably also has to assume that the person is experiencing a great degree of uneasiness or anxiety in the given situation and also toward the therapist. Only the very experienced therapist will be able to deal with this "negative transference" of the patient this soon and initiate therapy at all. It is very rare that something other than the flower motif appears in front of the patient's eyes. Naturally, we will accept anything at all that is imagined and we can say this to the patient when we ask him to imagine a flower. We formulate, for instance, "Everything else that appears before your eyes is fine too and please tell me about it." A peculiar and not rare form of disorder occurs when several flowers appear at the same time rather than one, which alternate with each other in the visual field, so that the person does not know which flower to focus upon. We try to have him verbalize this too and suggest that he wait and see which of the flowers finally remains.

End of Test

I conclude the test by asking the patient (with his eyes closed) to breathe in deeply first and then to open his eyes. This short period of imagining, which takes at most 5 minutes, can be followed by the most diverse reactions. When the patient opens his eyes, one often notices that he has some difficulty transfering himself back from the world of imagination into the actual situation. I deal with this and approach this reaction by saying to him that apparently he was "very far away" or "in another world." In addition, the person concerned is frequently impressed by the aesthetic quality and/or by the vivid impact of the flower. He is astonished at what he was suddenly able to do without suspecting at all how intensive his imaginal world is. As a third reaction, one frequently observes that a successfully pictured and pleasant flower motif is reflected in the mood of the person. After opening his eyes and finding his way back, perhaps he smiles or has a slightly happy facial expression, and if one asks him, he confirms that he feels well, is cheerful, and that the test was pleasant.

As stated, this flower test is usually quite a lovely experience for the patient. Here I must mention that I looked for a suitable test motif for a long time that has symbolically as little negative stress as possible due to the projection of problems and is experienced as pleasing. I owe the choice of a flower to a suggestion made by Günther Krapf in Munich, an intuitively gifted colleague whose work has been a credit to GAI.

Transition to Mental Imagery

Forming the bridge from the flower test to the introduction of symboldrama, which is obvious after this preliminary experience by the patient, can be undertaken in various ways. After the flower test, I express my appreciation to the patient clearly and in a routine, systematic fashion. I state my impression that he has a gift for visualizing or, according to the circumstances of the case, that he has a lively fantasy, and that we could put these attributes to very good use in the therapeutic method. I then suggest to him that we conduct the treatment possibly for long stretches of time in the form of mental imagery like this. If the product of his fantasy was less pronounced, I talk about "good beginnings of his capacity to visualize" or something similar. At the same time I indicate that, after some practice, he will develop even clearer visualizations.

It is to be noted in passing that this test is, of course, also well suited in general for determining the imaginal capacity of a research subject. Whereas I used to believe that there were various gradations in relation to this, I have learned in the meantime that there is scarcely anyone who cannot imagine a flower motif. If that is in fact the case, one can propose another motif instead, possibly a meadow or the house in which he lived with his parents. That usually works.

Beginning of the First GAI Session

When the patient comes to the next, the first GAI therapy, session, I remind him of the flower test and that I consider him ready to start the therapy from this point. I explain to him that focusing on the mental images works considerably better if he lies down on the couch and completely relaxes as comfortably and loosely as possible. If I am uncertain whether the patient has inhibitions about lying down, which occasionally happens with young female patients due to an inhibition in their capacity for self-abandonment when faced with a male therapist, I offer the alternative of continuing the mental imagery in a comfortable armchair and put my easy chair next to it. One should not overlook this possibility. If I have the impression that the imagination will work easily, I immediately begin with the meadow motif.

Setting of the GAI Session

As just mentioned, I prefer the couch position for the mental imagery phase. Figure 3b shows the arrangement (the setting) preferred for GAI. In contrast to the setting in psychoanalysis (Figure 3a) the therapist does not sit behind the patient, but next to his head. This is supposed to make clear the fact that the patient and therapist are together that is, that the therapist accompanies him in the mental imagery as an equal and the work in GAI is understood as teamwork on the unconscious conflicts. In the section about the transference situation in GAI I will go into the prevailing and desired psychodynamics in more detail. Please also pay attention to the placement of the window in the illustration. The position of the patient should in any case be arranged so that light does not shine in his face either from a lamp or from the window. During the mental imagery session, I try to dim the room a little or, in the evening, to dim the floor lamp in the room. However, external acoustical stimuli can also be disturbing, and it is

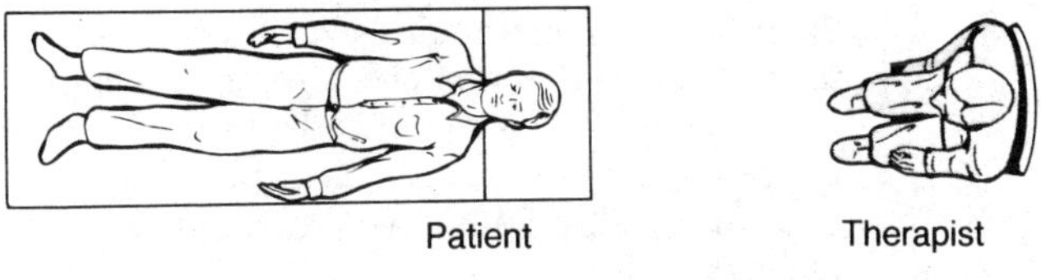

Fig. 3a: Typical couch position in the classic sense, as it is still used today in psychoanalysis.

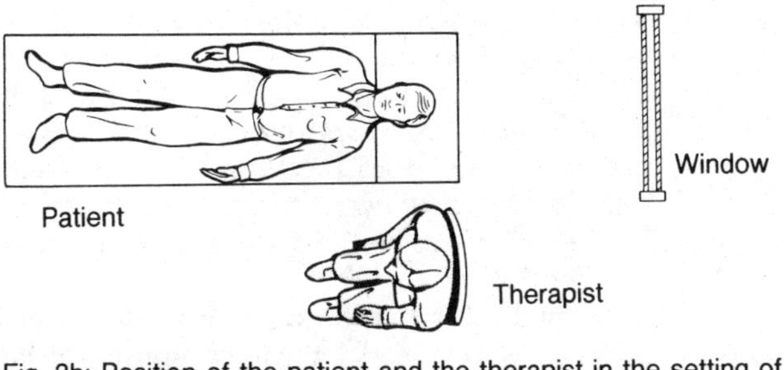

Fig. 3b: Position of the patient and the therapist in the setting of guided affective imagery.

important to create a quiet, relaxed atmosphere. Excluding incoming telephone calls is also a part of this.

Difficulties in Realizing the First Motif

Initial Difficulties

With some patients difficulties arise in realizing the first GAI motif. One naturally recognizes a disorder in this, which can bring about the impression that the person is not suited for the procedure at all. That is true only in very rare cases. I would like to tell you a few things about possible reasons for this first, and then give technical instructions as to how one can overcome these difficulties. Of course, that does not always work because hidden psychodynamic factors in the sense of transference and countertransference frequently enter into this.

Aids

Assuming the most frequently occurring case, the patient is instructed (for reasons of assuring the realization of GAI) to relax his muscles as I described on p.29. You offer him a suitable standard motif. Although you leave the option open to him that other motifs are also welcome and tell him to report any troubles to you that arise, at first nothing happens. The visual field in front of the patient really stays dark or black in the rarest of cases. Patterns or colors possibly appear or actually another image that is perhaps still vague. The patient does not have enough courage to talk about it because he believes he has the task of absolutely having to focus on the motif that you addressed. Sometimes it also happens that the patient has several images next to each other at the same time, possibly several flowers, and cannot decide upon the one or the other. Then it helps to ask him again to report everything he senses or perceives. Then you possibly also learn that he is presently disturbed by some bodily sensations. One can further encourage the patient to describe every small, perhaps insignificant impression. If such minimal sensations continue, (which rarely happens), the experienced therapist, having attended several courses, quickly finds a way to shape these minimal contents into imagery.

Repetition of the Flower Motif

If the patient cannot picture an image, possibly because the meadow motif is especially negatively cathected emotionally, I have him try another motif. An even surer way has proved itself, even when every attempt to focus on a motif fails or threatens to fail. Then I recommend concentrating on the flower motif from the previous session and proceed from this as follows. After the patient has described the flower again, I ask him to follow the stem looking downward to find out *where the flower is situated.* I I have him describe the spot exactly. There are *four* alternative *possibilities.*

Examples

The first is that flower is in a vase, which I also have the patient describe, and I then ask him to let his glance wander a little further and find out where the vase is located. It is on some piece of furniture. Then his view can gradually include the room. I ask him to describe it for me. When that has been largely completed, I insert the question whether the room is familiar to him or if it is a product of his fantasy. Both of these are possible. With uncertain and somewhat anxious patients, it becomes obvious that they adhere to what is familiar at first. The room is their own room or a room in their parents' home or in their grandparents' house. No matter whether this is the case or if it is a room created from fantasy, one can have the mental imagery expand from that point by having the patient look out of the window and describe the scenery or by asking him to leave the house and walk out into the open. In this way one can possibly lead him to the meadow.

The second possibility is that flower is in a garden. By having his glance wander, the patient possibly discovers the garden of his parents, of his own home, or one from his childhood that belonged to his grandparents. At this point a spontaneous age regression can quickly set in, that is, the patient relives a scene from his childhood. Good memories can soon open up here, and we have him report details about the garden to us.

The third possibility, a *modification of this procedure,* lies in encouraging the patient, who imagines easily and vividly, to expand on symboldrama, as was described here, immediately following the first performance of the flower test. In so doing I quickly convey to him a part of the desired assuredness in dealing with his imaginings while he is still sitting in the chair.

Transition from the Actual Situation

Another transitional technique, which is a little more prosaic than the previous one, takes place in the following way. At the first session of symboldrama, I ask the patient lying on the couch to develop the following image either immediately or after the one or the other motif failed to appear. He should imagine my office, in which he is lying on the couch. Moreover, he should try to get up and leave the room. Then I describe all of the additional steps: how he walks through a corridor, through my home or through the clinic, and follows a route that leads him outside. Depending upon the circumstances, I then offer him opportunities of going out into the country (on foot, by bicycle, by car, by bus.) and finding a meadow there in a more or less familiar area. Even that is not an absolute requirement for stimulating the learning process. At first it suffices, for instance, if he learns to imagine people and stores with displays aided by a stroll through city streets.

Reactions

It really is interesting that most of the somewhat motivated patients, even more so, the candidates in training, experience it as a success at the beginning when they have pictured relatively vivid imagery with accompanying feelings. The perception of this "other level," of the intense GAI, has a strange persuasive power completely independent of whether the contents can be immediately understood or deciphered or not. Conversely, inadequate success in imagining is often experienced as personal failure or as the lack of an important attribute, the latter above all in seminars for physicians and psychologists.

I usually do not continue with the four introductory techniques in the following sessions. Then it generally works better to approach a motif immediately. From what has been said, the fact emerges, and you should always bear this in mind, that the patient's introduction to GAI is usually connected with a learning process. The average person is not accustomed to expressing himself on the level of graphic imaginings and reporting about them in the same way that he communicates verbally. The learning process requires approximately two to five sessions. As becomes clear from these four examples, it is wise to support this learning process. Central to this is our effort to familiarize the patient with mental imagery and to teach him to refine both the imaginative perception and the observation of the accompanying feelings on this new experiential level. He should also be given the necessary assurance to extend the mental imagery beyond the initially restricted visual field, and he should be encouraged to move around in the continually expanding scenery. Here we wait to see what he undertakes independently, or rather what further imaginings appear to him spontaneously. Only when he becomes somewhat helpless or acts rather passive do we assist him in roaming further away into the distance, for instance, to describe the boundary of the garden or to look beyond it.

Learning Process

The technique of guiding the patient who has already completed this learning process is very different from that which, for the time being, is aimed completely toward unfolding the learning process.

Informing the Patient

One of the most frequent questions we are asked is how thoroughly should one explain the procedure to the patient, who is still unfamiliar with it. This is a broad field. Within the scope of this introduction I can give only limited indications as to how the therapist should proceed. I want to discuss the most important aspects, which are significant for introducing the patient and giving him information. The previous description of the transition was relatively straightforward. It did not explain to the patient why the mental imagery is being used and where the value and significance of GAI lie.

Extent of Information

Naturally the depth of intellectual information one provides depends upon the educational level of the individual patient. Basically it is desirable to treat the patient as a full partner, that is, we want to convey to him as little as possible the authoritarian impression that we "already know what will help him." Rather, I support the view that the patient should know as precisely as possible how a treatment basically works and what goals one can attain with it and where its limits lie. This ideal of an extensive clarification about psychotherapeutic procedure, of course, has its limits. With too much cognitive knowledge and too much insight into intellectual or even scientific interrelationships, the patient can be inclined to substitute this knowledge (which he can augment further with accompanying readings) for what is actually effective in the therapy, and in the course of further treatment prefer to move on the intellectual, cognitive level. However, that is exactly what we want to prevent. GAI is one of the few methods of a strongly *experientially sustained therapy*. That is its focus. This form of defense should be counteracted with those patients who tend toward intellectualization. In depth psychological treatment the rule of urging the patient not to read any psychotherapeutic material during treatment is in effect due to the frequent risk of premature intellectualization. Thus, I consciously also avoid giving academically educated patients too lengthy introductions to the procedure. With relatively less educated persons, I limit myself to asking them to wait until they have become familiar with mental imagery. Then they will realize that it brings them relief, and the insights connected to this will also become clearer and clearer to them. In the course of therapy I give hints now and then and try to work with the patient to acquire the larger connections.

Risk of Premature Intellectualization

Introduction of Intellectuals

With somewhat more educated patients and with professionals, I am reminded that Freud and later Jung, too, had discovered the great importance of dreams as the royal path to the unconscious and that in dreams unconscious material is expressed very precisely and frequently very clearly, although at first in coded form, that the dream is a compensation of the unconscious daily life and that human fantasy not only has an extraordinary range and a great wealth, but also has the capacity of leading unconscious problems to a solution in a creative way. In the course of mental imaginal therapy the person concerned will also perceive this increasingly clearly. In other words, I mainly refer to the self-awareness that can be expected, and my cautious support connected to it. If need be, I approach markedly intellectualized patients a little in some scenes of the mental imagery later on, by commenting on obvious and general positions of the contents and in so doing deal with their intellectual curiosity. However, I immediately emphasize the multiple determination of these contents and that I can only give vague points of reference. I make the further comment that only their personal feeling and their emotional experience can be the decisive factor in determining whether the hypothetically presumed connection captures the inner dynamics or not.

Dosing the Introduction

When I try to illustrate the breadth of meaning and of the emotional sustainment of the mental imaginal symbols in this way, it often initially meets with a lack of understanding on the part of intellectuals, particularly regarding the fact that the principle of contradiction is suspended in mental imagery. For that reason I give additional explanations to these patients in small doses, for instance, about the psychology of the primary process, the manner of experiences appearing there, the dreamwork. It nevertheless remains important that the therapist does not extend his *introductory explanation* too far, does not make excessive demands on the patient in so doing or direct him toward the intellectual track, which is to be avoided. I also expressly tell the patient that he can ask questions at any time in the future and should also have the courage to do that, so that I can find out in time what is still unclear to him. In this respect the opportunity exists to keep a dialogue going with him about technical problems of the therapy. With this, one prevents the patient from doing everything like a good child, so to speak, or accepting whatever one suggests (and then keeping a portion of inner reservations to himself anyway), which is due to the strong compliance frequently present in neurotic patients. On the other hand, it should be considered that prolonged discussions of this kind can also be an expression of resistance.

Discussion as Resistance

After having dealt with the practical introduction to the therapy in detail, I feel compelled to intervene for those of you who do not yet have the foundation of extensive psychotherapeutic training and experience (see also Zaro and colleagues, 1980).

Overall Significance of GAI

How Easy Is It to Use GAI?

The impression may have arisen that GAI is a procedure that is relatively easy to manage. At a first glance, that is in part correct. However, the more deeply the student goes into the method, the more he finds as with every psychotherapeutic procedure, that its practical application depends upon a *number of prerequisites.* I would like to mention the two most important of these and to add a number of comments concerning them.

Necessity of Self-Awareness

1. As emphasized previously, psychotherapy cannot be learned from books. Besides the given cognitive knowledge, it requires an abundance of practical experience and self-awareness, including practice in therapy. For GAI, this equipment is imparted in numerous advanced training seminars at home and abroad. Here it is particularly important for the candidate, who is advancing in his training, to treat a number of cases under regular supervision. For details, those interested can turn to the organizations listed in Appendix II.

Necessity of the Attitude Toward Perception

2. One of the *most frequent misunderstandings* arises in conveying a psychotherapeutic procedure due to the fact that those participating in seminars believe that conducting psychotherapy depends primarily upon knowledge of a method. The idea predominates that one only needs to have learned the method to soon be able to attempt one's own psychotherapeutic activity. Here the fact is overlooked that these methods are embedded in an abundance of psychological and

psychopathological approaches to perception, which are based not only upon the aforementioned self-awareness and practice, but also on a framework of solid knowledge. This extends on the one hand to the diverse psychic disorders and their symptoms. On the other hand, however, they cannot be understood only on the basis of their clinical pictures. Rather, the future therapist must have a command of well-founded knowledge and insights into the unconscious psychodynamics and related concepts causing them, that is, to know the general and specific theory of neuroses as well as psychosomatics and have assimilated them for use with patients. These fundamentals are necessary for competently leading discussions with the patient.

Unconscious Psychodynamics

3. Only those who have a command of the concepts, will be protected from making disastrous mistakes. The patient's material must be clarified into one or more concepts while collecting the list of symptoms, the triggering situation, the actual sociopsychological scene, and the genetic background to its character. In this way the wealth of data, which are to be collected from the patient, can be arranged according to the respective relevance. That demands extensive intellectual training, which has as its goal the assimilation of the depth psychological methods of thought and conclusions and their application to the respective patient. He must trace the contents of the GAI motifs in their individual form and learn to recognize the context of their meaning. Thus, he is supposed to follow the "significant train of thought" of the psychodynamics in the course of the therapy, that is, to read the "topography of the unconscious" in GAI better and better and to direct his interventions accordingly. Aspects of *prognosis* of GAI therapy must also be acquired with the purpose of recognizing the indication of the procedure on the elementary level for the respective patient and to coordinate it with the therapist's level of experience (see p.184).

Necessity of the Concept

4. Another important problem lies in the fact that during therapy the therapist is in a dyadic relationship with the patient and thus also brings himself in emotionally whether intentionally or not. The success of the therapy depends upon the therapist's emotional responses toward the patient. The problem of the variables relating to the therapist and of the transference and countertransference of feelings between patient and therapist becomes significant. I will deal with this later on.

Necessity of Control of the Therapist's Behavior

It seems questionable to me in any case, that—due to a lack of command of the concepts and their practical application in therapy as discussed here—a great deal of well-meaning effort and much helping investment in the patient can remain ineffective and failures then are charged to GAI. From the requirements for the training as a psychotherapist suggested here, a number of important technical and strategic steps can be derived for practice. At first, they apply, above all, to the introduction of psychotherapy.

Stretegic Steps

Introduction of Psychotherapy

Dealing with the Threshold to Therapy

A certain threshold must be overcome between the recording of the case history and the beginning of therapy. The observations and the data that the therapist has obtained from the patient need to be summarized and evaluated for the therapist to be able to lead a discussion with the patient, which is the final decisive factor for conducting the therapy. It serves two main purposes:

1. The therapist attempts to form a definitive opinion about the prognosis of treatment
2. The patient is informed of the result of these considerations. Either an offer of treatment is made, which is neither only positive nor negative, but can also be attached to certain conditions, or only a consultation without intending to have a therapy follow shortly

Judgment of the Prognosis

Which aspects should the discussion concentrate on in order to come to an opinion regarding the prognosis?

Patient's Expectations

1. *The expectations of the patient of the treatment.* The expectations are frequently placed excessively high, and the persons concerned believe their problems can be solved in a few days or weeks. In this respect the *dimension of time* must be straightened out, in particular, with the frequently impatient neurotic patients, and a provisional plan must be made regarding the duration of treatment and the frequency of the sessions. In fact it is surprising how many patients believe that sometime in the course of treatment "the big bang" will occur, through which the Gordian knot of the neurosis will be untied or another imaginary development will free him from his symptoms and personality problems practically from one moment to the next. Occasionally, a patient attributes superhuman and magical powers to the therapist, who is seen in the idealized role of the great healer, and by virtue of this "makes the patient healthy." ("You can do anything with me, Doctor, just make me healthy.") Here the patient is signafying that he is little prepared to take on the inner, often painful confrontation with himself, or active cooperation at all, which must be demanded, and to relinquish illusory expectations about the course of the psychotherapy. This is reminiscent of the topic of the motivation for therapy still to be discussed. The more unrealistic the patient's expectations are, the more problematic the prognosis of treatment becomes.

Goal of Treatment

2. The *definition of the goal of treatment* is related to this and should be worked out jointly with the patient. It is a prerequisite that he is informed by the therapist about the expected therapeutic steps, the applied procedure, and its accomplishments. This in turn presumes that the therapist has already formed certain notions about the prognosis of treatment with his patient. The definition of the treatment goal also depends upon whether all or which symptoms or behavioral disorders that the patient would like to get rid of and if the disorders can be successfully treated or not or, rather, with what likelihood.

Stress

3. The *dimensions of the burdens* that the patient will have to take on himself in the course of the treatment, whether they are of a temporal or financial nature or in the form of emotional stress, strain on his marriage or occupational situation, should be made clear to the patient

as well as the extent of the attitudinal change that will possibly be connected with the treatment.

External Conditions

4. Last to be discussed are the *external conditions of therapy,* such as frequency of sessions, scheduling, prospective duration and sequence of the individual periods, expected interruptions due to vacations, all of which determine the total duration of treatment. The question of the fixed termination of the therapy is also a part of this. This can occur by gradations, in the course of which subgoals are aimed for, in order to then make decisions about the additional steps and also about whether the therapy will be continued or not and with what frequency.

Termination

Establishing 15 to 30 sessions has proved to be extremely successful for short-term therapy. Here we are following the advice given by Malan (1963) and others to set a limit on the treatment at the outset. It was found that in at least two-thirds of the cases short-term therapy with the basic level of GAI does not take more than 20 or 25 hours, if clinical improvement is the goal (with limited restructuring of the neurotic personality), and I generally recommend making such an arrangement with the patient. Here I would like to stress that the problem of defining a *conflict focus* is not necessary in a short-term psychotherapy (Malan 1963, Dührssen 1972), which Roth (1976) particularly emphasizes. In this regard no selection of the cases for GAI therapy is necessary; its indicational spectrum is thus not restricted.

Short-term Therapy

Frequency of Treatments

5. We additionally agree upon the *frequency of treatment* with the patient, whether it takes place once or twice a week, possibly varying somewhat due to external factors. When only one session a week is held, the treatment can be intensified by asking the patient to paint one or two pictures of the imaginal contents at home. These are then discussed with him in the therapy session (Kulessa and Jung 1980).

Limitation and Further Treatment

6. The initial limiting of therapy does not preclude making a further arrangement after concluding the initially agreed upon period of therapy in those cases in which a *continuation of treatment* seems necessary or advisable. Either the treatment can be extended for a specific number of sessions (which are arranged in turn) or it can be continued as support for longer irregular intervals according to need. Another form of therapy can follow it as a supplement, for instance, group treatment. However, this supplementary agreement should not be made until the initial therapy plan has been completed.

The Patient's Motivation

7. The *motivation of the patients* for conducting the psychotherapy is the crucial point for the prognosis of treatment success. An inadequately motivated patient or one not motivated at all can almost never be motivated by the therapist later on, and will break off treatment sooner or later or carry it through due to compliance without any success. The experienced therapist is familiar with strategies that help him stimulate motivation within the scope of GAI. Motivation can be determined by:

1. Learning *how the patient* happened to come to us in order to ascertain to what extent his efforts to find a psychotherapy were influenced by others or self-determined
2. Finding out to what degree the patient is really suffering and to what extent this *"psychic pain,"* that is, his complaints or problems, is really impairing him in his conception of himself, in his happiness, and in his social situation or, rather, to what extent it is of secondary nature,

for instance, if parents, employer, spouses, or others have made the treatment a condition. Usually psychic pain decreases when a retirement pension has been filed for or likewise diminishes if the patient is awaiting a cure at a health resort or is intending to do so

3. The fact that the patient is prepared to take on *sacrifices,* such as a long traveling distance or conducting the therapy during his vacation speaks in favor of strong motivation. Also a part of this is the stated preparedness to undergo an inner development and readjustment or to temporarily do without a number of conveniences or rather to *separate from* agreeable *dependencies,* for instance, young adults with *problems of separation* from their parental home
4. The wish for more *independence* and self-responsibility also speaks in favor of good motivation, thus the development of a mature ego with the giving up of illusions, and the wish for a more strongly reality-oriented lifestyle and the mobilization of his own energies.
5. The motivation for psychotherapy is strongly dependent upon the *hypothesis,* that the patient has made *about the origin* or rather the cause of his illness. Is he *himself* convinced that only a psychogenesis is present and will he consider psychotherapy to be the correct treatment. The opposite is true if he believes in a somatic genesis. However, also with an intermediary form—if he recognizes (more or less out of compliance) and accepts a psychological cause, but keeps the view of an organic cause up his sleeve within easy reach—his motivation is ultimately limited. If necessary, one attempts to convince the patient by renewed organic clarification of the clinical picture. The adherence to an organic cause must, however, be interpreted as resistance and frequently has deep emotional roots
6. Patients who have no *clear idea* of what they expect from the therapy and what goal they are supposed to have (in my experience, this is approximately half of the patients) are naturally little motivated and frequently remain nebulous in treatment, too.
7. Sometimes patients are particularly well motivated for one kind of therapy but not for another that the therapist possibly considers more appropriate (for example, group rather than individual therapy). In such an instance the *patient's expectations* need to be analyzed and also to what extent illusory or realistic insights are linked with this. Attitudes of convenience, passivity, and the tendency for noncommitment or the opposite, the wish for a sorrowful period as the price to be paid for his improvement, can then become obvious.

Working Alliance

The aspects discussed here are in the broadest sense included in the concept of the *working alliance,* as it has been defined mainly for psychoanalysis. However, the gist of it can also be adopted by every other conflictually centered psychotherapy. I quote, "The working alliance is the relatively unneurotic, rational relationship between the patient and the analyst, which makes it possible for the patient to work purposefully in the analytical situation" (Greenson, 1973). Synonymous concepts are: "productive transference," "good rapport," "rational transference," "mature transference," "therapeutic alliance." "The clinical indications for this working alliance are: the readiness of the patient to carry out the various procedures of psychoanalysis and his capacity to work analytically with the resulting regressive and painful insights. The alliance is made between the rational ego of the patient and the analyzing ego of the analyst" (Sterba, 1934). "The significant event in this is a partial and temporary identification of the patient with the attitude and working method of the analyst, which the patient experiences directly in the regular analytical sessions" (Greenson, 1973). If we substitute the concept of applied GAI therapy for that of psychoanalysis, the relationships correspond to the conditions in our procedure.

Offer of Therapy

Offer of therapy or consultation: The offer of therapy to the patient results from the condensed *conclusion that the therapist has drawn* from all of the data. Naturally, a large amount of clinical experience is involved here. The formulation of a treatment prognosis depends upon diverse personal data of the patient, his early history, the type of illness and symptoms, his inner attitude, and many other things. Strictly speaking, there are three factors that are needed for making the prognosis:

Prognosis

1. The *kind of existing illness* and its symptoms
2. The *personality of the patient* and his attitudes and opinions
3. The kind of *therapy to be applied*

Duration of the Kinds of Therapy

With regard to the last point, we can develop relatively clear notions for symboldrama, once we know that short-term therapy of up to 30 sessions can achieve substantial gains with unspecified problem areas. For severe and exceptional cases, one has 50 to 60 sessions in mind; should a longer character analysis of persons older than 45 years be necessary, 100, 150 or more sessions may be required. The other two factors can only be determined through careful collection of the data, as discussed, from various points of view, and by a great deal of clinical experience. The well-known standard work in the German literature by *Heigl* (1978) gives important advice.

Patient's Independent Decision

Ultimately affecting the *therapeutic offer,* and in my opinion belonging to the most important strategies, is the patient's independent decision to carry out treatment in the suggested form or not (if various possibilities were discussed, then in the form selected by him) after all of the conditions and treatment possibilities have been explained. The therapeutic novice all too easily makes the mistake of believing that he must convince a patient, who still has doubts about the appropriateness of the treatment, and, as a result of wanting to help, pushes him into therapy. Such treatments, determined by others, are rarely successful. On the other hand, the patient's motivation is increased, or rather a lack in motivation becomes clear, when the patient makes the decision himself and this is also explicitly passed on to him. For this reason I dismiss each patient from the last preliminary interview with the request to *think over carefully* at home the questions raised and to let me know either by letter or by telephone whether he wants to enter the suggested treatment at all and specifically with me. If necessary, I make it a condition that he clarify his external circumstances if particular points still remain open.

Clarification of the Current Picture

If the *prognostic aspects* are not clear enough or if the patient is pressured by conflicts during the first interviews and is seeking additional discussions, I offer these at first in order to clarify the situation. I proceed in a similar way when the patient decides relatively commitedly, but I myself am still not clear about it. Usually I add another two or three sessions to refine the depth psychological case history. I am a supporter of the *"comprehensive case history"* because with its help it becomes much easier to recognize the relationship between the contents of GAI and the genetic data of the neurosis and to gain hints for the relevant centers of conflict to be focused on in GAI. If the patient is only half decided and/or it is obvious that he can only give up the *organic hypothesis* of his complaints with difficulty, but I nevertheless have the impression that precisely through the experience with GAI he has a chance to become convinced of the value of psychotherapy, I offer a compromise. I suggest a *trial run* of perhaps 8 to 10 sessions. Then both the patient and I have the liberty to decide whether the therapy should be continued or not. Here it is naturally important that the appropriate discussion really takes place in the tenth session and that it is thorough and that the patient is prompted to make a final decision as to whether he wants to continue or not. Since GAI usually brings relief soon and symptoms possibly improve, there is the possibility of convincing the patient of the significance of the GAI therapy in this way.

Trial Run

Session Thirteen: Temporal Structure Of The Therapeutic Session

Additional preparatory steps are necessary at the beginning of GAI therapy (possibly also before formulating the treatment offer) within the scope of the transition to the mental imagery technique with the help of the flower test. With good reason the question is asked again and again, what explanations or information one should give the patient before the first session with symboldrama begins.

Current Conflictual Situation

Current Conflicts Take Priority When Under Pressure to Talk

For me it belongs to the firm rules of psychotherapy to encourage the patient to talk about *his current situation* by making a short, rather casual comment after the patient has entered the room, we have greeted each other, and he has sat down. Particularly in GAI therapy, I consider it professionally irresponsible if the patient does not have the opportunity to talk about what is concerning him emotionally at the present time or rather what seems notable to him in his current problems since the previous session, before the beginning of the mental imagery phase. Here I, of course, do not mean that he is supposed to discuss his symptoms in great detail, to say nothing of complaining. However, he must have the opportunity for verbal release in one respect or another, if he is under emotional pressure or pressured by symptoms. If it concerns a repetitive description of symptoms, I let him know that I do not consider this to be the essential part of our work and soon direct him toward situations triggering these symptoms, to disappointments or frustrations, which he has experienced in the meantime and which can be important for these symptoms with regard to dynamics. If his need to discuss is very great, I am inclined to listen calmly even for a longer stretch of time. If the dynamic connections gradually become clearer, the time comes when I recommend that he try to focus on these problems in mental images, and I ask him to lie down on the couch so that he can relax better.

Explanations

In the first GAI session I explain to him that the mental imagery is intensified by relaxation and that the treatment begins with an exercise in relaxation in order to reach the level of GAI with relative certainty. I may also explain that he has surely heard that similar relaxation exercises, such as autogenic training, can be a help in treatments of nervous and psychic problems. Following this we continue the mental imagery, with which he has already become familiar during the fantasy exercise with the flower motif.

With the advanced patient, it suffices to ask at the beginning of a session whether there is something to be discussed or whether he is ready to begin with the mental imagery immediately. I leave it up to the patient whether he wants to conduct the initial discussion sitting in the chair or lying on the couch.

Dealing with Decisions

In a few rare sessions one must take into consideration that the patient would not only like to discuss a current problem in great detail but that decisions are also connected with this that must be elucidated with him from various aspects. This discussion is, above all, to clarify the patient's intentions, his feelings, and the pros and cons of a decision. As in all depth psychologically oriented treatments, the therapist is absolutely to avoid giving advice. This is also definitely true when the patient asks for it. By this, he is signaling his tendency to subordinate himself to the advice of the older person instead of making the decision himself once the situation has been clarified. In rare exceptions of particularly complicated situations, advice can be obvious. This holds true particularly if an external situation has to be changed because the therapy or its continuation depends upon it. Even then, however, the solutions are to be worked out jointly with the patient on the basis of *his* suggestions.

Experience gained in the past years has shown that such phases of discussion can be used productively in the course of a GAI therapy, if they lead to the depth psychological clarification of the problems at hand in the suggested way. They can also serve to clarify previous GAI sessions and the connections with current problems relating to personality or genetic problems. Here the breadth of the therapist's psychotherapeutic training is demonstrated when he makes use of these periods as far as possible without assuming an all too directive or even authoritarian position.

Short GAI Phase in Every Session

It is desirable that a GAI phase be inserted into every session, even if it is very short. If this does not work for reasons of time, then it must be abandoned in an emergency.

We have tried to determine the proportions of the average time of the discussion phases and the GAI phases related to the number of sessions. On an average, the relationship is one-third pure discussion to two-thirds mental imaginal work. This relationship also arises in part because the GAI session is dealt with verbally in the manner subsequently discussed. If one considers the structure of a treatment session in the course of a routine therapy,

Mental Imaginal Phase in a Session

the *mental imaginal phase* usually takes 30 to 40 minutes. Shorter phases are naturally also possible. On the other hand, longer ones wear the patient out all too easily and are only important if a pressing problem that is difficult to deal with is in fact to be brought to a certain conclusion in GAI.

Withdrawing the Relaxation

The mental imagery phase of the therapy session is ended by having the patient systematically clench his fists, bend and stretch his arms and vigorously using his muscles, repeating that three times, as if it were a strenuous gymnastic exercise demanding strong muscle tension. There are a number of reasons why it is absolutely important to conduct this "awakening procedure" which is derived from J.H. Schultz's instructions for autogenic training. The main reason lies in the following. In the course of symboldrama many patients sink into a relatively deep hypnoidal state without realizing it. This often has the consequence that, on the one hand, they are "disconnected" from the surroundings due to their intense concentration on the imaginal contents and are thus in a state of altered consciousness. On the other hand, a reduction in muscle tonus in the arms and legs is connected with it. This is frequently experienced as an extreme heaviness of the limbs and the attempt to bend the arms only comes about with a great deal of effort. In this connection I recall my previous statement that the relaxation exercise or rather analogous suggestions introducing the mental imagery are basically only a safety measure. The emergence of imaginings correlates to a high degree with a deepening of relaxation and the central "switching over" as defined by J.H. Schultz (1979). With the help of "awakening" this condition is supposed to be broken through by the patient's own activity. The intense muscle innervation, which frequently must occur with strong effort (which some patients shy away from), serves to activate the motoric portions of the cerebral cortex, which reacts upon the central activating system of the brain (formatio reticularis). The reduced degree of alertness during mental imagery is ended by this in the sense of having a waking effect. To advance the waking state further, I have the patient open his eyes and after a few minutes, during which he slowly finds his way around in the real world again, I ask him to sit up on the couch and let his legs hang down to the side. (Then he is sitting at a right angle to me.) The importance of this ceremony of "awakening" becomes especially clear during this period. The patient is frequently still occupied with what he experienced in mental imagery, with the mood and his feelings, which are still dominating him. He needs time to be able to orient himself to reality again, although he had, of course, maintained full reality control on the periphery. Nevertheless, the remaining state of submersion, a kind of inward absorption, is not terminated so quickly. Therefore I suggest to the patient that he remain in the waiting room for another 15 minutes after ending the session or perhaps take a short walk. However, he should in no case get behind the wheel of an automobile right away or walk in city traffic. This "inner absorption" shows individual differences, but needs to be taken into consideration.

Activation by Way of the Motoric Cerebral Cortex

Continuing Fixation on the Content of Mental Imagery

Follow-up Discussion

Rest Phase

Working Through

In connection with this, it is now easy to answer the question, in what form it is advisable to *deal with the material of the mental imagery* more thoroughly with the patient in the psychoanalytic sense and what do I personally think of this. At the end of the session, it is natural to approach parts of the frequently abundant mental imaginal material on the level of a more cognitive-rational outlook and insightful capacity in the same manner as in psychoanalytic work with dreams and to encourage the patient to make associations and to relate what enters his mind concerning the individual parts. This question answers itself, depending upon whether the patient is at all capable of doing this or only to a limited degree during the concluding stage of the state of altered consciousness as just described. The nonrealizable demand for a cognitive switchover is frequently all too easily experienced by the patient as unfair and can leave the feeling that the therapist apparently does not know what is happening inside of him.

What form, however, should the last 5 to 10 minutes of the session take after the conclusion of the mental imagery? As always in psychotherapy, no fast rules can be given; one must proceed individually according to the characteristic features of each patient. A small number of them have difficulty in remembering the contents of the mental imagery afterward, particularly during the first sessions. Here it can help to bring them back to the cognitive sphere, if the therapist tries jointly with the patient to recall individual scenes of the mental imagery. The greater number of patients know from experience that they are capable of remembering most of the contents again at the moment when they begin to write the obligatory protocol about the mental imagery at home. Then one can dispense with the recapitulation.

Letting the Mood Fade Away

Many years' experience has shown me that in most cases it is particularly valuable therapeutically to at first let the prevailing mood and the present feelings fade away in the presence of the therapist without disturbing them by direct questions. A phase of common silence arises in this way, in which the therapist indicates through his thoughtful attention nonverbally or by single, fitting comments that he understands the patient in his present condition.

Reinforcing the Emotional Tone

He can, for instance, say reinforcingly, "That touched you very deeply," "The experiences are fading away now" or "Give yourself a little time, let it all calmly fade away." A third group of patients is not strained emotionally to such a high degree in terms of mood. They either would like to have more information about some details or be given the opportunity to talk some more about the contents. In the latter case I ask the patient which contents seem most important, which impressed him the most, or I pick out some of these contents.

Answering Questions

If the patient is very familiar with the procedure, I possibly ask him if he sees a connection between the mental imaginal contents and the problem discussed at the beginning of the session or with another one that I then specify. It would lead too far afield to present a catalog of suggestions. The situations are so diverse, and the interplay of the interactions with the patient depends a great deal on the therapist's ability to empathize, for given situations have different effects on various individuals.

Individual Treatment

Only the broad training of the therapist in connection with supplementary training seminars and the supervision of individual cases can impart experience and confidence regarding which interventions are appropriate precisely in this refined phase at the end of the therapeutic session.

The therapist's behavior described thus far refers to a situation in which the mental imagery, particularly in its final stage, has run relatively smoothly and has faded out. However, the situation is totally different in those more rare cases in which GAI has aroused a series of intense negative emotions and moods, for instance, anxiety, uncertainty, depression, or a degree of helplessness. Usually that is the case if a scene in symboldrama could not be brought to a definite solution. The empathic therapist then correctly feels that he has to dismiss the patient from the session not only dissatisfied but also with a problem still remaining open. Particularly if the therapist has the impression that the patient will be somewhat burdened with this until the next session, he has the possibility of giving him a bit of assurance and confidence again through concluding interventions, without a seeming harmony having been forcibly brought about in the GAI scene. The aim is to again strengthen the ego defenses, which were relaxed by GAI. This can happen by the therapist's taking up the situation in question. Using an outside example (observations in another case) or even an example involving himself (description of a personal experience) or a more general explanation, he attempts to relativize the emotional uniqueness of the experience in the here and now. Further, it is often important and also helpful to call upon the defense mechanism of intellectualization. This occurs, for instance, when individual scenes or comments that touched the patient deeply are directly approached cautiously for their meaning. The therapist can also point out connections with previous experiences already familiar in GAI or form reality and thus demonstrate the cognitive fabric of the relationships of these parts to each other. In addition, direct questions as to the condition, the mood, cognitive details about the day, before leave taking—for instance, what the patient will do the rest of the day, whom he will meet, how he plans to spend the evening—have a relaxing effect through the feeling of the therapist's interest. However, the therapist should not be all that apprehensive and should presume that the patient's ego will compensate the uneasiness. A problem, which is not harmoniously concluded in GAI, is frequently followed by further therapeutically productive confrontations. I also go into this and suggest to the patient that he use this difficult but possibly productive situation from the point of view of the therapy and to write down everything that occurs to him relating to this theme in the meantime and bring it along to discuss in the next session. Naturally, it is important that the next session has already been scheduled. In an emergency, telephone help can also be offered for the interim period, which the patient almost never makes use of. With these empathic forms of intervention, needing coordination in regard

Concluding Interventions

Strengthening the Ego Defenses

Unsettled Problems Stimulate Confrontation

to details, it becomes possible to strengthen the patient's ego and to guide an excessive uneasiness rarely arising in symboldrama.

Journal

As already noted, every patient of mine is instructed, as a part of the therapy, to keep a journal of the mental imagery. He is to leave a wide margin on the paper, where I can make notes. When the patient comes to the next session, the current problems can be discussed more or less comprehensively to begin with, if necessary. Then I proceed to slowly read aloud in the patient's presence. Now that part of dealing with the imaginal material follows, which is commonly expected at the end of the previous session. I ask the patient both for ideas about parts and details of the journal as well as perhaps about possible connections with problems, which could be appearing in the record of the imagery on the basis of the problem discussed at the beginning of the previous session or one that has affected him in the meantime. Instead of the question, "Does something occur to you in regard to this?" which is common in psychoanalysis and somewhat stereotyped today, I choose more flexible and more varied formulations, such as, "What do you think of that?" "Do you have any ideas about possible connections?" "What do you think the one or the other part in this image means?" As the patient recognizes my interest in these questions and since at home between the two sessions he in fact did have mostly fitting ideas in reference to a theme of the mental imagery still affecting him, an amount of material becomes concentrated in this way. For one patient this is broader and he learns to utilize these ideas; for another it remains sparse and rendering the symbols of mental imagery into his outer or inner world remains closed to him for a longer period of time.

Process of Resolving

Ideas

Interpretation of the Contents of Mental Imagery

Here we again come across the question to what extent the therapist should interpret the contents of the mental imagery or whether he should provide additional information about them. The repeatedly asked question about interpreting contents of the imagery at all, here on the basic level, is connected with this. In the course of the further sessions the therapist is also supposed to stay relatively restrained in giving explanations about the meaning of individual contents and of the mental images. He should make it clear to the patient that knowing the diversely determined symbols intellectually does not help much. The technique of elucidation lies rather in asking the patient over and over again what occurs to him by way of his own intuition, his ideas and thoughts in reference to one or another of the contents based upon the knowledge of his problems and their background. The question then simply reads, "What do you think about it yourself?" The suggestion can be made that interpretations of contents by the therapist all to easily miss the core of the individual substance, that they have to be vague, and that in the course of the advancing therapy the one or other connection will become naturally more obvious and clearer to the patient. However, the situation in which clarity does not occur is also basically not a disadvantage; rather the effect of the mental imagery comes about first of all and most importantly on the level of experience. In fact, GAI on the basic level is predominantly an *experiential therapy,* as long as the treatment remains a short-term basis. The rule never to give direct interpretations, should in any case prevent the defense mechanisms of intellectualization and rationalization from being reinforced (see before). In the text about the entire procedure (Leuner, 1983) the more refined strategies, all the way to the interpretive aids while working through GAI, are presented in detail. In the approach to this, which is also valid for the basic level, the subtle clarification of the GAI contents, the accompanying feelings, and also the patient's possible thoughts or ideas about the material are the most important means of bringing the mental imagery out of the realm of the primary process and the archaic ways of experiencing into the realm of the reality-oriented secondary process and thus into the realm of reality and the preconscious close to insight.

Danger of Activating Defense Mechanisms

Clarification takes precedence

As for the rest, the therapist can be confident that most patients are—due to the immediate therapeutic effect of GAI (for example, the initial release of existing emotional uneasiness and pressing symptoms)—quite ready to follow the only semiexplanatory insightful path of the basic level. A part of this, in addition to dealing with the journal, which has proved especially valuable, is to have the patient sketch or, even better, *paint in color* one or two of the contents of his choice from the imagery session at home. He brings the pictures to the next session to discuss. Some therapists even insert a "special session" for dealing with the pictorial material, to which the patient can in turn bring thoughts and ideas to enlarge the field of understanding. In this way the patient's important creative capacities, still to be discussed, are developed using the material from the mental imagery on the basic level (see also Kulessa and Jung, 1983).

Painting the GAI Scenes

Therapist's Protocol

As far as technique is concerned, the question continues to be asked whether the therapist can or should make a written record during the session. In contrast to former practice, today all experienced therapists have discontinued this during the therapy itself. A very few, who still do it, claim that it serves to aid memory. I maintain, on the other hand, that it serves their own defenses from becoming drawn too far into the patient's emotional world by their empathy. I will address the topic of empathy later on.

Free-Floating Attention

The "free floating attention," that Freud (1912) recommended for psychoanalytic sessions is not compatible, or only with great difficulty, with the splitting of attention involved when the therapist is writing at the same time. The fine nuances of mental imagery, which can only be grasped through empathic resonance, concerning contents and above all emotions are all too easily lost, and the therapist no longer succeeds in making sensitive interventions in context. In other words, due to his

Regression with the Patient

writing he does not succeed in the necessary regression with the patient. He operates more strongly on the cognitive instead of on the emotional free floating level, because of which the guidance of the therapy suffers. For that reason I advise against writing

Tape Recording

during the session. Instead of this, we let a *tape recorder* run, with the patient's consent. There are rarely any objections to this, since today everyone is familiar with these devices. The patient's consent is easily gained with the idea that in this way the therapist can devote his full attention to the patient and his mental imagery. The tape recording serves as a check. With a suitable patient, one can even combine the advantage of allowing

Patient Listens to the Tape

him to listen to the tape in the office or at home in preparing the protocol. In so doing the patient perceives various subtleties afterward, and emotional fluctuations are triggered anew, which are lost in an account written from memory. Files of cassettes do not take up much space. The technical transaction of the recording creates no difficulties with the modern microphones, as long as these are brought close enough to the speakers. It is to be noted in passing that tape recordings are asked for regularly for cases supervised by the AGKB.

Session Fourteen: Structure and Guidance of the Mental Imagery I

In the following class hours, the structure and guidance of the mental image will be dealt with from various points of view. Again I point out that the technique of GAI naturally cannot be learned in a seminar course or by reading a book. The repeatedly emphasized self-awareness and participation in appropriate intensive seminars are of the greatest importance for practicing the style of guidance. However, these are not sufficient by themselves, because certain concepts, which the therapist must know, underlie guiding the mental imagery in a way that is therapeutically as favorable as possible. They consist partly of the psychodynamic knowledge of psychoanalysis and partly of the very extensive empirical experience in dealing with mental imagery. Naturally, they are limited to the basic level in this class. That has the two following consequences:

Role of Self-Awareness

Conflict—Semi-disclosing

1. Mental imagery is conducted primarily within the framework of symbolic disguise. Thus a protective style of guidance is pursued with the intention of setting aside stronger affective, discomforting, or depressing reactions in the patient and those experienced as threats in spite of centering on conflictual contents. Of course, this does not mean that conducting the therapy is to be markedly supportive and cover up conflicts
2. Focusing directly on conflict spheres and thus confrontational techniques are also set aside

These latter two methods, focusing and confrontation, are mainly the subject of the intermediate level.

Structuring on the Basic Level

To give you a survey of the individual points which I will deal with in the next hours involving this topic about the structuring and guidance of mental imagery on the basic level, I will list them now. It will become clear that the previous hours have been a preparation for the concepts. The external structuring of the session was already discussed in the previous section. Therefore the following deals predominantly with the *"internal" structuring.*

Therapeutic Strategies

For therapists trained in *Rogers* person centered therapy, I would like to mention that the topic here cannot be adequately described by the term "therapist's behavior." Rather, definite therapeutic strategies are described. Conveying them should in places be substantiated and discussed by illustrating the therapeutically effective components of GAI. In the larger context (Leuner, 1983) I point out in detail to what extent the therapist's basic behavior in person centered therapy can be used as a preliminary stage to the psychodynamic orientation in the scope of the basic level therapy.

List of Points

1. General style of guidance
2. Training procedure in connection with the standard motifs
3. Training procedure in connection with the fixed images
4. Creative development of spontaneous mental imagery
5. Conflict-free scenes and gratification of archaic needs
6. Pursuit of real situations
7. Orientation to therapeutically effective factors
8. Transference and countertransference

The material concerning the individual positions is of various dimensions. Therefore some of it is summarized in one instruction hour. For the sake of clarity and systematics, occasional repetitions from previous seminar hours cannot be avoided.

General Style of Guidance

The style of guidance in GAI is characterized by a friendly, reserved attitude on the part of the therapist. Initially, he suggests the individual motifs, as I have illustrated in the examples. Here he takes a wait-and-see attitude, in no case urging but granting instead, and he is cautious and reserved in his actions. He should in any case avoid taking on a marked position of leadership with too many requests for action within the imagery, that is, to do or to undertake one thing or another.

Learning Process

In this context I again refer to the factor of the learning process stressed on p.83, which the patient passes through in his first steps in mental imagery. In the course of this period of familiarization during the first sessions, the style of guidance is different compared with that during the fully developing therapy. Although actions are at first offered cautiously within the imagery, and questions are asked about details of image contents or about elements of mood and feeling, the therapist must also be capable of stepping in to provide more structure, if necessary,

Interventions

and possibly also undertaking decisive interventions. These can concentrate on getting the patient to stop doing something or on deciding to carry out a certain task.

The therapist's basic attitude should additionally allow the patient to sense that he is interested in the imagery contents, that he can reexperience and empathize with his feelings, and also how the respective scene moves the patient internally. However, this interest is not to be exclusively intellectual, to say nothing of

Empathy

scientific, but is supported by the *expression of human warmth and of inner togetherness.* In this respect the patient also regularly needs simple, usually nonverbal signals, on the basis of which he perceives the closeness of the therapist, the sincerity of his understanding, and his warmth. In critical, fearful, or seemingly dangerous scenes, the therapist is to express his *committed accompaniment* of the patient. Such behavior is definitely a part of the therapist's behavior in GAI.

Therapist's Behavior in GAI

The signs are generally limited to "hm, hm," "yes"—not to be given in stereotypic fashion—or possibly to the summarizing verbalization of one of the circumstances described by the patient. *Formulating the feeling tone communicated nonverbally by the patient* can be particularly important. It can be expressed in the imagined scene or in the feeling conveyed by the patient faced with this scene. If the therapist does not capture the feeling tone in his formulation as precisely as the patient expects, he usually reacts with a correction. However, in this way the prevailing feeling tone becomes conscious to him. It is verbalized, and this feeling is also neutralized in part by this. That is especially important with anxiety-laden scenes and wherever strong affects are involved that prevent the patient from returning to a well-tempered description of the subtler imagery contents. The therapist's interest and his empathy are also conveyed by loosely interspersed questions for details, whether they are about the imaginal contents or about the dominant feeling tone.

Verbalization of Emotional Contents

Empathy

In seminars, questions are frequently asked regarding the technique of the therapist's behavior. The participants are interested, for instance, in whether one should talk a lot or very little, if the patient should report continuously or only at intervals, whether the therapist's questions disturb or not. Of course, there are no general answers for all these legitimate questions about details. The interventions are completely different in each individual case and here again according to the passage of the imagery and its emotional quality. The *crucial criterion* for the *respective originality* of the *intervention,* in a manner of speaking the *key to all situations* in general, is *the empathic and inner accompanying indentification of the therapist with the respective scene of the mental imagery.* The matching technical term, which is used in a different way in psychoanalysis (from which it originates) as well as in person centered therapy, is "empathy." In psychoanalysis this means—and I would like to particularly emphasize this—a temporary, trial identification with the patient with the purpose of experiencing, either anticipatorily or internally accompanying, what the patient is about to do or what is happening inside him emotionally at the moment. Such kinds of identification for the purpose of understanding play a part in normal interpersonal relationships. They are based upon an archaic, holistic perception in the form of *imitative identification* and the *perception*

Identification

concurrently connected with it of *alteration of one's own person,* which this situation entails. Therefore both must participate in the empathy in symboldrama. Here the therapist identifies in part with the scenes, which the patient experiences in his mental imagery, and copies them in his own world of imagination on the basis of the patient's descriptions. His feelings likewise resonate with those of the patient, imparted by the sum of the patient's signals, whether they are the scenario of the imagery, the tone of voice, or the mimicking and bodily expression. If the beginning therapist follows this instruction strictly, a disastrous development can be in the offing, which must be recognized

Over-identification

clearly in time. Namely, it can happen that he falls victim to this identification with the patient almost completely and through this he scarcely perceives his own ego and its mechanisms of control. For this reason the *supplementary rule in connection* with the *empathic guidance of the patient* discussed here states that it is only supposed to be a *trial identification.* The inner closeness to the patient involved here is important, but it may only exist temporarily and for a short period of time. In the subsequent period of time therefore the therapist should withdraw from the closeness to the patient for an equally short

Empathy

time, during which the material he perceived by empathizing is critically and cognitively examined, studied in the context of his therapeutic knowledge and concepts. From this he makes decisions for further guidance. Such considerations result in simply contemplating whether to wait silently at a given point, whether to give a brief sign, whether to reinforce a shade of feeling or a part of the content, or whether to ask a directive or confrontative question. However, they can really only be appropriately applied in, so to speak, custom-made form to the patient's current inner scene, if the empathic process has preceded these considerations in the described manner.

The capacity to empathize in the way characterized here varies from person to person. We find therapists, who have a natural capacity for it from the start. Another group, frequently more strongly intellectualized and scientifically oriented persons, are, on the contrary, more accustomed to entrusting the guidance of the mental imagery to predominantly cognitive categories and can only do justice to the demands for empathy and emotional closeness with difficulty. A small group, frequently interested in psychotherapy, tends toward the opposite behavior. They have in part, a very good empathic capacity. They partly believe that in addition to this—or they do it more unconsciously—a high degree of self-denial in the midst of continual empathic closeness or identification with the patient can especially advance the therapy. At this point there arises the problem of insufficient

Over-identification

separation from the patient, that is, of *overidentification.* In another connection I presented this matter in detail (Leuner, 1983). These described undulation—between temporary, trial

Undulating Movement

identification combined with approaching the patient

Between Closeness and Reflection

emotionally, and the subsequent step backward away from the patient to examine the situation and plan interventions—prevents overidentification and maintains the necessary separation.

Accompaniment of the Patient

In this context, certain technical behaviors on the part of the therapist also prove to be unfavorable. Some young therapists believe, for example, that they should close their eyes during the imagery phase, relax, and let the images develop. That easily results in their regressing more strongly along with their patients. They then develop their own empathically analogous or slightly divergent imaginal contents, with respect to those of the patient. The capacity to structure the imagery in a cognitively clear fashion and to guide the patient is lost for them. Here the inexperienced person may become more and more quiet, still, and passive with an intensely depressed patient, and he becomes increasingly depressed during the imagery session while producing corresponding imaginal contents. The therapist has thus failed in his task (through insufficient separation), namely, to consider in what form he should structure the mental imagery specifically with this patient.

The interactional dynamics described here between therapist and patient usually become obvious when the therapist listens to a tape made during the session and the contents are discussed by a supervisional group.

Learning Theory

For the style of guidance in mental imagery, I would like to emphasize another aspect that is associated with *learning theory.* It is wise to support and encourage the patient at the completion of the mental imagery, all the more, when he is working with the standard motifs. This takes place by way of discreet, positive feedback (in the sense of praising). It can begin even during the flower test. This form of "reward" should, of course, be given cautiously so that it scarcely appears deliberate. I formulate it, for instance, by using the still very noncommittal "hm, hm" or "ah, yes," "I understand," "yes, you see," and I may repeat something that has already been said previously, but now put it more strongly in the service of rewarding reinforcement than to consider it as a sign of closeness, as was the case previously. One can intensify these reinforcements, for instance, "Pay close attention to what is coming next," "That is really important," "I find that interesting," "Perhaps you should look into that." Naturally it is clear that these signs or reinforcement, as I would like to call them, lead to the fact that certain contents or emotional aspects addressed by the therapist also attain greater importance for the patient, and then perhaps he steers his future imaginal productions more in the direction of these reinforced contents. Discreet processes of controlling the imagery are involved here, about which the therapist must be clear. He should in any case avoid bringing in his own preferences and tendencies too much and should reflect on the directions of intervention and predominantly subject them to the viewpoints of the therapeutic concepts presented in the following.

Conversely, situations can also arise in which it seems meaningful, precisely on the basic level, to protect the patient from certain actions in symboldrama or to prevent dangerous ones. Here we, of course, avoid statements that could be experienced as disapproving or punitive. More cautious directives should replace them, such as, "I am not sure if that is correct," "By no means try to" (for instance, actively attack an animal to kill it). It would be more cautious to formulate as follows: "I would prefer suggesting that you . . .," "Why don't you try . . .," "I could imagine that . . .," "If I were you, perhaps I would try . . .," or "How would it be, if you did . . . now." We in any case avoid such directions as, "Now do this and this," "Now walk along the brook." For the somewhat more mature patient, of whom we have the impression that he is completely capable of developing the mental imagery on his own impetus, we often ask what he would like to do, or give him the choice of taking up one thing or another next. In so doing we delegate to him a major part of the freedom of choice and the realization of his respective impulses and thus show that we believe he is capable of this. Frequently, this is an experiment with the patient to see if he responds to this or if he passively needs structuring by the therapist.

Protection

Formulations

In the discussion of the therapist's behavior, one specific direction must not be left out. The rule of abstinence has proved valuable, a rule that was proposed by Freud (1958), the figure many professional circles consider the main authority in psychotherapy, and in my opinion the rule of abstinence constitutes a very important mode of behavior in daily practice. Regardless of the form in which the psychotherapist proceeds or the technique used, he does well to observe this rule. In simplified form it states that *the therapist is not to enter into any personal or intimate contacts whatsoever with the patient during the treatment period.*

Rule of Abstinence

Personal Dealings with Patients

One is not supposed to become involved with the patient personally, which means that all social contacts, such as invitations, participation in mutual events, or other affairs are declined. The psychodynamic argument lies in the circumstance that, for the therapist, situations of psychological temptation can be connected with the initiation of personal contact, leading to uncontrolled countertransference feelings. There is no doubt that the therapist will treat his patient differently in the next treatment session if they have met on the occasion of a dinner party and been involved in conversation, danced, and perhaps become erotically involved, on the part of both. Conversely, hostile involvement may also occur. The patient also will have totally different expectations of his therapist than if the latter limited himself solely to his assignment as a psychotherapist and neutral and incorruptible helper.

I am well aware that recent innovations in psychotherapy, such as advances in therapy of sexual dsyfunctions, have expanded a great deal and contacts between therapist and patient are sometimes suggested. I have no experience in this direction at my disposal, although I am familiar, in part, with the literature. For the GAI therapist in training, clear and emotionally distinct conditions should in my opinion be set up from the start and in the long run be held to. This is done primarily in the interest of the patient to avoid all possible emotional entanglements in the area of transference and countertransference. The common task is the maintenance of cooperative teamwork in reference to the patient's preconscious and unconscious problems. An awareness directed toward this can only be maintained and intensified, if other kinds of emotional involvement through encounters between therapist and patient in the private sphere are avoided.

Treatment of Relatives

Naturally the rule of abstinence also applies to treating your own relatives or acquaintances. It therefore demands of you that you encourage neither your wife nor your brothers and sisters, your sister-in-law, or your children to form images in symboldrama. With the exception of fleeting attempts, such an action would have to count as a crucial professional error. First of all, I may remind you that it is considered medical tradition not to treat persons in one's own surroundings, in particular, family members. Physicians recognized that medical procedures performed on familiar or related persons are not free of emotional feelings and thus the diagnostic as well as the therapeutic capacity for making decisions and the technical assurance in the use of the therapy suffer. The temptation is often great, however, because the therapist believes that with GAI he now has the means at his disposal to help his intimate partner. However, here he sould consider that perhaps precisely the aggressive impulses of his partner, child, or other family member toward him are therapeutically valuable. These and many other impulses must naturally be suppressed by the dependent partner. Should they arise, the relationship runs the risk of being impaired if not totally destroyed by an unfortunate mixing of therapeutically released impulses, on the one hand, and the partner's expectations of loyalty, on the other.

Because I am familiar with the temptation of giving close relatives the "blessings" of GAI as, above all, the beginner sees it, I would like strictly and emphatically to warn against this. Regardless of what method is used, the psychotherapy of a partner always belongs in the hands of a third person for the

Protection of Impartiality

protection of impartiality and of professional competency. This does not exclude undertaking family therapy with third persons so that both persons involved can clarify their possibly emotionally disturbed relationship and can bring it to a new level.

Training Procedure in Connection with the Standard Motifs

Supervision Through the Panorama

The training procedure is the main technique in the sequence of mental imagery on the basic level. Training is equivalent to focusing on the individual standard motifs with the aim of completing the associated tasks and performances under the relaxed guidance of the therapist in one therapy session allocated to each motif. In this connection the question frequently asked whether only one or several motifs can or must be approached in one session and whether a certain order is to be retained in the sequence of the standard motifs on the basic level. To state it directly: It is usually neither possible nor does it seem meaningful to cover all five motifs of the basic level in one session. It is considered a rule that not more than one motif is focused on and dealt with per session. If it seems appropriate, the motif of the brook can follow that of the meadow (if the latter is only negligibly productive). If a motif cannot be exhausted in one session due to reasons of time, its continuation in the following session is completely permissible. This refers in particular to the time-consuming motifs of pursuing the course of a brook and inspecting a house.

Sequence of Motifs

The sequence of motifs is not meant to be rigid. It is elegant if the therapist takes up spontaneously arising motifs in the catathymic panorama and has them explored in more detail. Generally, the rule holds that it is not a matter of completing as many imaginal contents as possible. The therapist should exclude such an achievement factor from GAI, especially since the patients are well enough aware of the pressure to achieve from their family or everyday environment.

This does not mean that at certain intervals we should not press the patient to, in fact, run through the one or the other motif. However, of equal ranking importance is the free development of the individual images in connection with the basic motifs and here especially, the depth of the patient's inner involvement in what is happening, that is how affected he is in terms of mood and emotions in the face of the appearing imaginal scenes. In many respects I consider this more important than the appreciation of an abundance of imaginal impressions. The dimensions of what a patient develops during the imaginal phase of the session in one respect naturally depends on the length of the session.

Individual Psychic Tempo

In addition, we must take into account the individual's own particular psychic tempo, especially in reference to the capacity of developing fantasy contents and imaginations as well as formulating them. Persons with a sluggish and slow-moving temperament naturally tend to experience symboldrama more slowly, too. Elsewhere I dealt in greater detail with these very slow and inactive mental images presented, perhaps, in bits and pieces (Leuner, 1983). In any case it has been demonstrated very clearly that, also in these cases, the persons can definitely profit from the therapy, even more than expected as long as therapeutic patience and some positive feedback from the therapist is provided.

No Standard Course

From this and from diverse other observations, I have derived the rule that in teaching GAI to future therapists we must deliberately *abandon describing a kind of standard course* or *average and typical course.* Of course, this results in the aspiring therapists all too easily measuring the imaginal behavior of the patient against this average gauge and making premature, that is biased, judgments about the prognosis, which must be revised in a trial therapy. Our basic rule reads instead: *Every patient develops mental imagery according to his individual style, and it is the therapist's duty to accept this individual style and to adjust to it.*

Attention to Individual Style

This principle becomes clinically even more evident when comparisons are made to patients quite the opposite of the aforementioned. This group of patients develops mental images in lively fashion and goes through the individual passages quickly due to their lively temperaments, their extreme watchfulness, and frequently their capacity to think quickly. Please do not be deceived. This relative speed and agility, and perhaps the related colorfulness, in which these patients pass through the suggested basic motifs in no way indicates that they are at the same time emotionally involved and that the expected therapeutic success (precisely because they do seem so involved) is connected with it. If examined more closely, it can turn out that the emotions of these patients resonate defectively. They tend unconsciously to defend against the emotional side of their experiences, that is to ignore the emotional depths by means of their apparent enthusiasm for the beautiful contents. In this respect their ego is, in the final analysis, less involved therapeutically than that of patients with less brilliant, less impressive imaginal scenes. Persons, who are productive and especially gifted imaginally, thus initially offer an abundance of material, perhaps a very colorful world of appearances, that already surrounds them in the meadow. They can, nevertheless, be less involved emotionally in the depths of their person. I mention this possibility, because this group of persons are usually more strongly hysterically structured. A factor that can be playing a part with them, which at first does not occur to the therapist, is that these patients are very sensitive and find out what pleases the therapist. By means of their great adaptability and skill at roles, they can reach good terms with the therapist by unconsciously elaborating on their mental imagery in a way as lively, imaginative, and diverse as possible. After longer passages, one is able to discover that the actual emotional basis of their disturbance has not been restructured in the way, that it at first seemed to be.

Fast Pace and Emotional Involvement

Hysterical structure

Working with Details

In such cases one recommends a style of guidance with attention to the details of the catathymic contents, which he describes with increasing straightforwardness, verbalizes his emerging feelings, and does not let himself be carried away by all too much vivacity and enthusiasm. Patients in this group tend to overlook details, to deliver their description "with a big show," to jump from one thing to another, and to avoid even the small, realistic steps, which they have to perform, for instance, in climbing the mountain. Instead of this, they suddenly arrive at the top of the mountain, as if by a miracle. A style of guidance is presented to them, as stated, which urges them to subtle, detailed, and reality-oriented descriptions, and thus also ways of experiencing.

This hysterical style of behavior in mental imagery, somewhat exaggerated here, can, however, also be productive in a milder or personally more involved form. Only the experienced therapist will be able to gauge that. In any case, from a technical point of view, we will also take this expansive manner of experiencing, strongly conveyed by fantasy, into account by allowing the patient to develop in this form for the time being.

Development of Fantasy

Applied to the question about the sequence of the five standard motifs of the basic level, one can easily deduce that in principle one cannot insist each time that the patient strictly fulfill the assigned tasks. We nevertheless attempt to have him complete the series of exercises from one session to another. If he is inclined spontaneously to continue his individual catathymic contents in another direction, we will at first give in to this tendency for long intervals. Here I deliberately say "for long intervals" because it has proved to be important to take up the typical dimensions of the basic motifs occasionally and run through them to avoid biases. Later, within the scope of the intermediate level techniques, the therapist accrues greater freedom.

Systematic Guidance

Here, however, we still start from a systematically oriented guidance of the mental imagery and thus also want to prevent important circles of conflict from being avoided over a longer period of time due to all-too-frequent circumvention of the standard motifs. I am thinking, for example, that when the ascent of the mountain is continuously avoided, the connected problem of rivalry is also completely avoided by the patient over long intervals and is perhaps not properly dealt with at all.

Session Fifteen: Structure and Guidance of the Mental Imagery II

Training Procedure in Connection with the Fixed Images

Points of Conflict

Attention to those contents that signal certain *points of conflict* to us plays an important part in guiding the patient through the catathymic panorama, which is the reason for the previously stated standard motifs with their exercises, as was already indicated earlier. Points of conflict are recognized most easily in the aforementioned *fixed images* and, among them, particularly in the *obstructive motifs.* The last-mentioned are the most pronounced form of a neurotic problem in symboldrama and have particularly outstanding diagnostic significance. For the therapy itself, they offer the therapist an important orientation in every session, so to speak as junction or focal points, which he should note well and to which he should also direct the patient's perceptional attention in the imagery sooner or later.

Fixed Images

I am starting from the *generic concept of fixed images.* By this we mean scenes in symboldrama whose contents are characterized by stereotyping and thus fixation of the structures. One can return to them repeatedly, and they change only slightly in content if at all. They apparently represent decidedly firmly established, unconscious dynamic constellations, which signify a *pronounced problem* and are an expression of the immovable *rigidity as equivalents of the neurotic disturbance.* As in the formation of psychogenic symptoms, they arise from a compromise between a pressing impulse and the defense against it, in frequently quite complicated and multilevel form. I will subsequently present a number of these fixed images or obstructive motifs as illustrations. In the course of our further observations it became apparent that characteristics other than the purely stereotypic fixation are indicative of the conflictual character of imaginal contents, namely, strange contradictions in an image compared with the natural world, such as a forest that has both fall foliage and summery green leaves, extreme forms of expression, which we do not find in reality and which denote a special meaning through the kind of feeling tone they express or arouse in the person imagining them. Here one thinks of contradictory feelings, or the arousal of anxiety and fear, of coldness, of particular sublimity, bizarreness, or whatever the case may be. The qualities can be extraordinarily varied, the patient learns to describe them and should also render a descriptive account of the feeling tone. Only someone who is skilled in reading mental imagery and who is familiar with the symbolism will be able to throw light on the fine ramifications of this kind of conflictual contents. The following example is an illustration of this.

Neurotic Equivalents

Special Meaning

Example

Case 1 (15)

A 58-year-old woman, whom I have focus on a meadow as a trial run after the flower test, offers the following scenario. At first the meadow is very pleasant for her, the grass is high, she "places," as she says, a large number of dandelions into it. A brook flows through the meadow valley and this edifying view makes her happy on a gloomy afternoon. Without special request, she pursues the brook in the direction of its source. At first she is able to do this without any difficulty, and she is reminded of some walks which she regularly takes. However, she suddenly continues, for me relatively unexpectedly: "And now it is becoming difficult, I'm following the little brook through the thick undergrowth of the woods, it is tiresome. But, as usual on our walks, I naturally don't take a path, instead I wind my way through the thick undergrowth." This quoted statement appears to be an important fixed image. She decides not to search for a path and instead struggles through the underbrush. At the same time, it becomes clear that she goes on this sort of walk, which "cuts across," not only in this image but regularly in reality as well, instead of using the marked paths, as would be the obvious thing to do, even if they are only small trails. This emphatic "deciding against the marked path" is, by the way, strangely contradictory to the summery meadow defined by a happy mood. I see an additional fixed image marking a problem although somewhat played down, in her obvious disappointment regarding the expected source. She does not find an actual source. The water of the brook collects in a not very comprehensible manner, somehow diffusely, in the forest floor and suddenly becomes a rivulet. To this she says, "But that is not really a nice spring at all!"

Fixed Image

The two examples, simple as they may be, convey an impression of the peculiarity of fixed images as points of conflict.

I will now describe a few characteristic obstructive motifs, that can frequently be found in the first sessions of a short-term therapy on the basic level as signs of neurosis. Then I will consider how they are to be dealt with in order to make use of them correctly therapeutically and possibly from this to convey to the patient understanding and insight into his unconscious conflicts.

Obstructive Motifs at the Brook

Obstructive motifs can be easily studied *along the brook's course.* Very frequently we find the scene in which the brook is first pursued upstream for a stretch but then suddenly disappears into a big hole in the ground. The question arises, whether it continues to flow underground and later returns to the surface of the ground again. One can accordingly instruct the patient to look for this spot a few hundred meters away. Another kind of obstruction is present in the situation, in which the brook ends in a pond or village pool, thus in stagnant water, without flowing off again. The aim of pursuing the brook's course is to maintain the continuity of the flow by following it further. For this reason the therapist will leave nothing untried in such a case, so that the patient will perhaps somewhere find even the smallest trace of a continuation of the brook. Thus we have him look for a small outlet at the other end of the village pool or indicate that actually there must be one, not lastly with the intent of avoiding a stoppage of the water. The situation is more stubborn if the brook is suddenly dammed up by a concrete or wooden wall or becomes thinner and thinner gradually seeping away into the sand, and the bed of the brook continues but is empty. The sequence of such impediments is particularly characteristic here. Initially it is only a narrowing of the brook, then it drops down a small waterfall, later it flows into a man-made lake and does not come out again.

Mastery

The guidance of the mental imagery aims at allowing the patient in the obstructed situations to find a way out, trying again and again, in such a way that it could fit the nature of the motif. Here the patient's initiative and active motivation, of course, also play a part in finding this way out. A certain suggestive influence can be exercised when the therapist lets the patient sense his conviction that looking more closely or searching will result in the possibility of overcoming the obstruction. Naturally, there are absolute limits, too. Then they must be accepted, even if the patient is disappointed at first.

Example

Case 2 (16)

The previously mentioned obsessive-compulsive neurotic physics' student gave me a drastic example of the obstruction of the brook's course. At first he sighted a raging stream, which, however, quickly moved toward a rise in the landscape. Here it dropped down in a massive waterfall. The attempt to spot the end of the waterfall was not successful. Instead, it became obvious that the rift valley was severely eroded, and the water had to drop infinitely deep. On the way to the next, deeper plateau, it evaporated and thus did not arrive there. At first this circumstance was simply to be noted. I must admit that I was very impressed by this, and incidentally my patient no less so. It probably also seemed slightly splendid to him to be able to present such a powerful natural scene to me. The energy of the streaming water dissolved into itself, considered symbolically as an indication that everything was ultimately in vain, infinite, powerful, difficult, and could no longer be captured in the dimensions of nature as given. (This did not prevent me from decisively helping the patient in a long therapy.)

Another version of the obstructive motif with the brook can lie in the paradox that in the denial of reality the brook flows uphill or in waves, sometimes uphill, sometimes downhill. From this, at least, we can gather that the person concerned does not take the physical laws of nature all that seriously, and knows how to bend reality in poetic fashion or in other ways and thus tends to entertain illusory ideas.

Leading up to Obstructive Motifs

A part of the strategy for guiding mental imagery involves leading the patient up to the obstructive motifs or fixed images at intervals again and again, with the help of the standard motifs, even if cautiously and without direct and overly blatant confrontation. Here the therapeutic work lies in the exact description of the details, which are to be observed, in the attempt to have the patient describe the feeling tone aroused within himself or the mood content of the landscape motif. Ultimately, the patient should attempt, supported by suggestions if need be, to track down with the help of his own trial behavior how the obstructive motif can best be overcome. To compress it into a formula: Usually it helps further and further to point out to the patient some obvious detail, which he should observe very closely and describe in connection with this motif. A phenomenon of change then easily links with this, and in some way the possibility of a solution or of a path makes itself known, possibly after a vague prediction made by the therapist, in a way that the therapist himself had not expected. Thus, it is not the therapist who should find the solution nor who should make direct offers or suggestions concerning it, but by the path of subtly dealing with a detail of the fixed image, the solution adequate to the respective situation should be awaited. To illustrate this I would like to report the following example.

Trial Behavior

Awaiting Solutions

Example

Case 3 (17)

A female patient is crawling through a low tunnel as a brook flows from the right into the tunnel toward her feet. The dampness of the tunnel is unpleasant. She crawls further, gradually sees an opening before her, which she reaches. I have her look down cautiously and she perceives that the water plunges down in a waterfall deeply over rocks. She crouches there and does not know how she can go further. I have her look around and ask whether there is perhaps somewhere at the side of the hole a possibility for getting down: She says no. Then I ask her to describe the waterfall for me, very precisely and in every detail. Gradually, this works. Now she senses some of its natural beauty. In the next step I ask her to catch sight of the next, more deeply situated level, onto which the water is falling. Finally, this succeeds, too, and a landscape with a raging brook but which is otherwise green, productive, and pleasant opens up in front of her. Now she feels relieved and her situation, which she initially perceived as dangerous and precarious, has grown less critical. Now I urge her again to look at the slanting walls of the rock to the right and left to see if possibilities for a cautious descent might not be found after all. This succeeds now and she discovers that next to the hole some steps have been chiseled out and a rope is hanging down, which she can hold onto and slowly climb down the primitive steps, which later turn into a small path.

Naturally, it is a question of the patient's courage, whether she wants to follow this inconvenient and difficult descent. Another patient might possibly have dispensed with this out of fear. Actually, however, she scarcely has any other choice. I encourage her a little with the hint that in an emergency she can come back again, and incidentally indications already existed that there was a well-tested descent here.

Aids Given by the Therapist

The therapist should give these kinds of aids in a straightforward way, inspiring confidence but reality-oriented at the same time. He formulates his words as if the scene in question before the patient's eyes were totally real in all of its attributes. I consider this aspect to be very important. Here the goal is to encourage the patient to independent, mature action through trial behavior in this quasi-real scene, so that he learns to deal with reality in an appropriate form, to move within it and to stand the test. For this reason, in GAI we avoid as a matter of principle offering magical, illusory, or miraculous solutions, with exceptions in the early phases of therapy.

Conclusion

Signs of Change

Another reference to the guidance in GAI arises from this example. Naturally it is not very encouraging for a patient, when the mental imagery phase of the session ends at a point where an obstructive motif or fixed image exists and he feels hopeless without a solution to the problem. That is the reason we generally strive to conduct the session to the point where the patient can find a solution to his task and then return to a place of composure and contemplation; for instance, after climbing the mountain the patient naturally tends to return to the meadow from which he started. That is not a condition, but it has the advantage of comparing the more recent impression of the meadow with the first one at the beginning of the session. Phenomena of change can then be noted, partly in a positive and partly in a negative direction, and the changes give patient and therapist insight into how the elapsed session has been assimilated unconsciously. Here the significance of conflict-free areas is announced, which I will examine in detail later.

Danger of Instrumental Problem Solving

In dealing with fixed images and obstructive motifs in their plainest form, the attempt to prepare the way for very active constructive problem solving can be extremely tempting for the therapist. From the wish to help, to make the tasks easier for the patient, or to show him what kind of power the therapist can develop in the imagery (whatever the motives may be), the incentive can arise to intervene all too directly, too suggestively, or too instrumentally. In principle, we start from the fact that guiding the patient should be suggestive in the least possible degree, at most proposing and structuring. We have become very reserved regarding the question of giving the patient direct (instrumental) aids; rather, we try to give help only by hints, which are a stimulus to detailed description, and by certain

Role of the Therapist

Avoiding Direct Measures

statements that objectify or encourage (see before). We offer direct instruments of a technical kind only in rare exceptions. This refers particularly to aggressively destructive actions for overcoming difficult obstacles, for example, by using a powder charge, dynamite, a hand grenade, or whatever the case may be. The reason we strictly avoid such direct or instrumental interventions is twofold. On the one hand, the patient becomes dependent on us in this way and the therapist all too easily takes on the role of the magician of mental imagery. On the other hand, as a model for the patient, we do not want to teach him to strive for aggressive, violent, or unrealistic (that is, illusory) solutions to problems. He all too easily assumes what we suggest to him within the imagery later in his real life too and will try to solve pending problems, above all interpersonal ones, with similarly neurotic-impatient, spur of the moment settlements. It is important to me to increase the strength of the mature parts of the patient's ego by having him find possible solutions for himself. This finding-for-himself should arise largely from the patient's unconscious motivational system, his opinions and his experiential background, which the therapist cannot have a clear view of due to their complex structures. Direct measures, on the other hand, often have the quality of being taken by surprise. Some patients are inclined to undertake such daring solutions or acts of violence on their own in order to overcome obstructive motifs quickly and impressively. Usually this leads to spur-of-the-moment successes, which have no lasting value, or to a reinforcement of defenses and resistances, which are expressed precisely in the obstructive motifs. I would like to present an example of this, which illustrates the danger of the unconscious tendency to reinforce the resistances when the therapist proceeds operatively.

Example

Case 4 (18)

A 23-year-old patient had a neurosis with obsessive-compulsive structure and he had difficulty in making social contacts. During the first focusing, as usually is the case, he imagined a meadow with dismal, rainy weather. He found himself enclosed in a small square area, which was surrounded by a barbed-wire fence. Even after looking more closely, there was no gate or anything similar to be found through which the patient could come out. Diagnostically, one can conclude that he found himself in a situation not rare for compulsively structured neurotic patients. They feel very confined by their internal or external situation, as if locked up.

Here the question arises for the therapist—and he does not have so very much time to think it over—what he should do in such a perhaps harmless, but perhaps also relatively precarious situation. He will in any case refrain from ending the session in this frustrating situation, all the more so, as the scene was embedded in a gloomy landscape and the patient was affected rather strongly by being enclosed in such a way. There was, however, no distinct danger or anything similar to it. Our young colleague was quite smart now. He proceeded approximately according to the motto, "Obstacles are there to be overcome" and gave the patient a strongly suggestive aid. He told him that within the imagery he would give him wire cutters to simply cut through the wire. That worked, and the patient tried it. The result was, however, totally different from what either had expected. The fence unexpectedly turned into an approximately 2 meter high, solid wall. The unconscious psychodynamics of the neurotic confinement were apparently considerably stronger than could be so easily overcome by an instrumental action within the imagery (I refer to what is stated below). However, without realizing this and recognizing this sign as the intensification of resistance and taking it seriously, the colleague now introduced another method (continuing his direction of impulse, so to speak). He suggested to the patient that he now take a ladder and use that to climb over the wall. On the one hand, in his need, on the other hand, in his compliance, the patient followed this request of his smart therapist. However, at this moment, the wall grew to infinity and was insurmountable. The ultimate result appeared to be a hopeless situation for the patient and for the therapist as well.

Operation on the Symbol

I have designated the directive technique applied by the therapist as *operation on the symbol* (Leuner, 1957). If the procedure is employed in a logically consequent way and does justice to the symbol, the patient can be helped quickly with it, as the management models of nourishing and satiating and of reconciliation and tender embrace (p.95) have shown. The present example, however, did not lead to the desired therapeutic solution. That is frequently the case when attempts are made to solve obstructive motifs with purely technical means, thus instrumentally and perhaps directly or brutally. The intended effect on the patient achieves the opposite, a dramatic intensification of the defense mechanisms. The psychodynamics of the obstructive motif as the expression of an apparently deep-rooted defense mechanism of the ego were not considered in this case. The example shows all too clearly that the necessary change in the defense structures cannot be achieved by this simple instrumental intervention. In this regard it seems all too natural that the ego rejects accepting this brusk invasion endangering it by intensifying the obstructive motifs, thus its defense mechanisms.

Significance of the Ego Defenses

From this one can draw the following conclusion for GAI therapy. The deeper defensive structures must be considered first in each direct, offensive action against the obstructive motifs, that is, what significance they have in the patient's total system of ego defenses. As already stated, the therapist usually has only an insufficient grasp of the unconscious scene despite having recorded the case history and despite data from the therapy. Therefore we recommend the therapeutic strategy demonstrated before—to proceed cautiously by small steps, to call upon the patient's creativity and his own capacity to solve his problems, to give preference to dealing with details, and to await the individual developmental steps in accordance with the patient's unconscious motivational system. I call to your attention the example of the patient who had to look for a means to get away from the terrifying waterfall.

Protective Function

We must also bear in mind that a large number of the defense mechanisms—even if they are as grotesque as in the present example with the narrow enclosure surrounded by barbed wire—have primarily protective functions for the patient and therefore cannot be so quickly given up without more ado and are in many regards built into his total character structure in the sense of reaction formation. In other words, they frequently have a high degree of existential significance and have personal value.

Illusory Problem Solving

In this regard I want to finish by substantiating why such an instrumental technical solution to obstructive motifs cannot lead to the goal therapeutically. The same holds true for another variant of this, using a magic wand to overcome such obstructive situations. The idea stems from the imagery technique of the Frenchman Desoille. Thomas (1967) adopted this motif in the advanced level of autogenic training. As a therapist not sufficiently trained in depth psychology, he apparently overlooked the fact that in this way the therapist not only induces a magical solution in the patient, but that this is only possible in that he lends the patient his own phallic power in the form of the magic wand (which abandons the patient). The solutions are frequently highly dramatic, but do not stand up to the organic development of the therapeutic process in the patient, which we are striving for, and in my opinion lead to the wrong track of infantile, illusory problem solving, as the neurotic has generally inwardly expected for a long time.

Realistic Solution Through Details

After this discussion, we still have to think about what the better technique of proceeding therapeutically in our example would have been. It would have firstly been important for the therapist to have guided the patient, as previously mentioned, to deal in detail with the very aggravating and impeding motif of his fixed images. The therapist should have first prompted the patient to look at the barbed wire fence more precisely in detail and to closely examine its construction and details of its mechanism. In so doing he might have been able to insert a remark about his expectation that there was a way out of the enclosure or even more strongly: he could not imagine that no solution could be found. He could have formulated this somewhat cautiously, "I would like to assume that . . . , I cannot imagine that . . ., You ought to once try whether . . .." Here it also seems important to me that the therapist talks with the patient about his estimation of the possibilities for overcoming the obstacle and discusses details precisely. From this, the therapist learns the patient's inner attitude in the face of the problem. Is he optimistic about finding a solution, or does he quickly tend toward resignation? Is he perhaps afraid to take a risk? As previously stressed, the therapist should also encourage the patient to think about his own suggestions for solutions and to try them out. Even these can be discussed regarding their practicality in advance of the action. Lastly, the therapist could have given a few suggestions. For example, he might have called to mind that in similar situations years ago we, as children, had tried to lift up a barbed-wire fence, not drawn tight, to crawl under it. Another suggestion might be: somewhere there must be a spot, where the builder of the fence had twisted its two ends together and at that point one could untwist it, or lastly, perhaps rusty spots could be found where one could start gradually to wear out the wire. As stated, however, the possibility of a solution depends upon that part of the patient's ego activity, which the therapist cannot completely replace. He cannot, so to speak, "push" him into doing something that he is not prepared to do because of passivity or character defense. In any case such attempts must always start with the slightest and most subtle means and must begin with the detail. Each small attempt can be supported by the therapist, and usually such very simple attempts, starting from the details and conveyed by the patient's initiative, are worthwhile and in fact lead to a solution or at least a partial solution, which should be appreciated.

Behavior of the Patient

Stimulate Ideas

Details Once Again

The average patient is usually not familiar with the technique stated here. Therefore he needs the therapist's guidance at first, as was described previously. The therapist should always bear in mind that a patient's spontaneous tendencies for coping with an obstructive motif are not always the guiding rule and do not always contain the suitable solution for him. Patients (who react from their neurotic attitude) by no means regularly possess the "wisdom" about the best approach to a solution in their mental imagery. This is especially true of suggestion for overcoming an obstructive motif by means of destructive or instrumental actions at the first attempt.

Offering Strategies for Solution

Altogether, you see that the active removal of the obstructive motif is quite problematical. For that reason, it is also basically not advisable and in principle not a good strategy for solving problems either in imagery or in everyday life.

In connection with this, I would like to discuss a further technical possibility, which can be meaningfully applied in the present context. It requires the patient to be appropriately advanced and open to his unconscious impulses and the therapist must have already developed a certain independence in dealing with GAI.

Suppose that in the example just cited the discussed attempt of a trial solution to the situation had not been successful. The patient would have remained confined in his narrow area and if judged by the mood of the unfriendly landscape in the dismal, rainy weather, also remained quite depressed. Let us assume the most extreme case. In this situation the therapist would have had no other alternative than to break off the imagery. That would not be very fortunate therapeutically and not a real solution. Could there have possibly been another "initiative" to get further therapeutically? I would like to go into this briefly here. It would in fact have been obvious with this patient to approach this in my view very macabre and unfortunate situation in which he found himself in GAI more strongly from the emotional aspect. For that reason, I would have had him describe in detail the predominant feeling of being shut in, of not being able to get out. Then I would have asked him whether he was otherwise occasionally in a similar situation emotionally, recently, or in any other situation in his everyday life (that is, in reality). With this I am addressing the technique of stimulating ideas and associations described in detail on the intermediate level. In asking about the mood and feeling tone of the scene, a bridge to latent ideas and memories is formed, that is, between the imagery and reality, as the important task of connecting the two. In this way the depressing mental image would have encountered broader integration in the patient's already known, that is, familiar patterns of experience in his everyday world. Then it would also have sufficed at first to point out to him that apparently a central problem of his neurosis had been depicted in this image and that the planned treatment would in all probability lead to a relaxation or to a partial liberation. This dialogue could have been held during the imaginal phase or following it (in a sitting position). This kind of dialogue belongs to the previously mentioned type of a reduction of negative affects, which the patient takes out of the mental imagery along with him, if a problem involving a fixed image cannot be brought to a (partial) solution. Its negative character is relativized and the image as such is made more familiar.

Address the Emotional Aspect

Bridge to Ideas

Treatment

In the course of discussing the fixed images of this section, I hope it has become clearer to you that, as equivalent neurotic resistances and defensive processes, the obstructive motifs not only appear frequently and in relatively characteristic form, but are target points that, if stressed cautiously and with the help of certain tactics, can be therapeutically productive. The discreet developmental steps in the therapeutic process of GAI can also be documented in them most easily by means of the described phenomena of change. Some of the fixed images are of a superficial kind and change quickly; some are deeply established in the person as introjects (central referential person) or as stabilizing defense mechanisms of the ego. The *training procedure* as the central method on the basic level of GAI lies predominantly in the fact that the individually appearing central motifs do not have to be analyzed down to the last detail. The pointed, subtle analysis of the scene only becomes necessary

Productiveness of the Fixed Images

Analyzing the Scene

where fixed images arise. The concept "training procedure" is naturally a simplification. You have seen how relatively complicated and with how many various steps the patient is guided to work on the obstructive motifs in a differentiated manner. One can draw a close parallel between this technique, illustrated by a few examples, and the recognition of psychoanalysis that *the primary attention* should not be directed to the inhibited impulses pushing to get through (what the patient due to his naive notion would immediately like to do most); rather the attention and the subsequent working through are to be primarily applied to the *defense mechanisms,* that is, in GAI, the *obstructive motifs.* I remind you, for instance, of the various ways the course of the brook dams up and the ever-repeated attempt to find solutions at the point of stoppage, so that the water can nevertheless continue to flow. I also recall the patient, who at first hopelessly looked down over the waterfall and then gradually found a way down after all, by first drawing her attention to the rocky cliffs. It is far more important to work on the fixed images than on the material that embodies the impulses. This basically very important strategy can be best illustrated through the example of the patient trapped by the barbed-wire fence. The young colleague who advised the patient to cut through the fence with wire cutters wanted to *reinforce* the *impulse* (namely to get out) by introducing the shears. The result was the automatic reinforcement of the resistance. My approach, on the other hand, was to have the patient deal as thoroughly as possible with the resistance itself, namely, with the barbed wire, to get to know it better, to explore it and find out whether it had a weak point somewhere. I *centered his attention on the resistance* and thus accentuated a confrontation with it. According to previous experience, the resistance then gradually diminished, as already indicated, and the impulse found the opportunity to pass through the weakened resistance and to attain its goal, even if perhaps by circuitous paths.

Attention to Obstructive Motifs

I come to the conclusion of this chapter dealing with the treatment of fixed images, which we come across most impressively in the form of tasks to be solved by the patient while focusing on the standard motifs. I believe it has become clear that gradually coping with the fixed images or the obstructive motifs, even the step by step deferment of these structures, leads to the circumstance that previously unavailable stable imaginal impasses are gradually increasingly transformed into a flexible achievement. The greater degrees of freedom connected with this usually stands out clearly in the following GAI sessions and can also be traced by the onlooker. If a patient cannot complete some scene sequences in mental imagery due to initial obstructive motifs and also shows clear neurotic inhibitions and symptoms in his real life surroundings, these can be relaxed using the described techniques. The result is the neutralization of the obstruction itself. This is shown in the

Degrees of Freedom

Phenomena of Change

change of the obstructive motifs and equally in the previously discussed synchronic changes in the motifs of the panorama, for example, the all-round view from the mountain. This is a sure sign that the inner restructuring has started to move, that is, the change of the ego and its defensive structures. It is frequently connected with an improvement of the symptoms, from which the patient was suffering, and also of his disturbed social behavior, which we take up in differentiated fashion in each individual case. A great number of case study presentations are available concerning this (Beck, 1968; Koch, 1962; Henle, 1977; Holfeld, and Leuner, 1969), apart from the previously cited statistical and experimental psychological studies.

Individual Case Studies

Transfer to Actual Behavior

In experimental studies with GAI we have been able to show that an obvious transfer takes place from the patient's experiences in mental imagery to his actual behavior. This does not regularly require additional therapeutic steps to interpret or make conscious. I would like to exemplify this process through a case I treated. Not the least important reason for this is due to the fact that most of my psychoanalytic colleagues raise the question again and again, in what way in GAI therapy does this transfer from imaginal experiencing to action in reality take place. The transfer, when the technique is correctly applied, takes place spontaneously over long intervals apparently as an unconscious accomplishment of the receptive ego. The ego apparently has the capacity of transferring behavior in fantasy to real behavior.

The extraordinarily short treatment period in the following example is not supposed to astonish you. It is one of those rare cases, which show what the procedure makes possible in the sense of compensation of a subacute crisis reaction or rather of acute neurotic symptoms. It should be noted in passing that in this case it is not the patient himself who makes his way through the panorama in trial behavior (as is usually the case), but the form of his symbolic identification, the narcissistic portion of his ego, that undertakes this.

Example

Case 5 (19)

A 17-year-old high school student, who came from the German Democratic Republic, became ill after emigrating to West Germany with his family, showing the symptoms of an *autistic puberty crisis.* The possibility of a beginning *hebephrenic schizophrenia* could not be ruled out. He was taciturn and had difficulty in making social contacts; he spoke haltingly and with a rigid face as he reported his case history. He also complained about severe *headaches,* which could not be organically explained. Before the resettlement, he had been a very good student. In the new school he failed completely. The symptoms had begun 4 months previously, immediately after the assignment to a refugee camp and continued after moving out. In

GAI a cave spontaneously appears at the foot of a mountain. I urge the patient to stop in front of it (as we also do in the edge of the woods motif) and to observe the entrance to the cave. After a while, a fierce giant appears. However, he stops timidly at the exit from the cave and finally motions the patient to him. I encourage him to follow the giant. The latter leads him into his cave and shows him his world: a landscape with a river, vineyards, storerooms and a barn full of cows, practically a small, luxuriant paradise. I advise the patient to ask the giant his reasons for having withdrawn from the world. It seems that he had fled there because people had avoided him and laughed at him.

In the three subsequent sessions of GAI, each lasting three-quarters of an hour, the patient was repeatedly urged to lead the giant back out of the cave and into the world. The giant first encounters farmers in the fields. After overcoming all kinds of resistances, he is finally prepared to help with the work. Upon entering the nearby village, he hesitates timidly. I have the patient report details to me and encourage him to have the giant go in. Wandering through additional villages and through cities are suggested; wherever inhibitions, fear, or shyness appear, I have the patient voice these and I give him encouraging suggestions. In the course of these wanderings the giant's stature grows smaller from time to time. Having shrunk to the size of a child, he at one point lies down in the patient's childhood bed in his former apartment. I let him rest here. Soon, he appears again, all the more energetic, among the working farmers.

In the third session the patient reports about a striking synchronic transformation. Whereas the river had previously been sharply constricted by two rock ledges, these have now moved back. A wide street accompanies the river, and a hotel has emerged next to it. In reference to the patient's contact problems and difficulties concentrating in school, it seemed important to me to extend the training procedure to improving social contact behavior too. The giant's extensive wanderings and his cooperation with the farmers do not fully serve this purpose. I now suggest that the giant, who has shrunk to the size of a normal person in the meantime, apprentice himself as an errand boy in the hotel. Lots of people are going in and out, whom he must meet and whom he helps. In these situations, which the patient takes seriously, the giant gains confidence. The giant, who previously lived a secluded life and was not recognized by anyone, turns into a human being, who assumes an, although modest, nonetheless respected and socially useful role.

After the fourth session the patient reports that the headaches have disappeared almost entirely. Psychically, he now seems not only more open, more talkative, and emotionally more relaxed, but also has become more closely acquainted with his peers in his new class for the first time. Soon thereafter, he even participates in sports competitions and brings home good grades again.

Discussion

In this extremely short-term therapy, autistic seclusion and unrealistic expectations stand out distinctly at first, combined with wishes for omnipotence (the giant) as well as the rejection of competitive confrontation in the real world. One is nevertheless astonished at how the transformation on the level of the symboldrama is answered with scenes of synchronic transformation and a direct parallel to the change in actual behavior exists as well. During the first examination, the clinical picture was striking to a high degree; as far as that goes, the same was true of the change in the young man's behavior in the course of this very short therapy. Those trained in psychoanalysis will recognize that here only a very particular subsection of the patient's immature ego has been addressed; however, at the same time his object relationships have undergone a correction. The patient's situational response occasioned by the change of social milieu was compensated for the duration of a year. On the occasion of his approaching final examinations, he was again brought to the general clinic with a slight psychogenic paralysis of the arm. That is not surprising, because the patient's more deeply seated conflictual problems could not be treated in the short period cited. The patient was also not motivated to continue the therapy after the initial success. For the sake of completeness, it must be mentioned that the very obvious transfer in this illustration from the behavioral change in symboldrama to one in real life does not always take place that directly. More frequently, the outward adaptation lags behind or only small partial results are observed at all in this respect.

I recount such clinical examples of direct responses to symboldrama because the degree of evidence is especially high in these cases. However, this says nothing about how these processes are to be understood psychodynamically and what significance they have for the intended clinical "healing process" as a whole.

Session Sixteen: Creative Development and Conflict-free Scenes

Creative Development of Spontaneous Mental Imagery

This chapter is not extensive, although it is of great importance. I have formulated the chapter title accordingly, because there were several different reasons for which I was misunderstood in the first German edition of this book. At various points I had indicated that in guiding the patient it is important to let him stray from the standard motifs and their tasks and follow his own path in the mental imagery. In spite of this, apparently the idea was spread at that time that the therapist must complete one motif after another decidedly "systematically," always repeating this and in so doing hold the patient relatively strictly to the assigned task.

For this reason, it is a concern of mine to stress within the scope of the basic level techniques the possibility tested in various seminars of being able to stimulate the person's creative accomplishments in GAI. The patient can also develop his creative powers spontaneously or through some practice in symboldrama, just as the artist or scientist grapples for a solution. Along with Erika Landau (1984), I pursued these things and found, to a large extent, that the patient gradually becomes more creative in the course of the developing therapeutic process. This is expressed by the fact that the mental imagery is enriched in its contents, becomes broader and more colorful, and has more possibilities for action. In so doing, the development of creative solutions dealing with fixed images or obstructive motifs works better and better. Another form of creatively developing imaginal fantasies lies in their self-sufficient activity, which appears more expansive and is independent of the basic motif. I will return to both of these ideas later.

Stimulating Creativity

In what way can the therapist promote the creative development of mental imagery? If he conducts the training procedure in a predominantly methodical way, there is the risk that the patient's spontaneous fantasy productions will be suppressed. If after focusing on a basic motif, such as a meadow, a brook, climbing the mountain, or a house, he simply gives the patient the freedom to develop his images, which are spontaneously centering on this and allowing his behavioral wishes and perhaps even encouraging him to do so, the resulting creative elements become obvious to both therapist and patient. This can occur verbally simply through questions, such as, "What would you like to do now?" "Perhaps you would like to take a walk, where would you like to go?"

Encouragement

If we consider the creative arrangement of GAI, we can

Two Tendencies

differentiate *two phenomena,* in which the creative powers are manifested in addition to the self-evident expansion of the repertory in the imaginal material already mentioned.

1. These powers are manifested when the patient elaborates on the cardinal motif assigned to him in a spontaneously arising manner. The therapist must then grant him the freedom to stray even further, for instance, to take a walk starting out from the meadow, to adhere to details while pursuing the course of a brook, or to walk into the countryside, perhaps to let one's thoughts wander and to bring in thoughts from his own personal experience to the respective motif. Although the actual associative procedure as a technique of the intermediate level is clearly defined, one naturally should not prevent the patient from doing this on the basic level.

Creative Solutions at the Obstructive Motifs

The spontaneous creative attempts at problem solving made by patients in the face of obstructive motifs are especially interesting. In the previous section I cited examples of this in the scenes of a few patients. Guiding mental imagery therapeutically should focus particularly on problem situations at the fixed images. There I gave technical suggestions, as, for instance, concentrating on fine details with the subsequent phenomena of change, and the spontaneous development of images pointing to a solution. I believe that precisely for therapy the emphasis on creative manifestations lies in the spontaneous opening up of new possibilities for trial behavior.

Creative Expansion of the Panorama

In my opinion the therapeutically most productive, creative development occurs more calmly and is directed above all at the increasing expansion of the panorama, at its enrichment with elements of nature and the increasing existence of animals and humans. It is ultimately expressed in the subtle, individual therapeutic steps, in which the patient learns more and more to solve the problem positions at the obstructive motifs and fixed images in increasingly more constructive and more independent manner. In this regard one can observe a learning process in the course of therapy that is triggered not lastly by the therapist's example, measured according to how he has offered problem solutions in the face of fixed images. In the later stages of GAI, the problem-solving behavior will concern interpersonal relationships even more intensely. On the basic level this still predominantly occurs in the symbolic disguise of the landscape motifs. I recall the example of the young man's identification with his father (p.72), in which he climbed that mountain, which embodied the authoritarian paternal-masculine world (and thereby lost the rest of his speech disorder).

2. Creative abilities are also manifested when a small *group of especially imaginative patients* can only be held to the motifs of the basic level with great difficulty or not at all. Instead, they are to a large extent inclined to develop their imaginings in a more or less roaming fashion. The therapist will recognize the cardinal motifs only now and then. The most extreme form of these very productive imaginings is shown by those patients, whose imaginal contents are strung together in

Far-Ranging Imaginings

fragments, possibly in very brief snatches, allowing little or no relationship to a context to be recognized. The therapist, who is set on the standard motifs of the basic level, will be in an embarassing position here. That is understandable, especially since persons who imagine in this way represent a small and relatively extreme group. Nevertheless, the basic level therapist should be acquainted with this mode of forming images and know how he has to act in these cases. To come to the point, it usually concerns extremely severely disturbed patients, who do not have a particularly distinctive gift for fantasy but often also have a strongly hysterically structured neurosis. The pathological aspect lies above all in the fact that they are very tense internally or are in a constant state of emotional agitation, which causes them to quickly "spin out," so to speak, one motif after the other and thus to try to reduce the tension. If one pursues these fragments very carefully (possibly by means of a subsequent tape-recorded control), it becomes evident that the jumping back and forth from one content to another without any real internal consistency is determined by the following. Defenses that insert another image are very quickly formed against an appearing image so that the first scene does not need to be continued. From what has been said, it becomes obvious that these are actually tormented patients and that the concept of "creativity" applies in only a very limited sense.

Internal Agitation

Therapist's Behavior?

How should the therapist behave here? The simple fundamental rule reads: Intervene as little as possible, structure or direct as little as possible; rather, by first giving the person concerned full play, bring him to the point where despite possible flightiness and fragmentation of contents, he comes out with everything that presents itself and that is oppressing him. That may take a few or several sessions. In my experience being patient and showing a constant benevolent attitude are worthwhile. In the predominant number of cases, the field of imaginings gradually becomes better and better organized. Slowly, sometimes challenging the therapist's patience a great deal, the imaginings become structured into fully distinct scenes, which finally complement each other in their context progressively from session to session. In the predominant number of these cases it is clear that only the possibility of being able to imagine at all under the therapist's benevolent-granting protection and attention represents not only an emotional release but is actually therapeutically effective. Waiting patiently thus conveys its meaning in itself as long as a positive countertransference prevails in the therapist.

Waiting

Naturally, it is difficult to induce these patients to write a record of the proceedings or to talk about this material afterward. Here I assist myself by asking these patients to try to summarize the numerous contents thematically into a complex of problems as far as that is possible for them. The follow-up discussion possibly serves the attempt to form such interrelated topics. That may be vague at the beginning; however, from these prestructuring attempts, the patient naturally learns to organize the initially perhaps even seemingly chaotic field of imaginings

Forming Interrelated Topics

better. One must bear in mind that the inner haste and agitation that these patients radiate can be motivated at least in part by the high standard of accomplishment they have for themselves, and partially by the fact that they believe they absolutely have to offer something or demonstrate something to the therapist now. Basically, a great amount of therapeutic experience, of evenness of temper and confidence, are essential in dealing with them. The therapist must try to convey calmness, confidence, and stability to the patient through his own, even nonverbally perceivable attitude.

Nonverbal Influence

As already stated, these cases are not frequent, but the basic level therapist should also be prepared for them and to know that a different attitude than usual is required here. At a later stage it frequently becomes possible to suggest the basic positions of mental imagery and to let the standard motifs develop. This works the best when one makes use of their spontaneous emergence, for instance, of a house as a place of structuring a pause, which gradually leads also to setting the respectively appropriate task.

This excursion into the extreme positions of a small group of patients diverges somewhat from the actual core of creative imagery. However, it is more productive and also obviously more creative when the degree of fantasy development is more modest but nevertheless active. I would like to address this group of patients in the narrower sense as primarily creative.

In this connection the technical question arises of whether and when one should lead these patients back to the basic motif and the task associated with it. I have gained the following experience concerning this. If possible, one also allows a patient gifted with intensely pressing imaginings to develop very calmly. If necessary, one can even let his imagination turn in broad spirals and at first dispense entirely with returning to one of the basic motifs in the early sessions. Here the therapist's behavior should also be determined by the previously emphasized principle that every patient develops his individual mental imagery. In those cases, on the other hand, in which it is easy to bring the patient back to the standard motif, it is advisable, after a few digressions of 10 to 15 minutes maximum, to simply ask him the question, "And what is happening with the mountain now (brook or house, or . . .)?" With this we refer him back to the starting position, in which he previously stood, and ask him to continue at that point.

Return to the Basic Motif

That does not rule out our positive valuing of the creative and imaginative developments by means of accompanying symbols. I am of the opinion that disapproval or attempts to suppress impulses are ineffective in psychotherapy and should therefore best be omitted. From a psychodynamic point of view, one must, of course, consider that these digressions from the basic theme are possibly an expression of resistance. Also in connection with this, it has proved valuable not only to make these excursions possible for the patient, but if necessary also discreetly to encourage him in this. Some patients, especially adolescents, offer quite extensive excursions, for instance, all the way to floating in space or the transformation into an interstellar rocket, which races through space. After ample romping in these realms, possibly for several sessions, they gradually finally find their way spontaneously back to earthly regions and their realities. In other words, one should not be concerned if the patient makes digressions in his imagery and thus apparently fulfills a latent, pressing need. We patiently wait for the "dynamic satiation" achieved by the granting or even the reinforcing of these imaginings, because it will set in sooner or later. We make use of it in order ultimately to offer the basic motifs and the tasks set in GAI to the adolescent patient again upon his return to the base of facts.

Granting

Conflict-free Scenes and Gratification of Archaic Needs

The strategy of guiding mental imagery therapeutically, which has been made the central theme of this section, has its origin in the early psychoanalytic finding (Freud 1900) that not only inner conflicts and unresolved problems but wishful tendencies and their fulfillment as well appear in dreams and mental imagery. Our first concept of GAI therapy was, however, to proceed according to the general line of psychoanalysis in regard to the conflict portrayal and to have the patient experience the problem-laden scenes (fixed images) regularly during mental imagery in measured doses and in a form he can tolerate. They should be made more comprehensible to him, and he should seek solutions to conflicts in trial behavior with the therapist, whenever it seemed necessary and advisable. In other words we were moving predominantly in unconscious or preconscious conflictual circles, as presented in the previous chapters.

Wish-Fulfilling Tendency

In the course of the, in the meantime rather long, history of GAI and its stepwise development through clinical empirical experience, more and more doubts arose as to whether this strategy of focusing predominantly on the conflict-laden portions and dealing solely with them was correct. Ultimately, this seemed not only one-sided, but for some patients, particularly the severely disturbed and those with weak egos, it seemed to be in part overly stressful and to have the undesired effect of weakening the ego. In addition to this, contents completely the reverse of the problem-laden fixed contents also appeared temporarily, which spontaneously demanded attention from the patient. The *conflict-free scenes* stated in the chapter heading are the following. They appear in images of nature, for example, approximately in the sense of an increased inner participation in

Conflict-free Scenes

an aesthetic experience with nature, the feeling of well-being, the development of a pleasant, possibly even happy mood, and similar things. These moods can also be reflected in encounters with persons who emanate a positive emotional feeling, for instance, of reassurance and an easing of tension. Another area of gratification is connected with the various water motifs and patients' frequent need to deal with water from the brook, the spring, the river, or the sea. They drink it, they refresh themselves, they bathe or swim in it. I have already made references to the gratification connected with this, of in part very deeply seated and strongly regressive needs. How water is dealt with belongs quite obviously to the prototypes of opportunities for gratification and relaxation of particular imaginal scenes discussed in this section. The further pursuit of this effect of the imagery and the analogous observation of entire sections in therapy, which take place within the framework of conflict-free scenes and happy experiences of gratification, offer material collected by various therapists independent of each other, which finally led to the relatively systematic evaluation of the *second dimension of GAI* (in contrast to the first, which centers on conflicts).

Relaxation Through Water

Second Dimension of GAI

In the early period I believed that the conflict-free areas, which spontaneously appeared during the training procedure of the basic level technique, had a certain import. Therefore I recommended letting the patient's prevailing mood develop, for instance, in connection with the brook motif or with the edifying panorama from a mountain, and giving him the opportunity to abandon himself to the pleasant moment of experiencing this as far and as deliberately as possible. This also included, for example, the patient's wish to lie down in the sunny summer meadow, perhaps even to sleep (paradise symbolism) and other similar things. At first I understood these passages to be a kind of self-reward, which the patient prescribed for himself, and considered them according to the viewpoint of learning theory as a form of natural reinforcement. It therefore seemed wise to grant these occasions to the patient, wherever they presented themselves. Considered from the point of view of depth psychological theory, such conflict-free scenes could naturally signify nothing other than defensive processes in the face of suppressed conflicts or of anxiety and depressive abandonment, whose ultimate resolution alone could have made possible the desired maturation of the personality and its separation from childish behaviors. So that I do not go into theoretical details any further, it should be stated now that, on the one hand, mechanisms to cover up conflicts play a part here. On the other hand, the relationships are more complicated theoretically and extend all the way into the more recent theories of primary narcissism, which I cannot go into here (see Pahl, 1980, Leuner 1983).

Gratification—Defense Against Conflicts

The actual breakthrough to our new understanding

concerning the gratification of archaic needs and the consequent and exclusive focusing of conflict-free scenes occurred in the case of short-term therapy of 15 sessions of a diversely disturbed female patient, that Wächter and I studied in detail (Leuner and Wächter, in preparation). In the following I present this example in somewhat more detail, because for the first time it in fact completely drew our attention to this "second dimension of GAI" in its therapeutic significance.

Example of the Therapeutic Significance

*Case 1** (20)

The patient was 39 years old, married, and had two children. The reason for the referral to our consultation was the symptom of excoriated acne located on her face and particularly severely on her back. The symptom had existed for a year. In addition, she had sleep disturbances, gallbladder complaints, spastic pains in the epigastric region, and depressive states. She easily became nervously agitated and had the obsessive fear of dying. Most of the symptoms had been present for 9 years and had been triggered by the birth of her second child. On the way to the hospital she believed that she would die there and would not go home again. In recording the depth psychological case history it was striking that the patient could contribute scarcely any relevant data. Current conflicts were rejected, and it was obvious on a broad front that the patient was accustomed to covering up. In her behavior she gave the impression of being somewhat schoolgirlish-childish. Her handwriting was reminiscent of that used for a school essay, and this somewhat childish-playful impression was confirmed in GAI, when she had little paper boats swim in the brook and threw pebbles in the river. The GAI was characterized by meadow motifs and other landscape images, which were definitely friendly, full of flowers, and bathed in sunshine, thus not only without any problems but practically embodied a "children's picture book world," as participants of one of my seminars worded it. She liked to lie down in the meadow, enjoyed the friendly scenery, or fall asleep. While inspecting the house, she found a large haystack in the attic, in which she lay down to sleep, and while focusing on a scene outdoors with her family, sheer harmony and friendliness prevailed. In other words, all attempts at bringing hidden problems into view failed. It was therefore very obvious that the patient could not be introduced to a conflict-centered therapy. I supervised this case as was true of all of the cases in Wächter's research program, and he introduced the case to me as "not suited for the program." I formed the hypothesis that the patient was apparently following a strong inner need, not only in covering up, but she herself unconsciously staged the various

---

*** This case was a part of *Wächter's* research program (1980). The patient was treated with the basic level technique.**

satisfying experiences in a clearly excessive form in mental imagery for reasons unknown to us. I advised my colleague Wächter, who had developed a negative countertransference with this patient, to adopt a granting attitude in the future and to wait and see in what form the mental imagery would develop. However, nothing changed in the style of the imagery or in the patient's attitude all the way to the end of the therapy. After 15 sessions she was discharged from the outpatient treatment as had been prearranged. Wächter and I were extremely surprised about the results of the therapy. The patient experienced herself subjectively as extremely relieved and relaxed. The spastic epigastric pains and gallbladder complaints no longer existed, the sleep disturbances were considerably improved, and the mood swings were also slighter and shorter. Even the obsessive fear of dying had disappeared. The excoriated acne had in part remitted well in comparison with a series of previous findings. During the postobservation period conducted for more that 3 years, there was no relapse. The psychological tests, which were carried out, correspondingly showed a reduction of the psychosomatic complaints (Giessener list of complaints), and the values for neurotic tendency in the Brengelmann test and the ones for manifest anxiety in Taylor's were considerably reduced (Leuner and Wächter, in preparation).

Commentary: It is remarkable that psychosomatic symptoms, which existed for 9 years, underwent a sustained improvement by means of this conflict-avoiding therapy with GAI. Even more astonishing is the fact that the psychic symptom of obsessive fear, which is reputed to be very obstinate not only in the present case but also in clinical experience in general, was likewise decisively influenced. Finally, the long-lasting success is surprising in comparison to the short therapy.

As I stated, a number of other therapists can report similar treatments having proceeded in conflict-free milieu, which were striking due to their very short duration of ten or fewer sessions. There too, the good results were unexpectedly stable over several years time.

Theoretical Background

As already mentioned, I cannot go into the interesting theoretical and psychodynamic background in this class. However, we had to draw the conclusion that the dimension of conflict-free scenes and of the gratification of archaic needs, however one wants to explain it, represents a new therapeutic component of GAI that is to be taken seriously. In any case it seemed desirable to expand on it further in detail and if possible to study it systematically and also to apply it.*

*** Considered from the psychoanalytic theoretical viewpoint, we observed imaginal contents, which indicate a regression either on the primary narcissistic experiential phase or on a more orally accented, but rarely an anally accentuated phase of gratification. I have presented some theoretical explanations in connection with this elsewhere (Josuttis and Leuner, 1972).**

The mode of effect of a therapeutic component or a strategy going in the same direction can be most easily illustrated by a model, in which a clearly defined clinical experience characterizes the mode of effect. To what extent this can be transferred to longer term therapies with successful termination and lasting therapeutic success is another question. As important as it is, I do not want to extend the subject of the gratification of archaic needs too far in the scope of this seminar. Therefore I am restricting myself to two additional clinical examples of this kind. Conducting this technique on the broader scope must be left up to the advanced therapist, but wherever spontaneous signs announce themselves in the catathymic panorama of the basic level, the therapist must be prepared for them and must know that there is considerable therapeutic potential in focusing on conflict-free scenes. In conclusion I will explain what can be done technically in this respect on the basic level. First I will present the two examples.

Openness for Spontaneous Conflict-free Scenes

Example

Case 2 (21)

This case demonstrates the calmative and autonomically strongly sedative effect when using the water symbolism.

A 50-year-old physician became a patient after undergoing an appendectomy. The operation came very unexpectedly for him and afterward he had the impression of having escaped an existential threat. The quite characteristic experiencing of an intense personal helplessness is related to this. He feels uneasy, suffers from sleeplessness, and, although he was confined to bed after the operation, his blood pressure increased to 170/120 mm Hg in contrast to preoperative levels of 130/80 mm Hg while lying down. The patient, who has practice in autogenic training and in GAI, subsequently makes the following attempt. After employing autogenic training to relax, he imagines a scene in which it is possible for him passively to abandon himself to his surroundings. He imagines that he is swimming on his back in the slowly moving water of a river. Soon he senses physically that he is being carried by the water and surrenders himself to the feeling of an increasing fusion with the surrounding water of the slowly flowing stream. The image completes itself in a large wide river, which is filled to the edge with water, divides into two branches, and is surrounded by green meadows. The person strives to yield to the feeling of a swimming suspension in the water for a longer period of time (roughly 15 minutes), which turns out to be very pleasant. He repeatedly focuses on this image several times in the same day. In so doing he experiences considerable general relaxation and relief, which also influences the existing sleeping disorders positively. His blood pressure measured on the next day is now at a level of 130/80 mm Hg.

Commentary: The speedy effect influencing the autonomic

nervous system is surprising. It also becomes evident that exercises, in which autogenic training is connected with a characteristic catathymic image gratifying archaic needs, can gain great significance for a deep sedation of the autonomic system without medication. Its dimensions become clear in reference to blood pressure inasmuch as the diastolic rate also undergoes a decisive reduction. This example shows a certain parallel to the use of water by the patient (pp.60–61), who was ill due to hyperthyroidism. In the meantime Przywij (1983) has made three case histories available in which, under quite different conditions of illness, striking and lasting therapeutic successes through focusing upon an imagined bath are described.

Example

Case 3 (22)

This second example shows how the contents, which lead to archaic gratification, can be focused on in very individual ways and also shows the danger of letting the patient practice on his own.

I was summoned to the University Medical Clinic to see a married female patient of approximately 40 years of age, who was there because of a severe, recidivistic ulcerative colitis. I was already acquainted with the patient and her family because of previous treatment in a similar acute state. I met the patient, in a very agitated state in her hospital room, hastily making several telephone calls in order to settle from her bedside the affairs of her six children staying with various friends and acquaintances. In the conversation I at first let her tell me about her current problems. It gradually became obvious that she was afraid either someone would alienate one of her children from her and/or her severe illness, which had not been controllable for years, would have fatal consequences for her. The excessive activity was the obvious attempt to defend against these hidden but panicky anxieties. She slept restlessly and only very little, could scarcely eat anything, and, in spite of the pharmacotherapy by an internist, she had frequent and bloody stools. An effective psychotherapeutic crisis intervention seemed absolutely necessary. Unfortunately, I had little time and an out-of-town appointment in 2 days, so that I had to try to make the best of the situation. The patient, as stated, already knew me and trusted me. My previous cautious attempts to treat the extremely disharmonious marriage and the patient's severe neurotic stress in a conflict-centered therapy had failed due to the patient's general resistance and her intense flightiness. At first I tried to get her to realize the fact that at the moment the most important thing for her was to calm down internally in order to be able to look at her situation more objectively, more calmly, and thus also more realistically. In her role as a patient she could not also be obligated at the time to take care of all the concerns of her family personally.

Crisis Intervention by Focusing on an Individual Scene of Gratification

After she was able to accept that, and my pronounced calm attitude was also in accordance with a transference expectation, I aimed at a crisis intervention with GAI. I asked her if she could recall a situation in her life, whether in nature, or in her relations with people, in which she felt especially good, secure, calm, and harmonious. After thinking a little, she described a scene to me in which she is lying in a deck chair in her garden on an afternoon in summer and the sun is shining diagonally across the roses blooming there. It reinforced my opinion that this scene had the experiential qualities for her that I wanted to touch on. Subsequently, I gave her a few suggestions for relaxation, which I deliberately dealt with in detail, and asked her to imagine this scene before her eyes. I restricted myself to very brief verbal statements from her to be sure that the image had been realized. Then I advised her to surrender herself completely emotionally to this scene, to let the prevailing mood and its emotive value fill her, in a certain sense to soak it up totally into herself and to stay in a meditating attitude in this world of hers for as long as possible. The exercise took approximately 15 to 20 minutes. Then I had the image fade away but asked her to continue to indulge in this mood of expanding inner calmness and relaxation, which she was sensing, and I quietly left her hospital room. The next day I found the patient considerably calmer, more relaxed and at ease, and from her bed she greeted me with a friendly smile. The actual situation seemed to have calmed down. Her family had also arranged various things without her.

She had slept well that night, had an appetite, and ate her not very attractive, special diet. The agitated peristaltic movement in the intestinal region had subsided. Altogether, I detected a striking and rapid change in the overall psychic attitude and autonomic system of the severely ill woman. I conducted the exercise again and instructed her to focus on this imaginal motif on her own in a quiet hour or at night before falling asleep, because I could not come the next day. When I returned on the day after that, she continued to feel quite well. The attending internist was quite satisfied. However, now she told me that a somewhat unpleasant incident had occurred during the exercise on her own, which I had suggested. After having focused on the scene with the deck chair for a while, she had begun to shrink physically and had become smaller and smaller. At the end she had felt as if she were an embryo that had been lying abandoned in the deck chair. That had made her uneasy but had not had a fundamentally negative influence upon her. I continued the exercise in my presence on the following days and held dialogue sessions about current questions to relieve stress. The patient stabilized over the next 8 days. She was now able to take with composure and with practically none of the initial depressive and desperate mood the news about the very severe ulcerative findings of her intestinal illness, which she then

Spontaneous Incident

received and which indicated an operation. (To finish the example for the sake of comprehension: A further psychotherapeutic treatment was not possible with the patient and would have had no more significance with these extreme organic findings. After she was operated on, I tried to help clarify the marital problems with both partners. Finally, the patient accepted responsibility for her life, separated from her very difficult husband, and built up a new and, according to her description, quite positive life for herself.)

Discussion

Commentary: Here GAI also has no other function than that of a crisis intervention. The strong influence on the entire autonomic nervous system becomes clear through the first session. An encouragement of the patient as well as a strong advance in trust in the therapist is connected with this. The technical path of focusing on a completely individual, need-gratifying scene becomes clear, with which the therapist cannot be familiar, particularly for differentiated persons. It is essential, since even the water motif can by no means be globally used as free of conflictual material with all patients. Rather, in each individual case one must clarify in the initial contacts what a subjectively satisfying scene of the narcissistic, oral, or possibly anal drive (or wish) gratification involves for the individual.

Archaic Drive Gratification

With this patient the small incident is particularly informative, in which the archaically gratifying (narcissistic) scene suddenly changes into a partially anxiety-laden one. I do not need to go into detail regarding the contents of the inclination to become smaller, since the tendency toward embryonic regression becomes all too clear. Ordinarily one can never predict when and in what way a satisfying image of this kind obtains a negative accent or even turns into a negative anxiety-laden one. For this reason such exercises on one's own are not to be recommended to patients. Archaically satisfying images should only be undertaken in the therapist's presence, who can guide the contents and take up any deviations therapeutically. Incidentally, this "upset" is quite characteristic, and the therapist must be prepared for it when a particularly gratifying motif is focused on for a longer period. For further examples and conclusions see Leuner (1983).

Second Dimension in the Routine Therapy

The experiences described here of the *second dimension of GAI therapy* can be used in two different ways in the routine therapy with GAI on the basic level.

Lack of conflictual Material

1. If, contrary to all expectation of the therapist, the patient does *not present any conflictual material in GAI* but adapts himself extensively or exclusively to pleasant and harmonious, agreeable contents in the panorama, the therapist should not attempt to prevent him from this or to search emphatically for conflicts or to provoke them. Bearing this new piece of knowledge in mind, he will take on a granting attitude toward the patient and let him experience these predominantly positive contents in the mental imagery. He will preferably accentuate them and now and then reinforce them whenever particularly marked scenes of

this kind present themselves. The therapist can, with a great deal of certainty, presume that this procedure will also have an important clinical therapeutic significance for the patient and that he will be able to help him by this means. The path of the help does not, however, go in the direction of an internal confrontation, of a maturing of the personality particularly in the face of his initial referential persons and his environment. This expectation can be entertained only conditionally here, although we have examples at our disposal still to be analyzed, in which a maturation of the object relations also occurred upon completion of the experiential categories. However, such a goal cannot be obtained by force. Nevertheless, through the improvement of symptoms, which can last for years, these patients are helped without a doubt for the time being within the scope of a short-term therapy of 10 to 20 sessions.

Reinforcement of Spontaneous Conflict-free Scenes

2. If the therapy of the basic level proceeds relatively routinely in the manner described in this class with the fade-in of fixed images and other conflict-related contents, the therapist will attentively register, on the basis of the knowledge of this new therapeutic dimension, especially consciously, *all of those conflict-free scenes* that the patient experiences in mental imagery in the course of the usual procedure. He will additionally try to reinforce these passages experientially in the patient,

Offering Motifs of Water

whether by offering him water motifs in connection with this to moisten his feet, hands, or face, to bathe in it, to swim, or drink from it. He may also ask the patient to absorb within himself lovely, pleasant, harmonious scenic images wherever they appear, and while meditating to enrich and "soak up" the mood. It is insignificant whether it is the view from the summit of a mountain, of a meadow in a valley, or other scenes. Of course, the same holds true for all scenes in which spontaneous meetings with a friendly animal or with a pleasant or generous person materialize. Usually it is even advisable to end the session with such a scene, provided that it has been savored enough. The theme, which has now become conscious, and the mood experienced can resound in this way. It is in fact remarkable what degree of inner calmness and stability patients can gain from this part of therapy. In the further sessions in GAI, phenomena of change become connected with this, which in no way regularly indicate a covering up of

Control Through Phenomena of Change

the prevailing problems, but frequently also denote a strengthening of the ego with an openness to new things and with increased courage to new solutions in mental imagery and frequently also in coping with reality. The second dimension of GAI described here can be placed under the category of "anaclitic therapy" (of the supportive type). Seen from the perspective of drive dynamics, its basis is a primary narcissistic and oral regression.

Session Seventeen

Pursuit of Real Situations

In GAI the primary consideration was, in accordance with the depth psychological dream theory of no matter which school, to bring unconscious material to the level of the dream symbols. The forms of the application of mental imagery, which were conceived of in Europe, are similar to each other in this. Through the therapeutic successes of GAI and the seemingly feasible forms of graphic concealment of the impulses and conflicts released from the unconscious, it also seemed quite "elegant" to at first leave them on the preconscious level by means of the symbolic encodement. This was supposed to prevent the patient with a tendency for intellectualization from plainly cognitively recognizing what subject is under discussion. As is generally known, it is an advantage of projective test procedures in general that for long periods of time the patient cannot know what purpose the test serves and what kind of psychic material is being addressed. The preference given to symbolic representations as the projective expression of unconscious problems seemed additionally to have the advantage that a broad range of ambivalent tendencies or a compromise between impulse and defense as well as into the depths of gradated emotional experiences is expressed in contaminated form in the one image in the symbol. The frequently very high level of involvement in mental imagery can apparently be explained from this. During the intensive occupation with this symbolic world and its empirical study, the idea remained in the background for a long time that imaginal contents from the concrete everyday situation could also be of interest and perhaps productive for the therapeutic process and helpful in gaining insights. Focusing on scenes from reality was always at the fore in the schools of behavior therapy and behavior modification of the American version. Whereas for the working hypothesis in GAI and its precursors (also for instance in the advanced level of autogenic training), it was regarded as an unspoken rule that the appearing imaginal contents are "more than themselves," "mean," or symbolize something, in other words, the mental imaginal scenes emerging within the relaxed state can never be comprehended without simultaneously considering the quality of their symbolic meaning. The American schools of behavior therapy (for example, Wolpe, 1958) do not subscribe to these kinds of ideas at all. The imagined object or the imagined person is itself the real thing and nothing else. For our area, it can be recalled that in night dreams we also often experience very real scenes. When applied to GAI, we can thus ask ourselves, what actually prevents us from taking a conflict we are focusing on within a situation from reality closer to consciousness rather

Symbolic Encodement

Behavior Modification

Real Scenes in Night Dreams

than concealing it symbolically, for instance, in the form of landscape motifs or representations of animals. The presumption would be that the therapist is familiar with his patient's pending current conflictual situations from discussions with him. For instance, with a young person one thinks of a problem in his relationship to his mother or to a mother substitute figure. We know, for example, that cows occasionally spontaneously appearing in the meadow symbolize a certain maternal quality, as is likewise the case in the scenotest, and can therefore also act as a substitute for the mother. We can track down such a conflict through the image of a cow very precisely. Particular qualities are of interest, whether the cow is emaciated or fat, clean or dirty, whether the udder is flaccid or full and how the cow behaves toward the patient, when he approaches it: with animosity or in a friendly manner. Does he experience the cow as being friendly, calm, easy going or the opposite, dumb, gaping, rejecting, boring, chewing its cud to itself. Why should we not have his own mother also appear instead of this (we practice such encounters in the intermediate level techniques of GAI, too)? Then he is requested to observe the mother's behavior precisely, how she is dressed, whether she conforms to her age, how she greets him, in a friendly or unfriendly manner, arrogantly or in an excessively mothering fashion. The subject's feelings are likewise to be described in view of his emerging mother. Finally, for patients with a certain degree of practice, attempting to talk with the person in question can also succeed. The results vary. With some patients this works; with others, it does not. This is the limit.

Focusing on the Actual Referential Person

Focusing on actual scenes probably has the most important significance therapeutically when the concern is dealing with phobic situations, such as the stage fright of an actor, a musician, or a speaker. One subjects these persons precisely to the imagined scene, in which they find themselves faced with a large audience. Taking up this example as a typical model (we could also consider a snake phobia or another kind of phobia), we then follow technically the described rules of dealing with the fixed images in GAI. As the first step, we have the patient describe the anxiety-determined situation and the anxiety-arousing object in minute detail, that is, all of the nuances, and the same for the patient's own emotions and the feelings originating from the anxiety-producing object. Then we try to find a way of making the patient more familiar with the scene or the situation. This can occur if he cautiously approaches the situation step by step or if he begins a fantasized dialogue or, as we present it on the intermediate level later on, if he undertakes a role exchange and places himself in the position of the fear-arousing figure. The experienced reader clearly sees that we are approaching practices of behavior therapy with this. Independent of it (behavior therapy did not yet exist at the time GAI was conceived), we pursued the stepwise approach toward

The Phobia Model

Procedure as with Fixed Image

Role Exchange

the fear-arousing object from very early on (compare the technique of symbol confrontation, Leuner, 1957). In this way a certain gradation of the dosage of anxiety can be attained. In psychoanalysis the release of anxieties under the protection of the therapist has also been an important therapeutic measure from the beginning.

Dosage of Anxiety

As far as the phobias are concerned, there are some attempts with GAI to deal with the respective anxiety through focusing on the actual scene. Strangely enough in these cases, there has not previously been much success in keeping the patient on the real level within the imagery. On the contrary, fantasy soon spontaneously took over and suddenly disguised the scene symbolically. I cannot account for why this has been the case. Perhaps it is due to the fact that patient or therapist or both were already too far involved with the mental imagery technique. Perhaps it is because our patients tend more strongly than American patients to place fantasy-born contents in the foreground. I would like to follow-up with a suitable example to illustrate this strange development of a session that was focused on primarily as a scene from reality.

Symbolic scenes fade in

Example

Case 1 (23)

In one seminar a female teacher has the following complaint. She is highly afraid of the principal of her school. In his presence she is extremely self-conscious, anxious, and cannot speak freely. We subsequently agree that in GAI she will very precisely imagine the scene, how she enters the room of the omnipotent one and sees him sitting in the usual manner behind his desk. She should then try to find a way of establishing contact with him and beginning a conversation. Perhaps I ought to mention that the teacher has a relatively lively imagination and a certain eidetic gift without, however, standing out above the average of this group of persons. In GAI she experiences the following (in summary form).

After she has entered the principal's office, she sees him, gigantic and massive, sitting behind the desk. However, it is not the actual appearance of the man; instead she recognizes to her astonishment that the figure is made out of newspaper. In the follow-up discussion she finds an explanation for this: This metaphor "out of paper" is very appropriate, because he actually is a person, for whom a great deal in his official, school, and apparently also private nature is just "paper." In the scene in which he is sitting overly large behind his desk, the patient shrinks to a tiny form of the size of Tom Thumb. (We recognize the symbolic representation of tininess and the feeling of personal powerlessness in the face of this all-powerful figure.) In this moment of hopelessness and helplessness something quite unexpected happens for the subject. Little "green men," who are no bigger than she is, come from the various corners of the room as if to help her. All of a sudden the little green figures, together with her, make a kind of assault on the desk by way of running past its legs. In this moment the figure of the paper principal collapses and now under the desk is just as small and inconspicuous as the teacher and her helpers. She is very surprised and has to laugh about this sudden and unexpected turn.

Regressive Solution

Commentary: Elsewhere (Leuner, 1983) I discuss this example in connection with the capacity for creative problem solving on a regressive, childish level of fantasy. The symbolic manner in which the meeting takes place and how the tension of anxiety toward authority figures is related is unmistakeable. In contrast to an attempt at solution through imagination in behavior therapy, in which the real scene is instated by the therapist and is played through step by step according to his standards; here the teacher creates the scene in accordance with her own motivational system and the solution also occurs in a form apparently adequately corresponding to her at that time. In this I would like to see an advantage. Here it is noteworthy (and in my opinion also characteristic based upon analogous clinical experience; see for example, the recent discussion of the crisis intervention) that this 30-minute session had sufficed to take away a large part of the teacher's fear of the principal. She was now able to encounter him more composed and calmly.

Individual Solution

Apart from treating phobic problems in the form of scenes from reality, focusing on such scenes has also so far proved successful in another much less dramatic area. The possibilities dormant within it have probably not yet been exhausted. I am thinking of the setting up of banal scenes from everyday life, in which the patient behaves as he usually does. We can have him describe in the usual way, on the one hand, the details of the imagined visual perception and, above all, on the other hand, the feeling tone, that emanates, for instance, from the landscape, the rooms of living quarters, the encounters with people and those with whom he lives. It has been found that in the state of deeper relaxation, which almost everyone slips into during continued imaginings (without needing to be induced to it directly, as I emphasized earlier), the respective scenes from daily life are experienced emotionally much more densely and precisely than in reality. In confronting scenes of his daily life in GAI the subject receives in a manner of speaking the answer to the question, "How do I experience unconsciously my everyday surroundings in terms of feelings?" If one does in fact allow such scenes to run their course, it can happen that the person not only gains insight in this direction, but he also experiences this exercise as a kind of confrontation. An abundance of unconscious, previously repressed attitudes, aversions, or their opposite, inner likings, can be made perceivable and thus conscious. In the preceding example this became obvious in a

Confrontation with Everyday Scenes

very extreme way by the fact that the school principal was made of newspaper, and a component of the teacher's emotions with regard to her unconscious, refined perception of his human qualities was expressed in this. I would not like to leave it unmentioned that the great precision of the subliminal emotional perception of actual situations can be traced to a capacity of man discovered very early. O. Vogt, the well-known brain anatomist, who spent a great deal of time working with hypnosis at the turn of the century, formulated it: Hypnosis can be understood as a microscope of the psyche, that is in the hypnoid state intrapsychic processes are "magnified" as if through a microscope and are thus grasped more clearly and precisely. Now the example.

Emotional Precision

Example

Case 2 (24)

The female patient is a 38-year-old secondary school teacher, who comes to me for treatment due to diverse psychosomatic symptoms. She has taught for several years at a well-known convent school, and her small apartment is also in the area of the school. At first, she had felt very well and safe there, as far as she had perceived the situation before therapy. Toward the end of a necessarily very long therapy due to its personality changing effect, I dealt with the question with her, how she would probably feel upon returning to the milieu of this school and the living situation of the convent. It was important to me to prepare her for this and to make it possible for her to test whether and for how long she wants to continue to live under the same conditions. In other words, it was my goal to have the patient experience the emotional aspect of this living arrangement from the current standpoint of that time. In this process the following takes place, reproduced here in simplified and somewhat free form.

To reach her apartment, she walks through the courtyard, which is arranged like a garden and which she definitely loves; the sky is overcast, the garden looks meager, the foliage and the flowers seem somewhat too wilted to be able to give off that natural freshness that she had formerly appreciated so much. She enters her little apartment. She allows the effect of the rooms to work on her. Now they seem very small and narrow to her. She scarcely finds room to walk between the pieces of furniture. The atmosphere in the rooms is musty and gray. She is shocked about this. This is the reason I think I should give her verbal assistance in saying perhaps for the time being she should view this impression as only a momentary mood without something final having been expressed about the value of her apartment. Then she looks out of the window into the courtyard garden again and has the impression that the buildings surrounding it have moved closer together. The area seems cramped, and the entire scene expresses a degree of confinement, which makes her shudder and evokes a strong feeling of aversion and also of anxiousness.

"Microscope of the Soul"

Commentary: The "microscope of the soul" instituted here in GAI to assess the actual scene in emotional terms was not only successful but also gives relatively concise answers. The element of confrontation lies in the circumstance that the patient finds herself faced with an entirely changed emotionally charged scene when compared with the actual scene viewed soberly and remembered much more positively.

An explanation seems necessary to me. In view of one of the experiences described in this example, while the actual situation is being focused upon, a patient and a therapist with little experience might subliminally or uncontrollably pursue the notion that the scene described and its emotional quality express something equivalent to "a truth" about the imagined object. Therefore it would serve as a kind of yardstick or judgment about it, in this case about the convent school and the patient's living situation. The idea that "the unconscious" is incorruptible and imparts "truths," as has occasionally been naively assumed and also described, does not hit upon the core of the matter.

Evaluation of the Emotional Impression

What is then expressed in this example? Nothing more and nothing less than the momentary, emotional assessment of the imagined real object (or the imagined human figure). This assessment is dependent to a large degree upon the present, that is, current mood of the person, upon the influences that he is subject to at the time. That can be the current influence by another person or a discussion held with the therapist or it can be due to other circumstances of the frame of mind. In a resigned mood, for example, an imagined object will have an entirely different emotional tone and the proportions will be shifted very differently from those imagined by the person in a happy, expectant mood.

This goes to prove that it is a matter of an emotional assessment, which must also be explained to the patient. Moreover, it is determined by the state of tension, by a high level of sensitivity, and thus is also frequently excessive. In therapy it is therefore advisable to focus on such scenes from

Repetition is Advised

reality at repeated instances in different moods, especially if they have a greater degree of involvement for the person, such as a living arrangement or a partnership situation. Nevertheless, this unconscious emotional assessment of the scene gives clues to hidden currents and emotional relationships of the person concerned, which he learns to perceive in this way. He can check up on them more often through repeated focusings. If they recur, he can examine relationships to people, institutions, living areas, or he can arrive at a readjustment, for instance, of greater distance or of liberation from dependencies.

Gaining Material

A third advantage of focusing on actual situations lies in the fact that a great amount of material can be gained in regard to the case history and also, above all, to the patient's current social relations in his surroundings. I am thinking, for instance, of the circumstance in which one has a young patient return to his parents' home in GAI and run through scenes of encountering the relatives or interactions at the dinner table. The intake interview by itself can probably never indicate as many characteristic features of the family's interactional dynamics as such a scene in GAI. With many patients, symptoms are then even revealed about which they had never spoken, as, for instance, an agoraphobia, among others.

The technique of the procedure is not difficult. However, the therapist should know that to focus on actual scenes the patient must be advanced in therapy and must have acquired a certain amount of stress capacity, since occasionally powerful emotions can be connected with this, as is evident in the last example and in other places (Leuner, 1983).

Session Eighteen

Orientation to the Effective Therapeutic Factors

In this session some important technical aspects will be reproduced in context, which were scattered here and there in the directions presented for guiding the mental imagery or were occasionally briefly mentioned in some of the motifs. The recapitulative description is meant to accentuate their great importance, particularly since they are usually so refined that they are either taken for granted or the therapist's style of guidance passes over them without expressly taking note of them. I would like to summarize them briefly:

1. *Focussed exploration of the imagined scenes* and their emotional tone with the goal of their cognitive penetration and formulation
2. *Objectification* and transferral of the contents from fantasy to reality by the *patient's* spontaneous *interpretation of the contents*
3. *Liberation of feelings and affects* to the point of catharsis
4. *Feedback effect* of the objectified conflicts, and facilitation of the creative process.
5. *Control* of the steps of therapeutic development *through phenomena of change*

These individual positions are difficult to represent graphically. I must ask the reader's indulgence for occasionally expressing myself abstractly because of this. I believe, however, that you are now well prepared to be able to follow and understand this summary on the basis of the clinical examples described previously.

Cognitive Penetration

Focused exploration of the imagined scenes and their emotional tones with the goal of their cognitive penetration and formulation. The title of this first technical aspect seems somewhat awkward. It specifically concerns the following. The perception of the catathymic images can, in marked form, come close to the perception of real objects. The first action that the patient therefore carries out within the imaginal process is the visual perception as such. What he then does with the apprehended object or the scene itself remains open for the time being. Is he only able to grasp it in passing and then drop it in favor of the next one repetitively by rushing, so to speak, from one scene to another? It is considerably more effective therapeutically if the therapist's style of guidance aims at having the patient gradually learn to bring a single imagined scene fully into his present experimental world in terms of its total contents.

This is first of all promoted by the instruction to describe the scene as comprehensively as possible in all of its details. This involves a cognitive penetration, that is, analysis of the "perceptual" field, which can be carried quite far. As already mentioned occasionally, this subtle penetration and focussed visualization leads to the circumstance that the scene is augmented by broader surroundings and by all sorts of details, and completely new elements can appear. In terms of technique, the therapist should ask the patient more frequently at the beginning to describe the scene as precisely as possible and to go into detail. In so doing he should at first avoid too many detailed questions, above all those that can be answered by "Yes" or "No" and are thus "narrowly" framed.

Emotional Tone of the Scene

Open questions are better, such as, "What else do you see?" "Can you look a little more closely?" "Please try to describe details to me, I would like to get completely into the image myself." I should like to point out that a learning process can be stimulated in the patient here and in this way one can train him, in a manner of speaking, from session to session to experience the catathymic scenes more and more broadly and precisely in terms of cognitive contents. However, in the actual sense of the concept, this educational task is not accomplished until the patient likewise learns to perceive and at the same time to verbalize the emotional tone of the respective scene. Two aspects are to be noted here. On the one hand, there is the *emotional tone emanating from the scene as such;* on the other hand, there are the *patient's feelings themselves,* to which it is necessary to pay attention.

The Subject's Emotion

In the former case it is then, for example, the mood of a landscape, of a room, the qualities which a mountain, a wooded scene, or whatever else radiates. To direct the patients to a finer perception of them, the therapist can offer the choice of a few qualities, in order to make it clear to them what is meant by this, namely, a relatively naive, somewhat childishly oriented perception of the simple emotional impression. In the second case one would ask about the feeling situation in which the patient finds himself. Frequently, he gets into the frame of mind of catathymic scenery more slowly or more quickly, and the mood it radiates and his own mood blend into one. However, that is not usually the case. The opposite can also occur, and a patient refuses to accept the negative atmosphere of a catathymic scene and disassociates himself from it. In both cases the question arises of how he feels about the scene emotionally. Does he experience it as pleasant or unpleasant, pertaining to him or foreign. It is thus always helpful to verbalize the feeling tone, particularly when faced with fixed images.

Relatedness to Reality and Personal Interpretation of the Contents

Objectification and transferral of the contents from fantasy to reality by the patient's spontaneous interpretation of the contents. Objectification as a basic form of dealing with mental imagery has the aim of gradually bringing the conflict represented in the symbolic image or even the conflict-free scene and the accompanying feeling tone out of this form of its representation. It is the expression of the strongly regressive experiential level under the principles of the primary process. Step by step, this formulation is also to be grasped intellectually by means of verbalization and the analysis of the cognitive contents. In this way the imaginal contents gain, on the other hand, more and more strongly the quality of an object, of a comprehensible object, which does not merely stop in the realm of emotions and magical symbols. On the other hand, as the therapeutic process advances, the meanings of the symbols gradually become clearer, and the patient's interpretations of them correspond more and more to reality-oriented categories in the sense of secondary process. A good example of this was the short-term therapy of the 17-year-old high school student, who gradually led the giant emerging from the cave into the real world and the giant successfully adapted to the conditions prevailing there. For the therapeutic guidance, this objective means that wherever any too imaginative, too contradictory, and too unreal scenes emerge, the therapist will give preference to a somewhat pointedly objective form in choosing the statements of his interventions and in the tone of his voice to influence the patient toward the goal of getting him to perceive this fantasy material in a more pragmatic way (but by no means in an authoritorian "correcting" manner), to visualize it and to describe any exaggerated feelings as precisely as possible. In other words, even the greatest monstrosities, as for instance a wildly snorting dragon that is emerging from the woods, are observed, visualized, and described in the same minute way, in which one would investigate a highly technical apparatus. This objective tends toward a shifting of the circumstances of the wishfully oriented primary process to the reality-oriented secondary process. Finally, the possibilities for the patient's own spontaneous interpretation of the contents and for drawing the patient's attention to sudden ideas, as sparing as we still are with them on the basic level, are also a part of the increasing cognitive penetration of the scenes.

Secondary Process Orientation

Objective

Liberation of feelings and affects to the point of cartharsis. The realization of the feelings, which is strived for under the first technical aspect discussed, naturally leads to the circumstance that the patient increasingly learns to perceive the feeling tone of the scene more clearly, and this all the more so because he has refined his inner perceptions in a state of relaxation. Moreover, stronger feelings and affects are also occasionally released; they can be of a negative kind, such as anxiety, uncertainty, terror; they can be of a positive nature, such as calmness, joy, or being intensely aesthetically impressed, to name only a few. The release of these feelings to the point of abreaction in the sense of mild or even stronger motoric catharsis with reactions in breathing, the facial muscles, as well as with marked verbal formulations usually has a liberating quality. It should be supported by the therapist, just as is the case with breaking into tears or perhaps

Refined Inner Perception

Abreaction

the long, terrified crying on the occasion of a helpless scene or of a sad loss. He has to accept the shame that is frequently connected with this. At the same time, such a situation can make it clear to the patient that the therapist is understanding of these reactions, and the therapist can show him that he values them as "therapeutic release." The result of catharsis, perhaps

Microcatharsis

only of a "microcatharsis," is an emotional neutralization of initially emotionally cathected GAI contents. These change in the process, and the patient gains greater cognitive clarity about the meaning of the contents, growing knowledge regarding interrelationships, and clarity in decision-making processes, which was not possible for him before abreacting these cathexes as a result of the regression connected with them. The release of affects and cathartic reactions are thus not ends in themselves,

Gaining Cognitive Clarity

but means to an end, in order to heighten the greater cognitive clarity already stressed under the two previous technical aspects precisely at those points that, fixed images, for instance, have produced interference. In explaining this, it is to be noted that very intense cathartic reactions are rare in GAI and are difficult to trigger. They appear when early childhood or other traumatic scenes are relived anew, which very rarely happens within the framework of the basic level technique.

Feedback Effect

Feedback effect of the objectified conflicts, and facilitation of the creative process. As a result of the deciphering of catathymic contents in the course of the therapeutic process and even through the mere visualization, the conflicts portrayed in the imagination are projected from the individual's own ego and appear a meter or more "in front of" his closed eyes. The conflict as "tangible object" thus moves farther into the distance.

Object Character of the Conflict

This object displaced to the outside, as a part of the individual's own conflictual ego, can now be observed and critically examined, especially if the visual imagery has been produced in addition. Structures not noticed or recognizable until that time can then be perceived in joint exploration with the therapist (or with a group), classified and examined for their feeling tone. However, even if visual detail is not at hand, the experiential contents projected outward can be dealt with as an object. Its presentation in one or another of the stated forms naturally has an immediate retroactive effect (feedback) on the ego. Therefore not only the spontaneous urgency to create by projecting the individual's own emotional conflict outward as a natural element of the self-healing tendency (as also in night dreams) is relevant, but also this secondary act of the retroactive effect, the feedback of what has been created upon the individual's own, perceiving ego letting itself be impressed upon anew has therapeutic significance. This is to be verified later. A circular process materializes through this retroactive effect, which provokes a

Preconscious Confrontation

more unconscious, preconscious, or even cognitively clearer inner confrontation that continues constantly. Depending on which level the penetration of the created images takes place, this process stays more in the graphic realm, half preconsciously and half unconsciously, or it is carried out consciously to the point of gaining cognitive insights. This applies particularly if clarification of the meaning comes about through the individual's own interpretation of the symbolic connections and through sudden ideas relating to details of the images. To understand the therapeutic effect of GAI on the basic level, it is thus important to keep the following in mind. Already on the preconsious level, which for most patients maintains precedence in the scope of a short-term therapy, the process of inner confrontation is promoted and again and again receives new impulses to develop the mental imagery further. This is then expressed in the repeatedly mentioned, expanding, and developing creative imaginal formations, whereby the initially scanty and pale scenes become more lively, richer, and more populated by man and animal; broader worlds open up, and the patient learns to resolve the initially difficult and scarcely to be surmounted obstructive motifs in investigative actions. This also gradually becomes looser, freer, and less problematical. The preconscious feedback effect, remaining with the image for quite a long time, thus has a certain independence which one should not underestimate. Under some circumstances, it can lead further as an emotionally conveyed confrontation than if the therapist is in principle aiming at dealing with the affective imagery in cognitive and intellectual terms too soon. The approach "to wait patiently in the image," which Boss (1953) demonstrated in the existential analytical treatment of the night dream, allows one to comprehend better the image as metaphor in its entire scope and complex meanings and to understand it more completely than if a conceptual analysis takes place. The factor of focussed exploration emphasized under the first technical aspect is so important for this reason. The therapist can reinforce it by also guiding the patient to let an imagined scene work on him longer and in a somewhat meditating way and to observe it very calmly. A transformation can possibly already be at hand that gives notice of the experiential retroactive effect as a therapeutic act. This applies for the conflictual contents as well as for those that are conflict-free. The feedback effect can even be intensified by the therapist's conscious focusing of the perception and visualization on a specific part of the contents for some time and firmly holding the patient to it. There is a kind of confrontation in this if conflictual contents are concerned. The process of the psyche's confrontation with itself can be decisively set and kept in motion in this way. A peculiar oscillating back and forth between the diffusely emotional sensing of preconscious emotions, on the one hand, and the visible concise image as displayed object, on the other, characterizes this process.

Independent Emotional Confrontation

Boss' Phenomenological Approach

Intensification of the Feedback Effect

At another point, we thought about this retroactive effect and acquired a number of indications for the unexpectedly great binding character of this process. Experiments have verified this.

Binding Character of the Process

They have proved that a close functional unity can exist between the symbol and the unconscious emotional conflict behind it. The one presupposes the other. The influence upon the symbolic image, whether through the therapist's intervention or through the described feedback, has an effect on the nonverbal, regressive level in accordance with the unconscious dynamics of the conflictual structure. We rely upon the process of preverbal confrontation over long intervals within the framework of the basic level as an important therapeutic component of symboldrama. This process seems to stand in particular contrast to the cognitive process of clarification initially stressed under the second technical aspect. However, in most cases both processes operate parallel to each other; the one dealt with here frequently in the first phase of therapy, the cognitive clarification discussed being more in a later second phase. However, both processes of clarification can, as already stated, also run simultaneously and mutually enrich each other. That may seem somewhat theoretical at first but is only the attempt to abstract the functions of symboldrama described in the various technical directions and examples belonging to them in the previous chapters.

Preverbal Confrontation and Clarification

Control Through Phenomena of Change

Control of the steps of therapeutic development through phenomena of change. I can keep this section brief. *Phenomena of synchronic transformation,* which appear in the course of the advancing GAI therapy, for instance, in the *increasing development* of the stream's course, of the landscape in the view from the mountain, or the small discreet transformations emerging after each session and after many a therapeutic step due to therapeutic interventions, represent not merely a possibility of control for the therapist. What is more, for the patient they are a bit of encouragement and confirmation when they are brought to his attention and are occasionally focused upon. The therapist should also comment upon them for this reason and occasionally strengthen them verbally under the rubric of "reward" (reinforcement) as preparation for the patient's own perceivable gaining of insights, of therapeutic release, and improvement of his symptoms. These appear later than the phenomena of change, which can be noticed early. The failure of phenomena of change to appear, which were expected by the therapist, is also important in this connection. On the basis of this he can judge diagnostically whether the therapeutic process is not presently advancing in general or at a particular spot, whether ego defenses or resistances are existing here or a transference problem is bringing the treatment to a standstill. It then becomes necessary to search for an explanation. There is the possibility of illustrating the stagnation to the patient at this point. In connection with this I would like to add another diagnostic motif to the basic level. It allows one to recognize the stagnation of the therapeutic process with an astonishing degree of logical consistency, which at the same time expresses the particular degree of simplicity of the projective functions of mental imagery. The therapist who is still unsure can check on the progress of the treatment process with its aid.

Checking on the Therapeutic Process

In my early experiments with symboldrama I discovered that *focusing on the motif of building a new house* is especially suitable for this purpose. Here the patient is urged at particular intervals, that is, after several sessions or at a fitting opportunity in the catathymic panorama, to imagine a "new building" independent of the subject being dealt with at the time. What is specifically meant by "new building" is left completely open. With great regularity, a dug out excavation site appears at the beginning of therapy. In the course of further treatment one can observe various stages of construction, for instance, that the basement has been closed in with masonry, the first floor, the rough construction of the second floor, and that the roof has been completed. Then the typical steps of the interior work follow, until at the end a completely furnished house is standing. Here, too, it seems as if (as previously mentioned) the psyche had the capacity to develop an inner measurement for a completed therapy, when the inner curve of development has been rounded to the extent that a certain degree of confidence and internal completion has been achieved. Conversely, scenes in which the construction is not continued are particularly concise, for instance, a workers strike. Faulty solutions in the form of illusory expectations are also expressed during the construction of such a building, for example, if a multistory building with a complicated concrete construction or something similar is put up instead of a residential building and then is perhaps left when only half completed. The immature (often narcissistic) designs of the individual's grandiose ego emerge in this and are reflected as illusory expectations from the therapy. Here matters, of course, become more complicated, and the analysis of the patient's faulty expectations needs to be dealt with. Only the very experienced therapist, well trained in depth psychology, is able to handle this. Nevertheless, these scenes can have an important feedback effect on the patient in the sense of impending insight and corrective adjustment.

Faulty Developments

Session Nineteen

Transference and Countertransference in Guided Affective Imagery

Therapist's Behavior from a Technical Point of View

Up to this point in the course, I have tried to present the supervision of mental imagery and the interactions connected with it as well as the therapist's style of guidance more from the technical point of view. This is thoroughly appropriate and is also supportable for long intervals of time. Nevertheless, we cannot ignore the fundamental knowledge, which psychoanalysis gained decades ago, about the emotional relationship between the patient and his therapist. For this reason I must examine the problem of transference and countertransference feelings in order to then discuss the particular conditions that are found in GAI in regard to this.

Transference of Feelings

From psychoanalysis, we know that in every psychotherapy the patient transfers feelings onto the therapist sooner or later and in more or less pronounced form. They correspond to those that he had toward important referential persons in an early stage of his childhood. These may have been mother or father figures or others, who played an important emotional role in his life as loving persons either temporarily or continuously. He was also afraid of them and had other negative feelings for them. It is debatable whether these feelings are constantly involved in therapy, and are thus to be paid attention to, or only intermittently and only when they have increased to a certain level and have noticeable consequences in the treatment. If these feelings are of a more positive nature, one cursorily speaks of a "positive transference," which can possibly have a high level of liking and even a portion of genuine amorousness in it. If negative feelings are mobilized in this transference situation, such as insecurity, nervousness, anger, or protest, one speaks equally globally of a "negative transference." By studying the prevailing transference feelings at the time more closely, it can be made evident that they are determined by the emotional relationship to a particular person from early childhood. One then speaks, for instance, of a "father transference," a "mother transference," or the transference of the relationship to a grandmother, and so on. Psychoanalysis has made dealing with the patient's transference feelings into an instrument of the therapy itself, provided that it is not just a matter of a short-term psychotherapy of 20 to 30 sessions (which is usually the case in the basic level of GAI). Freud correctly recognized that the infantile neurosis resurges in these transferences and is revitalized in the "here and now" of the therapeutic session of the adult, that is, is experienced and becomes resolvable therapeutically. This condition is called the *transference neurosis.* In psychoanalysis, the process of striving toward its resolution can stretch out over very long periods of

"Positive" and "Negative" Transference

Transference Neurosis

time, over weeks and months. It is at the same time regarded as a principle that a transference analysis can naturally only be performed when these feelings have reached such a high pitch that the patient perceives them or that they have assumed a character, which is disturbing the therapy. This aspect of interference of a negative transference can in fact be a considerable handicap for a psychotherapy in symboldrama, too. It distorts the therapeutic process, hinders its progress, or questions it in general. For this reason the basic level therapist must be familiar with this problem, too. If, for example, a patient develops such a negative transference toward his therapist in the sense of early childhood fears of his strict father, the consequence can be that his insights slacken off, his anxiousness makes him shy, and he no longer brings any real material into the therapist. The experienced and qualified analyst will then try to analyze the patient's transference feelings. Something else can

Countertransference

also take place, however, the counterpart to that, the transference on the part of the therapist. Instead of confidently using his analytic tools, he can possibly react emotionally to this negative transference of his patient if he has an emotional problem of his own with relationships that has not yet been sufficiently resolved. He can, for instance, be annoyed with a patient who stops imagining. That is the situation of countertransference. It is based upon the fact that the therapist transfers, that is, projects onto the patient, his own incompletely resolved negative early childhood relationships to a referential person. The communication between the two suffers reciprocally with the consequence that the therapy stagnates.

Interference in GAI

Experience has shown that one of the most frequent difficulties in conducting GAI therapy successfully emerges in those cases in which a negative transference of the patient arises or, conversely, an unresolved countertransference of the therapist obstructs dealing with this problem. Only through subtle analysis of the situation in a supervisional group (or individual supervision) is it possible to make the therapist's countertransference reaction conscious and generally in this way to also continue the treatment.

Special Situation in GAI

How do transference and countertransference work specifically in GAI?

Compared with psychoanalysis and other predominantly verbally oriented forms of psychotherapy, there is a specific kind of emotional relationship between the two participants. Stated globally, the transference of the patient's early childhood emotional relationships onto the therapist during treatment is largely insignificant for long periods of time and can generally be rated unimportant as an interfering factor that must be dealt with in detail. However, it cannot be excluded entirely. In two situations it moves decisively to the fore:

Two Forms of Interference

1. If the negative emotional transference onto the therapist occurs during the first meeting, for example, in the course of recording the patient's history or during the first attempt to introduce GAI. I am thinking, for instance, of the circumstance in which a patient is primarily shy, anxious, or distrustful toward the therapist and the therapist is not able to reduce this sufficiently by means of his manner of guiding the dialogue, which is open and inspiring of trust.
2. If a pronounced, regressively accentuated negative transference emerges in the course of the GAI therapy of a patient, who turns out to be severely disturbed, perhaps due to a narcissistic or borderline personality structure. Then countertransference reactions are also mobilized all too easily in the therapist who is not fully trained. The relationship of the two to each other is unavoidably influenced negatively in spite of the therapist's best efforts.

In both cases the therapist, who has not received training beyond the basic level, has reached his limits. He then has the choice either to refer the patient to a more experienced therapist or to submit the case to careful individual or group supervision (case study seminars of the AGKB), if possible within the scope of a permanent regional supervision group.

If we disregard these two unquestionably extreme positions for the time being, global statements about the particular position of GAI in connection with the problem "transference and countertransference" require a psychodynamically substantiated foundation. I would like to discuss this in the following.

Reasons for the Special Conditions in GAI

One can state three reasons why the transference and countertransference relationships generally play a relatively minor part in symboldrama as far as it concerns an interference of the process of therapy that has begun positively. To avoid misunderstanding, however, I must emphasize again that the patient's transference feelings (and conversely, the therapist's) also are constantly resonating in symboldrama and can influence the treatment. On the intermediate and advanced levels, the more extensively trained therapist should learn not only to perceive the patient-therapist relationships but also to deal with them in a therapeutically productive way. The three reasons are:

1. Therapy on the basic level is generally limited to short-term therapy
2. The patient's transference feelings are mostly projected into the level of mental imagery
3. The setting in GAI reduces the risk of child-parent projections

Short-term Therapy

1. A pronounced transference neurosis seldom appears in the psychoanalytic short-term therapy of 15 to 30 sessions; instead a positive level of transference predominates (Loch, 1972). That is a relatively global and not more precisely substantiated statement.

Projection screen of mental imagery

2. The projective energy of the patient (pressure to project), with which he transfers early childhood emotional relationships onto the therapist, is to a large extent absorbed into the projective screen of the mental imagery in GAI. The mental imagery provides an important and in the patient's consciousness far more apparent projective screen than the therapist sitting next to him, who in psychoanalysis and other verbal methods is the only receiver of projections available during the therapy session. As is generally known, the external constellation (the setting) of psychoanalysis is even specifically arranged in such a way as to encourage the transference neurosis.

Explanation

I would like to include an example to illustrate the different situation in GAI. Elsewhere I described the scene in which an adult patient with a depressive neurosis experiences an age regression during a GAI session. He relives a scene very intensely in which at the age of 11 years he was led into the room with Christmas presents and his father informs him that the favorite present that he had been expecting is not for him but for his brother, who was also there. This scene is, however, not experienced only as a pale memory or a mere regermination of the corresponding feelings of horror, helplessness, but very clearly as the interaction at that time between the 11-year-old and his father. The horrified reaction of the boy in the imagined scene is naturally a condensation of the already disturbed father-son relationship. This relationship revitalized in GAI has therefore as such been actualized "in origine." In this moment the patient's entire attention and his emotions are bound to this scene. He will most likely project this scene from reality, making him helpless, not only onto the mental imagery but onto the total present surroundings and onto the therapist sitting next to him as well. At the same time, however, he will not be able to evade the corrective knowledge that there (in the imagery) his father is involved and here his therapist. The therapist clearly indicates his understanding, his support, and his readiness to help the patient in the critical situation. Thus, the primary direction of projection of the father-son relationship is aimed at the projection screen of the imagery, which is experienced as being approximately 1 meter in front of the patient's closed eyes. Due to the complete inner involvement with the dramatic feeling, by which the patient is almost totally occupied in this moment, a part of the projection can be directed at the surroundings and thus the therapist. Two sketches (Figures 4a and b) are meant to illustrate this. For the present, it must be left undecided how strong this "auxiliary projection" is and to what extent it distorts the, in reality helpful, therapist in his role at this moment and allows him to be experienced just as hostilely as, for instance, the father. One can only say with certainty that the main projective direction is the level of mental imagery and only auxiliary projections, which at times can temporarily disturb the relationship with the therapist, are directed toward him. Within the scope of the progressive training to become a GAI therapist, the person should learn to perceive and to deal with these transferences. To repeat it again, the "auxiliary transference" is probably always resonating and, in a refined analysis of the imaginal contents, can frequently also be traced from them; it is sometimes also very pronounced without, however, hampering the progress of therapy.

Special Setting in GAI Compared with Psychoanalysis

3. *The setting in GAI compared with that of psychoanalysis* offers further reasons for the relative constancy of the transference relationship. Here I am again starting from some psychoanalytic conceptions. More strongly than in practically all other forms of psychotherapy (with the exception of hypnosis), the patient in the imaginal state is on a regressive, that is, ontogenetically, very early emotional level of visual symbolic experience. Since this regression in GAI is deliberately introduced therapeutically and also terminated

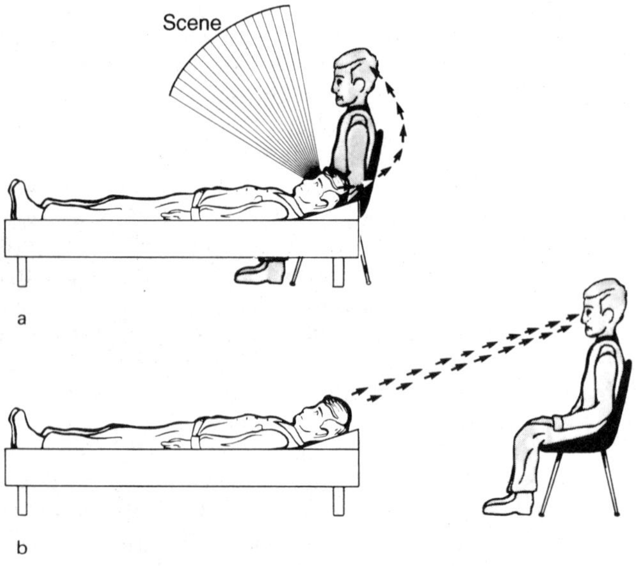

Fig. 4a and b. The projective transference relationships in guided affective imagery (a) differ from those in psychoanalysis (b) predominantly due to the fact that in GAI the main projective dynamics are manifested imaginatively on the projective screen of the mental imagery. Thus, they are not only phenomenologically distinctive and concise, but occupy the consciousness of the patient. A more or less strongly pronounced "auxiliary projection" can be directed at the therapist. In the case of psychoanalysis (b) the therapist, who is present and experienced mainly in the reflecting position, is the only object present toward which the transference projections can be directed.

again, and because its focus stays relatively constant due to the continuity of the mental imagery (imaginal consciousness), we speak of a *controlled regression.* In other words, the patient's ego in part adopts the role of a small child or an infant. In this respect a mother-child relationship exists very predominantly with the therapist sitting next to him. The patient's major emotional attitude in it is of the *anaclitic dependent type* (Spitz, 1956). This dependency can be considered in several different directions: dependency upon the therapist, upon the emerging imagery, and upon the feelings liberated by the mental imagery. If we look at this offer of anaclitic transference made by the patient, which is also stimulated by the therapist through relaxation and inducing the imagery, then the assumption that the therapist agrees to this offer is obvious. Thus, for his part, he assumes—at least as long as he does not keep a check on himself—the complementary protective maternal role in the sense of a particular attitude of taking care, the so-called diatropic attitude. With therapists who are not fully trained this in fact often initially occurs very spontaneously. However, there is an important reason for not continuing the pronounced mother-child relationship. The overall relationship is characterized by a peculiar "both . . . and." Under the protection of the therapist, the patient receives the instructions to explore the imaginal contents by observation, to develop several different activities within the mental imagery, even to accomplish things and occasionally to face up to difficult situations with adequate supervision. This role contradicts that of the exclusively passively surrendering small child. One could say that the patient's ego is split within the mental imagery. It displays, on the one hand, the regressive traits of infantile dependency and the more mature position, on the other hand, in exploring and verbalizing the imagery. Here, the more mature portions of the ego are addressed distinctly and successively more and more intensively in GAI, which can come into action *at the same time* due to this *ego-splitting.* The therapist, who, on the basis of the technique of GAI, is called upon to direct the activities, cannot assume solely a diatrophic attitude of taking care, which, as we know from experience, hinders the development of the person's independence. He must instead continually initiate various, even if small, steps toward maturing the ego through independent activities in the mental imagery (see earlier). This is one of his functions. It can be noted in passing that the therapist's anaclitic protective function is important in helping the patient to give up in part a number of defense mechanisms developed late, for example, intellectualization and rationalization, fears of arising impulses. Nunberg (1932) pointed out the significance of the therapist's presence, which is, incidentally, one of the reasons why exercises with GAI on the patient's own are problematical and rarely successful and why imaginal techniques, in which the patient practices on his own, such as on the advanced level of autogenic training and with active imagination (Jung), show different results from GAI and have their own problems. Symboldrama is very emphatically *a dialogical method.*

Controlled Regression

Ego-Splitting

Model of the Diver

I have chosen an image as an analogy to illustrate this relationship of the dialogical dynamics between patient and therapist in symboldrama, which was sketched here with concepts of psychoanalytic theory. The situation reminds me of a diving expedition of previous years. A boat goes out, a diver jumps into the water. He is closely and vitally related to the boat in that he is connected to it by a rope, by a tube that supplies him with air to breathe, and by a telephone line. The latter serves the close contact with the head of the expedition. The head of the expedition and the diver are working on a common task: the exploration of things at the bottom of the sea. However, in doing this they assume very different roles. The diver is, on the one hand, completely dependent on the head of the expedition, but on the other hand, he is essentially on his own in exploring the ocean depths (his unconscious). By means of telephone contact, he tells the leader of the expedition what he encounters on the ocean floor and what difficulties he has in solving the task assigned to him. Conversely, he receives advice from the leader of the expedition as to how he might proceed further and perhaps instruments are also handed to him to reach the goal.

The analogy between this image and the described dialogical relationship exists in three aspects: dependency of the diver-patient, his independent activity apart from this, a certain amount of protection, and care embedded in a teamlike cooperation. In this, each is dependent upon the other in order to carry out the common task of exploring the deep sea. There is no superordinating or subordinating relationship, no relationship between adult and child, but only between two largely equal persons, characterized in psychotherapy with the English concept of peer situation. Set in relation to the language of psychoanalytic concepts, the vector of dependency of the diver-patient refers to the strongly regressive infantile portion of the ego; the vector of the peer relationship refers to the portion of the mature, actively participating ego of the diver-patient.

Peer Situation

With this I arrive at practical considerations. Conducting therapy of the basic level according to the described behavior and style of guidance is ordinarily sufficient most of the time. I see a great advantage of this procedure in the circumstance that the transference-countertransference relationship—difficult to comprehend in symboldrama—can be largely neglected at first for the therapist who is not yet fully trained. The treatment is facilitated by this and makes limited demands upon the therapist's training, at least for the first steps. As already mentioned, progressive training beyond the basic level sees to it that the therapist receives instruction in perceiving transference and countertransference if possible and can incorporate it therapeutically. Within the scope of the basic level, he should at least, however, be acquainted with this and know that difficulties and the breaking off of GAI therapy are usually the result of transference or countertransference resistances. He should have such cases supervised. Otherwise he will have to recognize his limits in such instances and advise the patient to change therapists. I deliberately do not want to go into the various possibilities of the interfering transference reactions of the patient here because it would remain too theoretical.

Limited Demands on the Therapist on the Basic Level

A Frequent Transference Reaction in GAI

Just *one aspect of the transference reaction* of many patients seems noteworthy to me, because it is apparently connected with the characteristic quality of GAI. Patients to whom imagining at first seems strange and possibly like a demand to accomplish something can experience the task of developing mental imagery as if it were a situation in school, particularly if they are still relatively young. There they were continually asked to produce something. The school situation is possibly extended even further back to the relationship to a parent, who had demanded high accomplishments in school. The technical way to bring these or similar situations closer to a solution lies almost completely in having the patient verbalize his current feeling, that is how he feels toward the therapist in the given situation. Perhaps one can additionally discover of what this momentary situation reminds him.

Frequent Countertransference Position in GAI

If we look at a few of the therapist's countertransference feelings, which initially emerge most frequently, they lie in two directions. The one already mentioned is the unconscious emotional identification with the role of an overly caring mother or of a powerful protective father, perhaps due to guilt feelings at exposing the patient to certain unforeseeable scenes or even dangers of the mental imagery. This so-called *protective attitude* is well known and is usually not particularly advantageous for the psychotherapy. It is discussed in supervision seminars and should also be researched in more detail. The other direction of countertransference concerns younger therapists who in view of the knowledge of the new procedure and its possibility for use let themselves be influenced by the feeling of supposed superiority and even of greatness. They possibly experience themselves in the role of a magician of the unconscious realms and like to enjoy the feeling of their "power" for a while. Naturally, there are also pitfalls for the course of a psychotherapy in this. As already stated, only the frequent participation in supervision (case control) seminars is suitable for giving the person concerned insights into these, his *unconscious* faulty assessments.

Session Twenty: Indications and Contraindications of the Basic Level

Problems of Delimitation

An important consideration is what indications and contraindications a therapeutic procedure has. As far as psychotherapy is concerned, it has long been known that one usually runs into problems making brief statements about these two points. Everyone who has been involved in the treatment of neuroses knows that in attempting to state indications it does not suffice to start from diagnoses or clinical syndromes. On the contrary, a number of other aspects are brought into the assessment, so that various factors are taken into consideration for the treatment prognosis of a psychotherapeutic procedure. I would like to enumerate these very briefly in the following to then bring forth an additional viewpoint.

Duration of the Symptoms

The severity of the neurosis has to be considered. Clinically this is measured in a very simplified manner according to the duration of the symptoms and by whether the patient already had neurotic symptoms (primordial symptoms) as a child. The social environment in which the patient is at the time and the possibility of changing it are also important for the prognosis. The assessment of the patient's personality is additionally significant. This is measured, for instance, according to how extensive the psychoneurotic portions of the disorder are, or, expressed in another way, his adjustment or maladjustment to his social milieu. Also, the abilities of the person, such as to solve problems, to assert himself in difficult situations in life successfully and persistently, the proved capability of starting a family or building up a profession, are important factors in assessing the personality of a patient, which have an influence on his treatment prognosis. The same applies conversely to the tendency toward passivity and dependency upon people.

Adjustment to the Social Milieu

In the attempt to determine the therapeutic indications in an individual case on the basis of these various factors, a number of *criteria for prognosis* were developed and published in the literature, which I would like to reproduce here (in greatly simplified form). They are not specific to GAI, but are applicable to every form of psychotherapy.

Criteria for Prognosis in Guided Affective Imagery Therapy

1. Kind and degree of symptoms do not influence prognostic judgment whatsoever
2. The duration of the symptoms is an important factor in deciding the issue. If the symptoms go back beyond 3 years, the prognosis is surely burdened by this, but even cases

with symptoms existing for 5 to 10 years could be successfully treated with the basic level

3. A certain amount of psychic pain is prognostically favorable; an absence of psychic pain is unfavorable
4. The longer a person has stood up to the vicissitudes of life without symptoms, the more favorable is the prognosis
5. A passive, submissive expectant attitude toward the therapist, an inclination for convenience exhibited during the initial interview or, conversely, immediate uncritical agreement indicative of strong compliance is unfavorable
6. Signs of being overindulged and of passive dependency (according to the case history), the emergence of neurotic lies and swindling are signs of "neurotic neglect." The same applies for addictive behaviors, for escaping into bluff and dishonest techniques in working and living. Neurotic impatience and pedantry are also assessed unfavorably
7. On the other hand, the prospects are favorable for persons who are completely honest and accustomed to active and difficult work
8. The impossibility of changing a severe external social and fateful situation impairs the prognosis
9. The strongly finalized neuroses occupy a special position. An extreme case is the retirement pension neurosis. The prognosis is very unfavorable if claims for compensation have already been granted or if the prospects for payment are good. (The same applies for criminals in prison or for neglected persons in corrective educational institutions)
10. A prerequisite for a successful psychotherapy is the patient's absolute commitment, in which a part of the responsibility for the success of treatment can be transferred to him

Contraindications

The following clinical aspects and diagnoses are signs of poor prognosis and thus also *contraindications* for symboldrama:

1. Deficient intelligence with an IQ lower than 85
2. Psychoses of an acute or chronic nature or near psychotic states
3. Organic brain syndrome
4. Severe depressive mood (also of a severe neurotic kind)
5. Insufficient motivation, even for a simple nondisclosing therapy
6. Expressly hysteric neuroses
7. Borderline and narcissistic syndromes

In assessing the contraindications one additional factor must finally be taken into consideration, which strangely enough is forgotten in such lists, namely, *the level of training* and the ability and *experience of the therapist.* The therapist also enters very strongly into the totality of what occurs in GAI therapy. The successful outcome of the therapy depends upon his artistry in guiding the patient, on his clinical experience, his self-awareness, and upon the special qualities of his character in the sense of sufficient sensitivity and training in empathy. I have dealt with the problem of the style of guidance in great detail elsewhere (Leuner, 1983).

Nosological Viewpoints

General Clinical Indications Described According to Illness Categories

1. So-called neuro- or psychoautonomic disorders and psychosomatic syndromes of a moderately severe nature
2. Decline of the functional or psychic components in internal or other illnesses
3. Anxiety states and phobias
4. Neuroses with predominantly psychic manifestation of average severity with the exception of obsessive-compulsive neuroses
5. Neurotic character disorders of adjustment
6. Psychoneurotic and neurotic character disorders in childhood
7. Adjustment disorders in puberty and adolescence

Treatment goal

Finally, another word concerning the intended goal of treatment with GAI. On the basic level one will naturally have to be content with somewhat more modest results. This especially concerns the treatment of character or personality disorders in the second half of life, from about age 45 years on. Relaxing the character armor with the repertory of the basic level usually succeeds to only a limited degree, particularly in neurotic patients who have difficulty making social contacts, are inhibited, have an obsessive-compulsive structure, or are schizoid. The treatment of severe phobic anxieties also has its limits. The borderline cases, seen more frequently today, are a special category by themselves. These patients do not in part conform to the behavioral pattern that we are familiar with in neurotic patients. For this reason contacts with them are difficult in the first place, and one must expect arbitrary behaviors and short psychotic-like episodes. There is very little practical experience to indicate that treating them with GAI can be promising. In some cases they are very capable of imagining. This group of patients as well as that of the more severely narcissistically disturbed belong to the *contraindications* for the basic level therapist (they resemble each other in many respects and cannot be clearly differentiated from each other). Unfortunately, their diagnosis is difficult in some cases, since these disorders can occasionally be masked.

Criteria According to the contents of GAI

Criteria of Prognosis in Accordance with Guided Affective Imagery

As is generally known, symboldrama has a diagnostic aspect. Utilizing it systematically can be scientifically interesting, but is in contradiction to the therapist's behavior necessary in treatment, described in detail in this volume. Nevertheless, we frequently gain a large number of diagnostic clues from the special quality of the fixed images and from the dimensions of their regression as early as the first four sessions, without stressing a diagnostic attitude. There are a number of typical signs of neurosis and a number of signs in GAI that make a statement about how disturbed a patient is, at least at the time of conducting mental imagery. Occasionally, they are almost highlights, which flash and can particularly impress the therapist due to their powerfulness. From long experience, however, we have become wiser. These "highlights" of pathological contents in the first sessions can only be more clearly defined in their genesis if they are brought into relationship with the patient's current problems, that is, his current social situation and the dimensions and particular characteristics of his symptoms. Current crisis situations can simulate a severe disturbance. For this reason, one must conversely also take into account the degree of ego-strength, of the patient's capability to cope with social stresses, crises, and symptoms. As we know today, in forming the prognosis it is also necessary to include the healthy parts of the ego in the considerations. In other words, dramatic and archaic contents in the first GAI session do not absolutely signify a poor prognosis for treatment. Recording the psychological case history in depth must also be brought into relationship with the contents of symboldrama and the stated current situation.

I will cite a number of typical, extremely pronounced GAI contents that can be regarded as very unfavorable signs for prognosis. However, please also realize that relatively inconspicuous contents and a seemingly smooth progression of the imaginal scenes, which are in no way unimportant, either say nothing about the prognosis or say a great deal, inasmuch as they actually contain too little relevant material about the prevailing problems in connection with the patient's history and social situation. In other words, there is a conspicuous discrepancy here. I would like to illustrate this with an example.

Risk of isolated view of GAI contents

Example *Case 1* (25)

A professional man just under 50 years of age was referred to me by a colleague who had already conducted 30 sessions of GAI with him. The patient seems suited for it, but the colleague had the impression that the case was "too complicated" for him without giving any reasons. The imagery does in fact proceed clearly, precisely, a little too orderly, but by no means free of some neurotic signs and indications of the not entirely resolved relationship to his mother and his wife, of the inhibited aggressiveness and the tendency toward resigned-depressive withdrawal. However, when I looked at all of the prognostic factors, I came to the conclusion that the treatment would be very lengthy, and I could not be all that optimistic about reaching at least an important subgoal of therapy.

The central symptom is an amotivational syndrome designated as "depression." The patient continually feels exhausted and weak, has to rest for several hours after working at his desk for a short time, is consequently unable to work, or rather he is threatened with premature retirement, and he is a burden to his environment. The disorder has existed for almost a year. It came to light only much later that the occupational conditions have led to a strong aversion toward his current field of activity due to a change of superiors, demotions, and an overload of work. The patient is married, the marriage is described as "very good," but it is striking that his more energetic wife tends to reproach him for his passivity and above all for not consumating the marriage due to primary impotence. For this reason, they adopted children and created a family life to a certain degree. The patient's attitude toward the therapy is positive, on the one hand, but more of a secondary kind, as he fears financial losses if he does not become able to work again. The clearly indicated passive attitude is an equally bad prognostic sign, as are the pronounced counterdependency of his mother, the dependency on his wife, and his relative helplessness in the current overall situation, from which he has withdrawn into his weakness syndrome. With this he is unassailable to everyone. Other factors in this are the primary impotence, which has practically become a characteristic feature and the strong submissiveness and reaction formation connected with it, which have caused him to develop a definitely solemn appearance. Structurally, depressive traits are in the fore, which are uncharacteristically mixed with other, in part, compulsive traits. He has a strong tendency to regress with respect to hypochondriac self-observation and to a tendency, to which he has yielded for years, to have himself "built up" in cures at spas due to a slight compensatory cardiac defect.

The GAI therapy, which was conducted with lengthy interruptions, reached its goal after 150 sessions. However, the therapeutic technique demanded a decidedly psychoanalytically oriented guidance partly on the basic and partly on the intermediate or advanced level in order to treat the marked problems in the personality structure of the patient, which were made even more difficult by certain ideological-religious commitments. From the beginning, I limited the treatment goal to the treatment of the amotivational syndrome, the improvement of the marital relationship and of the patient's ability to assert himself professionally and excluded the treatment of the primary impotence, secretly hoped for by the patient. One could be satisfied with the overall results. This was supported afterward by occasional follow-up counseling of the patient. The example is meant to show that considering the contents of a GAI in isolation does not suffice for making a prognosis. Rather, it is the discrepancy between the dimensions of the personality deformation and the concealed social problems in symboldrama that initially actually seems to be relatively unproblematical and that first allows a statement about the prognosis.

Extremely Distinct Forms in GAI

Now I come to a few characteristic extreme forms of the catathymic panorama that prompt one to examine the prognosis cautiously and which indicate a pronounced current disturbed state of the patient.

These are present if, for example, the GAI contents are predominantly of a depressive nature at widely different spots: the meadow is dried up, the brook is empty, nature is meager, or it is raining, the meadow is a swamp, it is a concentration camp in which half-starved figures are found. Attempts to find a positive motif in the same or another session in a possibly more distant geographic location, for instance, visiting a beach on the Mediterranean, likewise lead to no change. It is gray there, too, the sea is leaden, the beach empty, far and wide no one to be seen, and so on. If one focuses on a brook, it can be dried up; no water at all or only a few drops come out of the spring or the brook is dirty and brackish, soon dammed up and no possible outlets are found. In the mountain motif, strongly distinctive disorders usually are manifested by the inability to climb the mountain, whether due to its extreme height or because it is so steep, or consists of smooth rocks on all sides or is made of an artificial material, for example plastic, which makes the ascent impossible. Flying to the mountain by plane is rejected, does not work; it is extremely cold on the summit, stormy, and very negative feelings are triggered, a view into the distance is not possible. The prognosis is at least dim, and it certainly requires great therapeutic expenditure if the landscape shows nothing but dense forests all around without a sign of human settlement. The motif of the edge of the woods can indicate a severely disturbed state if considerable anxieties arise upon approaching the woods.

Abstruse, bizarre, and fantastical formations in symboldrama most always indicate a severe present disorder (if it does not concern the total personality), which scarcely permits treatment on the basic level. Here I always pay particular attention to whether irreconcilable stylistic incongruities appear in the landscape, for instance, those in which one part is a central European landscape and the other is an exotic or foreign one. I refer to Figure 1, page 77, where this kind of scenery is reflected. More approachable disturbances appear in the catathymic panorama in the incongruity between parts of the landscape, which are in the summer and others in the autumnal phase, or in a very rapid change of day and night or from summer to winter during one session. An example of this is the sudden beginning of a snowstorm, which completely covers the landscape, thus a "stormy" repression due to a current problem.

I would like to be content with these relatively few descriptions, which can be regarded only as examples for the diversity of extreme expressive creations of symboldrama. If one goes into details, it is the multiplicity of obstructive motifs or of fixed images, one following the other, that illustrate the dimensions of the acute conflict defenses and make the prognosis dim.

"Noisy symptoms"

In conclusion, I would like to mention one important experience in the therapy of neuroses in order to eliminate occasional prognostic misunderstandings concerning the severity of symptoms as well as the drama of an imaginal scene. It has long been known from experience (Dührssen [1962] occasionally referred to this) that so-called "loud, noisy" symptoms, with a correspondingly dramatic GAI, do not absolutely have to speak *against* a good prognosis for treatment. They are mostly hysterically structured patients, who have hyperexpressive tendencies and styles of representation and like to put themselves into the limelight for their own sakes and that of their audience as a distinctive form of their communication. Extremely configurative subject matter in symboldrama may possibly in part have poor prognoses, when one also includes all the factors of the current sociological situation and of the patient's history. However, from this one may not conversely conclude that discreet contents in GAI and discreet symptoms, such as psychogenic headaches or character-armored personalities, are prognostically favorable.

Risks of Guided Affective Imagery

Risks and Masked Contraindications

At the close of this session I would still like to talk about the risks of GAI on the basic level. As long as the procedure is conducted according to the principles described here and in accordance with the guidance by a therapist with adequate advanced training, it actually presents no risks. The contraindications should naturally also be taken into account. In our experience, difficulties can only arise when a neurotic structure with brittle defenses or a concealed narcissistic or borderline personality is not recognized in good time, and through the use of this procedure regressive or infantile portions of the patient's ego flood him with archaic imaginal material and consequently, among other things, trigger anxieties and depressive reactions. Beyond this, the main points of risk are, on the one hand, extremely hysterically structured patients or those with a mixed hysterical-depressive structure, which usually is already apparent in the clinical behavior and in the first GAI sessions. On the other hand, they can be found in intensively neurotic-depressive syndromes, above all, in patients whose ego is still immature, who have not yet proved themselves in life and are very dependent on relatives, and who have possibly concealed their lack of independence through a symbiotic relationship for a long time. In this connection, it becomes particularly obvious that in using GAI the psychotherapist must have sufficient clinical, as well as diagnostic experience at his command also to be able to determine the indication for the procedure in view of the diagnosis, as is done in every field of medicine.

Importance of a Supervision Group

If we are cautious in making the prognosis, we favorably observe that the therapeutic results are generally good with the basic level of GAI, too. They encourage the therapist to further involvement with this procedure, above all, if he follows my repeated advice and joins a supervision group, in which he can discuss his therapy and which broadens the horizons of his views and experiences. It has frequently been shown that even in the case of a doubtful prognosis, attempting treatment with GAI is only rarely harmful and possibly brings clarity very quickly as to whether the treatment prognosis can be considered positive in an acutely disturbed case. The longer the therapist involves himself with symboldrama systematically, that is, also with therapy conducted in a clear and logically consistent manner, the more confident he will be to refine his capacity to judge the prognosis and the selection of his patients (with the support of supervision). In connection with this I may remind you that another principle in psychotherapy starts from the fact that accepting a patient for treatment is not, least of all, also dependent upon whether the therapist can bring forth the necessary empathic attention for his patient. If an *a priori* obscure antipathy toward the patient exists, with the negative answer to the naive question put to oneself, "Do you like this person and do you believe that you can work together with him therapeutically?" this should prompt the therapist to refer the patient to a colleague.

Appendix I

Survey of the Additional Levels of Guided Affective Imagery and Their Instruments*

Intermediate Level

Supplementary Standard Motifs

Sixth training motif for focusing on *referential figures:* Referential figures, that is, father, mother, siblings, superiors, spouse, and children, can be focused on as actual persons or symbolically on various levels of object representations. The appearance of the figures as actual persons can possibly trigger defenses that are avoided through concealment in symbols. Location of the encounter can be actual places or instituted in the meadow motif. The symbolic concealment can occur in landscape motifs (as frequently happens spontaneously), in the motif of the mountain, the spring, the brook or in the form of trees, whether it be a tree standing alone or in accordance with the three tree test (Klessmann, 1978). The attribution made to the trees among each other usually reflects the emotional tone of the family interaction. The concealment in the form of animal figures succeeds more or less purposefully, for instance, an elephant as father, a cow as representation of the maternal element. The behavior of the animals toward the patient in his attempts to approach them, touch them, and talk to them is revealing and allows one to discover unconscious attitudes toward the referential figures.

Seventh training motif for testing *sexual attitudes:* With female patients, we suggest riding in a *car* as follows. The patient is wandering through the countryside on a lonely road and is tired. A car appears, stops, and the driver offers to give the patient a ride. A great number of behaviors with diverse forms of defense become apparent in distortions of the situation and reflect relationships with partners. For male patients we use the symbol of the *rosebush* at the edge of the meadow, based upon the poem by Goethe: "The Hedgerose." After looking at the rosebush, the patient is asked to pick a rose. The distinctiveness of the flowers, the patient's hesitation, his fear of pricking his fingers give important information. The motif can be of crucial importance in the treatment of sexual disorders. Focusing on the scene of an apple or cherry tree and requesting the person concerned to pick a piece of fruit (motif of the Garden of Eden) is more intensely symbolically concealed and is suitable for both sexes. The patient's behaviors provide information, which is, however, usually quite well concealed.

Eighth training motif for exploring attitudes toward *aggressive impulses.* A lion is focused upon as an expression of freedom and independence and the capacity for expansive and/or aggressive behavior. It can be imagined in a cage, performing stunts in a circus, or moving freely along the edge of the jungle. It can be mild and friendly like a teddybear, expressing marked aggressive inhibition. The lion's behavior toward an adversary of the patient can additionally demonstrate the extent of aggressive inhibition toward a specific person.

Ninth training motif for determining the *ego-ideal* as an authority, which

---

*** In connection with Table 1 (p.97)**

develops from the idealization of the ego and the identification with the parents and collective ideals. It is a model that the subject tries to conform to. (The problem of identity is closely related to this). The patient is asked to think of the first name of someone of the same sex and then to visualize the person to whom this name belongs. Usually a person appears, whom the patient knows and who has particular qualities that the patient would like to have.

Therapeutic Techniques

III. Associative Procedure

In contrast to the relatively highly structuring training methods of the basic level, GAI is handled very freely here and the therapist abandons his protective behavior. In part, starting from a standard motif and, in part, totally independent of this, the therapist lets the scenes developing freely in the patient's imagination build associative chains. This only works with patients who have enough creative fantasy. In this process the contents quite often converge on early childhood traumatic memories or on scenes before the psychic trauma in frequently highly emotionally conveyed age regressions. The associative procedure is not only restricted to imaginal contents, but also covers the stimulation of associations that reach partly into the past and partly into the present. Here the arising feeling tone or emotion has the function of a bridge in stimulating these sudden ideas. Under the therapist's protection traumatic scenes are spontaneously relived and endured, often with the release of anxieties and other affects.

IV. Reinstatement of Night Dreams

A night dream or fragments of it can be used as a starting motif in the expectation that the dream will be continued in GAI in one version or another and can be brought to an end, which offers solutions.

V. Focusing on Acute Conflicts

At the beginning of the session, the patient is requested to verbalize an urgent acute conflict, in the process of which emotions are usually released. When the theme has reached its highpoint, the patient is asked to visualize the problem in mental imagery by the therapist's offer of a motif as best suited as possible. Usually the problem then appears vividly and revealingly in the patient's imagination and can be played through in dry rehearsal form on the symbolic level.

VI. Inspection of Bodily Organs

With psychosomatic illnesses, it has proved useful to have the patient visualize the afflicted organ or the affected area of the body and to indicate that a change will be found there. Two techniques are possible: (1) the capacity to view the organ from the outside, as if it were exposed or could be observed through glass, for instance, the inside of the skull or body cavities; (2) the patient shrinks to the size of Tom Thumb and enters through the mouth moving along the natural path to the organ, for instance, the stomach, the intestines, the heart, the lungs. This technique offers information about the object relationships, which are symbolized in the afflicted organ. The scientific value of exploring psychosomatic syndromes (Zepf, 1983) as well as the therapeutic value (*Eibach,* 1982) are documented.

VII. Striving Toward Resolution in GAI

For the technique of resolving the repetition compulsion in patients with severe personality disorders or wherever this component is to be treated in psychosomatic illnesses, GAI has a number of imaginative strategies at hand that substantially supplement the techniques of clarification and interpretive offers in the psychoanalytic sense, such as: symbol confrontation, association, focusing on fixed images, reliving and enduring anxiety, and other negatively emotionally cathected scenes, (See *Leuner,* 1983).

VIII. Analysis of Transference

In contrast to the basic level technique, in which the therapist's behavior is taught primarily from the viewpoints of a normative behavior, the therapist on the intermediate level should be able regularly to follow, address, and interpret the patient's transference relations in GAI and in the same way to perceive, reflect, and work on his countertransference. In this way mounting interfering transference and countertransference relations can be recognized in time and resolved. This applies especially for long-term therapy in which neurotic personality disorders are treated.

Management Models (Operation on the Symbol)

Inner Guide

Positive symbolic figures, which either appear spontaneously in the catathymic panorama or are also occasionally chosen by the patient, are used to assume the leadership through the panorama. They usually lead the patient to fixed images and induce creative solutions on the symbolic level. The image of the therapist, which has become an introject, is often symbolized in leadership figures.

Confrontation with the Symbol

In the scope of the management model of symboldrama, this technique is one of the most outstanding ones and is very effective in dealing with especially regressive infantile object relations. The confrontation usually occurs with hostile symbolic figures, which either appear spontaneously or can be elicited using suitable standard motifs. Through subtle visual analysis and describing in detail how they are perceived as well as the accompanying feeling tone, strong emotions can be liberated, relived, and endured under the therapist's protection. Their neutralization then appears in transformations of the symbolic figures from primitive to more highly structured ones. Usually the principle of reconciliation and gestures of tenderness are added here to attain an assimilation of negatively cathected introjects.

Advanced Level

Standard Motifs

Training Motif 10a: Cave; Motif 10b: Swamp.

Both motifs are characterized by their connection with the earth's interior. Starting from their symbolic significance as sites of deeper unconscious layers, symbolic figures, which have mostly archaic characters, are set free from both openings when the patient observes them in GAI. Whereas the cave motif personifies the female genital element in the sense of the mouth of the womb and the cave itself, the uterus, the swamp is symbolically closely associated with the theme of the immature or strongly infantile sexuality in the sense of anal eroticism. Symbolic figures emerging from the swamp are generally related to the oedipal problem: in female patients to the paternal sexual world, in male patients to the maternal sexual world. However, the anal theme as such in the sense of excrement and dirt in its highly ambivalent meaning must also be considered, on the one hand, as the opposite of cleanliness, and on the other hand, as having a productive and beneficial effect. The motif of the swamp, just as that of the volcano, has only minimal significance for routine therapy.

Eleventh Training Motif: the Volcano.

Visualizing a "fire-spewing mountain" only has significance when a patient is under the pressure of strong aggressive impulses in a current situation, usually due to being severely offended. If the volcano is active in the imagery, a relatively fast discharge of the impulsive pressure, frequently connected with an ego regression, can be reached in order to deal with the situation in a more mature way afterward. The motif does not exclude aspects of self-destruction, for instance, if masses of lava destroy surrounding villages.

Twelfth Training Motif: a Book.

This motif is usually less archaically cathected; however, material is also produced from the depths here by unearthing an old illustrated book (a Bible, for instance) that is frequently very symbolically coded. The motifs of the volcano and of the book are supplementary motifs, which are rarely significant for routine therapy and can only be meaningfully introduced in special situations.

Therapeutic Techniques

IX. Combination with Conventional Psychoanalysis

The patient develops *free associations* in connection with the imagery, that is, the contents of GAI are dealt with as dreams are in classic psychoanalysis. Following the imaginal contents, the *conflictual focus* appearing symbolically in them is taken up and discussed with the help of the patient's ideas. This is of special importance in resolving the repetition compulsion by means of the vividly appearing neurotic maladjustments. This is the most frequent way of expanding GAI in the direction of a verbalizing analytic technique.

GAI is used in the framework of a conventional psychoanalysis, if the patient is *unable to dream,* or other forms of resistance arise, which are difficult to analyze, particularly in the sense of a transference resistance.

Management Models (Operation on the Symbol)

e. Exhausting and Killing

This procedure demands exceptional experience on the part of the therapist. It takes up latent aggressive and hate impulses and also those already being realized and gives them a chance to be expressed in imaginal dry rehearsal. They are mostly of an anal and more rarely of an oral nature. Since guilt feelings naturally arise when aggressive hate impulses are released, the delayed principle of "exhausting" the symbolic figures is preferred. With the therapist's help, the patient brings the symbolic figures to the point of exhaustion by means of nonstop motoric action. This appears in phenomena of change, which indicate strong neutralization. Similarly to the case in symbol confrontation, rapid behavioral modifications can be obtained here, if this management model is used appropriately and empathic attention is shown. However, it can be misunderstood as self-destruction and should not be employed against crucial object representations (referential persons) of the patient.

f. Magical Fluids

As illustrated in the imagery of GAI, it became obvious that the use of water has an effect on psychosomatic disorders that cannot be explained rationally. Diverse experiments with bodily fluids, such as saliva, human milk, and urine, have shown that correspondingly imagined scenes can have highly explosive effects, for instance, upon hostile symbolic figures. Parallels to magical or natural medicine became obvious here. However, the systematic use of this motif has not been tested for routine therapy with GAI and is also difficult to administer in proper doses due to its irrational content on a regressive level.

The advanced level is not taught within the scope of the GAI therapist's training. It can be neglected to a large extent in the practice of therapy. Only the very experienced therapist, who is well-acquainted with the use of the GAI intermediate level in practice, can work in the area of the advanced level on the basis of the literature. For this, however, advanced training in psychoanalysis and many years of psychotherapeutic experience with GAI are required.

Appendix II

Addresses of the organizations that promote seminars to train therapists in guided affective imagery or that arrange for participation in seminars.

1. Association for Guided Affective Imagery (AGKB), Friedländer Weg 30, D-3400 Göttingen, Federal Republic of Germany, Tel. 0551–46754
2. Austrian Association for Guided Affective Imagery (ÖAGKB), Bayernstr. 19, A-5020 Salzburg, Austria, Tel. 06222–85435
3. Swiss Association for Guided Affective Imagery (SAGKB), Buchenweg 22, CH-3012, Bern, Switzerland, Tel. 031–237494
4. Svenska föreningen för Symboldrama (SFS), Lyckestigen 7, S-35244 Växjö, Sweden, Tel. 0470–11258
5. Parent organization:
   International Society for Guided Affective Imagery and Imagery Procedures in Psychotherapy and Psychology (IGKB/ISGAI), Friedländer Weg 30, D-3400 Göttingen, Federal Republic of Germany

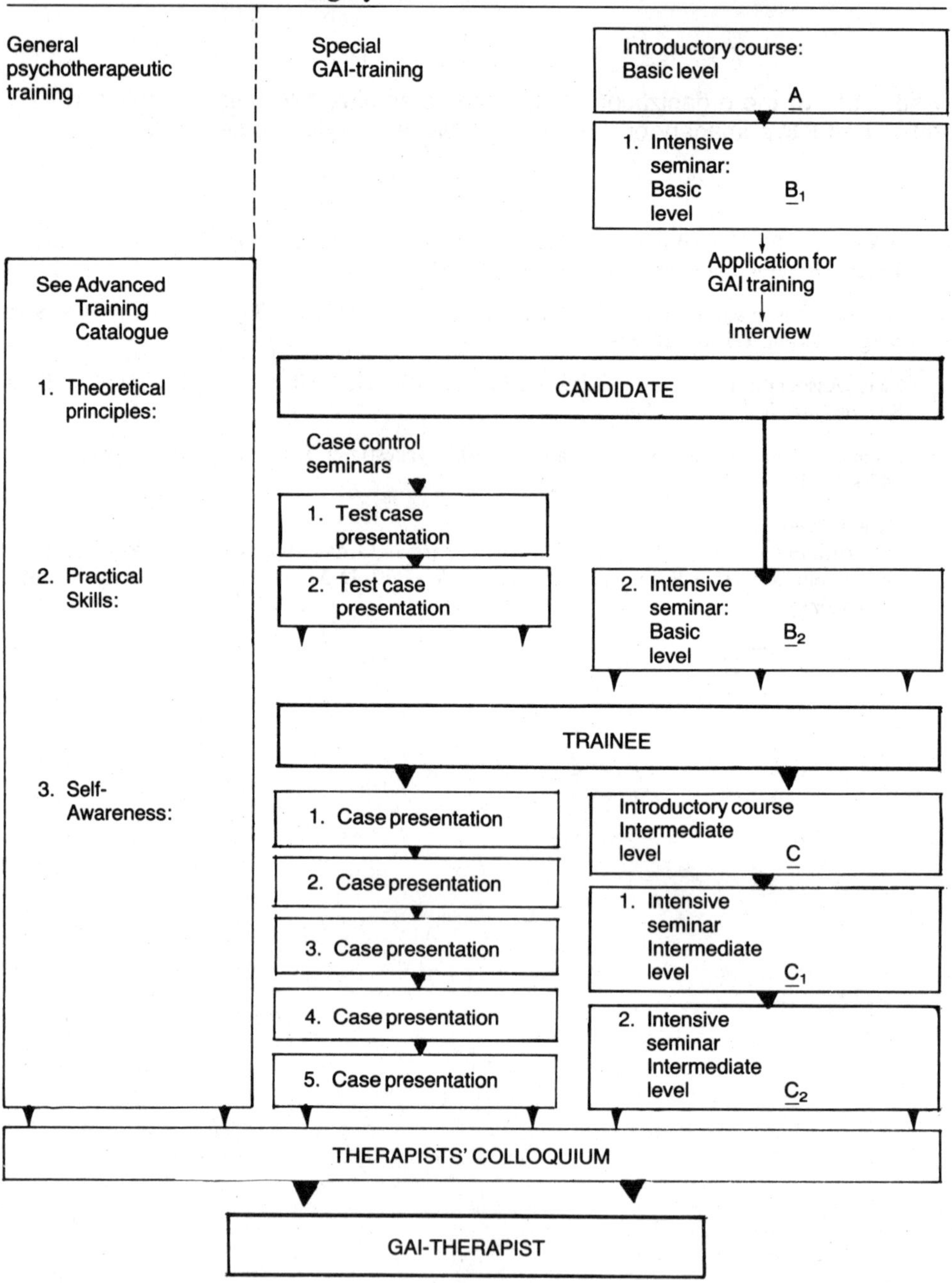

Advanced Training for Therapists: Advanced level seminars
Case control seminars
Special seminars

Appendix III

A list of the original works of the author on GAI (in chronological order).

Leuner, H.: Kontrolle der Symbolinterpretation im experimentellen Verfahren. Z Psychother Med Psychol 4:201, 1954.

Leuner, H.: Experimentelles Katathymes Bilderleben als ein klinisches Verfahren der Psychotherapie: Grundlegungen und Methode. Z Psychother Med Psychol 5:185, 1955.

Leuner, H.: Experimentelles Katathymes Bilderleben als ein klinisches Verfahren der Psychotherapie: Ergebnisse. Z Psychother Med Psychol 5:233, 1955.

Leuner, H.: Symbolkonfrontation, ein nichtinterpretierendes Vorgehen in der Psychotherapie. Schweiz Arch Neurol Psychiat 76:23, 1955.

Leuner, H.: Symboldrama, ein aktives nicht-analysierendes Vorgehen in der Psychotherapie. Z Psychother Med Psychol 6:221, 1957.

Leuner, H.: Das Landschaftsbild als Metapher dynamischer Strukturen. In: Stolze, H. (Ed.): Festschrift zum 70. Geburtstag von E. Speer, Lehmann, München, 1959.

Leuner, H.: Die Verifizierung der existentiellen Bedeutung des Symbols durch Symbolprovokation. In: Aktuelle Fragen der Psychotherapie, vol. 3. S. Karger, Basel, 1960, p.45.

Leuner, H.: Leistungen, Indikationen und Grenzen des Symboldramas. Z Psychother Med Psychol 10:45, 1960.

Leuner, H.: Das assoziative Vorgehen im Symboldrama. Z Psychother Med Psychol 14:196, 1964.

Leuner, H., K. Nerenz: Das musikalische Symboldrama und seine psychotherapeutische Wirkung. Heilkunst 77:330, 1964.

Leuner, H.: Guided Affective Imagery (GAI): A Method of Intensive Psychotherapy. Am J Psychother 23:4, 1969.

Leuner, H.: Das Katathyme Bilderleben in der Psychotherapie von Kindern und Jugendlichen. In: Biermann, G. (Ed.): Handbuch der Kinderpsychotherapie. Reinhardt, München, 1969.

Leuner, H.: Über den Stand der Entwicklung des Katathymen Bilderlebens. Z Psychother Med Psychol 19:177, 1969.

Leuner, H.: Katathymes Bilderleben—Unterstufe—ein Seminarkurs. Thieme, Stuttgart, 1970.

Leuner, H.: Indikationen zur Psychotherapie. Ringelheimer Biologische Umschau, part 5, 1970.

Leuner, H.: Das Katathyme Bilderleben in der Psychotherapie von Kindern und Jugendlichen. Prax Kinderpsychol Kinderpsychiat 19:212, 1970.

Leuner, H.: Therapeutische Möglichkeiten mit dem Katathymen Bilderleben (Tagtraumtechnik) bei RM-Konsumenten. Ref. Fortbildungsveranst. Nervenklinik, Tubingen, 1971.

Leuner, H.: Grundzüge der tiefenpsychologischen Symbolik (unter Berücksichtigung des Symbolismus im Katathymen Bilderleben). In: Ausgewählte Vortrage der Zentralen Weiterbildungsseminare der AGKB, Göttingen, 1974.

Leuner, H.: Die Bedeutung der Musik in imaginativen Techniken der Psychotherapie. Vortrag gehalten auf dem Ostersymposium der Herbert von Karajan-Stiftung, Salzburg, 1972. In: Revers, W.T., Harrer, G., Simon, W.C.H. (Eds.): Neue Wege der Musiktherapie Econ, Düsseldorf, 1974.

Leuner, H.: Imagination als Spiegel unbewussten Seelenlebens. Angelsachsen-Verlag, Bremen, 1974.

Leuner, H.: The Role of Imagery in Psychotherapy, In: Arieti, S., Chrzanowski, G., (Eds.): New Dimensions in Psychiatry: A World View. John Wiley & Sons, New York, 1975.

Leuner, H.: Stellung des Katathymen Bilderlebens (KB) im Rahmen der aktiv-klinischen Verfahren der Psychotherapie. Referat gehalten auf dem 1. Internationak Congress für

Aktiv-Klinische Psychotherapie, Innsbruck, 1975.
Leuner, H.: Guided affective imagery: An account of its development. J Mentl Imagery 1:73, 1977.
Leuner, H., G. Horn, E. Klessmann: Katathymes Bilderleben mit Kindern und Jugendlichen, 2nd ed. Reinhardt, München 1978.
Leuner, H.: Basic principles and therapeutic efficacy of guided affective imagery. In: Singer, J.W, Pope, K.S. (Eds.): The Power of Human Imagination. Plenum Press, New York, 1978.
Leuner, H. (Ed.): Katathymes Bilderleben—Ergebnisse in Theorie und Praxis. Huber, Bern, 1983.
Leuner, H., H.-M. Wächter: Kurzpsychotherapie einer Acne excoriee mit chronischer Neurose mit dem Katathymen Bilderleben (KB). Ein Beitrag zur„ anaklitischen Therapie" In press.
Leuner, H.: Lehrbuch des gesamteu Katathymen Bilderlebens. Huber, Bern, 1984.

References

Amann, A.N.: Aktive Imagination. Walter, Freiburg, 1978.
Boss, M.: Der Traum und seine Auslegung. Huber, Bern, 1953.
Brengelmann, J.C., L. Brengelmann: Deutsche Validierung von Fragebogen der Extraversion, neurotischen Tendenz und Rigidität. Z Exp Angew Psychol 7:291, 1960.
Breuer, J., S. Freud: Studien über Hysterie. Wien, 1895.
Desoille, R.: Introduction à une Psychotherapie Ratronelle. Paris, 1945.
Dührssen, A.: Analytische Psychotherapie in Theorie, Praxis und Ergebnissen. Vandenhoeck & Ruprecht, Göttingen, 1962.
Ehebald, U.: Stellungnahme bei der Diskussion des Plenums der 8. Norddeutschen Psychotherapietage. Lübeck, 1979.
Eibach, H.: Ein Fall von Herzneurose (zugleich ein Beitrag zur Frage der endlichen Analyse). In: Leuner, H., Lang, O. (Eds.): Katathymes Bilderleben—Ergebnisse II. Huber, Bern. 1982.
Frank, L.: Über Affektstörungen. Berlin, 1913.
Freud, S.: The Interpretation of Dreams. Standard Ed., Hogarth Press, New York, 4:241, 5:383, 1953.
Freud, S.: Recommendations to Physicians Practicing Psycho-Analysis. Standard Ed., Hogarth Press, New York, 12, 1958.
Freud, S.: Observations on Transference Love. Standard Ed., Hogarth Press, New York, 12:162, 1958.
Greenson, R.R.: The Technique and Practice of Psychoanalysis. Volume I, Indiana University Press, New York, 1964.
Happich, C.: Das Bildbewusstsein als Ansatzstelle psychischer Behandlung. Zentralbl Psychother 5:633, 1932.
Haronian, F.: The ethical relevance of a psychotherapeutic technique. J Relig Health 6:148, 1967.
Heigl, F.: Indikation und Prognose in der Psychoanalyse und Psychotherapie, 2nd ed. Vandenhoeck & Ruprecht, Göttingen, 1978.
Heiss, R.: Allgemeine Tiefenpsychologie. Huber, Bern, 1956.
Holfeld, H., Leuner, H.: Die Behandlung liver chronisch rezidivibender pshycogenen Psychose unit dem Katathymen Bildbleben. In: Leuner, H., Lams, O. (Eds.): Psychotherapie mit dem Tagtrauma. Huber, Bern, 1952.
Josuttis, M., H. Leuner: Religion und die Droge. Kohlhammer, Stuttgart, 1972.
Jung, C.G.: Über psychische Energetik und das Wesen der Träume. Rascher, Zürich, 1948.
Klessmann, E., H.-A. Klessmann: Ambulante Psychotherapie der Anorexia nervosa unter Anwendung des Katathymen Bilderlebens. In: Leuner, H., Horn, G., Klessmann, E. (Eds.): Katathymes Bilderleben mit Kindern und Jugendlichen. 2nd ed. Reinhardt, München, 1978.
Kornadt, H.-J.: Experimentally excited images as function of dynamic systems. Proc. XIII. International Congress of Applied Psychology, Rome, 1958.
Kosbab, F.P.: Selfanalysis in Guided

Affective Imagery. Arch Gen Psychiat 31:283, 1974.
Kretschmer, E.: Medizinische Psychologie. Kretschmer, W. (Ed.). Thieme, Stuttgart, 1922, 14th ed., 1975.
Kulessa, C., F. Jung: Effizienz einer 20stündigen Kurzpsychotherapie mit dem Katathymen Bilderleben im testpsychologischen prae/post-Vergleich. In: Leuner, H., (Ed.): Katathymes Bilderleben—Ergebnisse in Theorie und Praxis. Huber, Bern, 1983.
Landau, E.: Kreatives Erleben. Reinhardt, München, Basel, 1984.
Landau, E., H. Leuner: Seminare uber Katathymes Bilderleben und Kreativitat. Göttingen, 1976.
Leuner, H.: Kontrolle der Symbolinterpretation im experimentellen Verfahren. Z Psychother Med Psychol 4:201, 1954.
Leuner, H.: Experimentelles Katathymes Bilderleben als ein klinisches Verfahren der Psychotherapie. Z Psychother Med Psychol 5:233, 1955.
Leuner, H.: Symboldrama, ein aktives nicht-analysierendes Vorgehen in der Psychotherapie. Z Psychother Med Psychol 6:221, 1957.
Leuner, H.: Das Landschaftsbild als Metapher dynamischer Strukturen. In: Stolze, H. (Ed.): Festschrift E. Speer. Lehmann, München, 1959.
Leuner, H.: Grundzüge der tiefenpsychologischen Symbolik. Mat. Psychoanal Analyt Psychother 4:166, 1978.
Leuner, H. (Ed.): Katathymes Bilderleben—Ergebnisse in Theorie und Praxis. Huber, Bern, 1983.
Leuner, H.: Lehrbuch des gesaunten Katathymen Bilderlebens. Huber, Bern. 1984.
Leuner, H., H.M. Wächter: Kurzpsychotherapie einer Acné excoriée und chronischer Neurose mit dem Katathymen Bilderleben (KB), zugleich ein Beitrag zur „anaklitischen Therapie". In press.
Malan, H.D.: A Study of Brief Psychotherapy. Tavistock Publications, London, 1963.
Murray, H.A.: Explorations in Personality. Oxford University Press, New York, 1938.
Nerenz, K.: Das musikalische Symboldrama als Hilfsmethode in der Psychotherapie. Z Psychother Med Psychol 19:28, 1969.
Niederland, W.G.: River symbolism. Psychoanal 25:469, 1956.
Nunberg, H.: Allgemeine Neurosenlehre auf psychoanalytischer Grundlage. Huber, Bern, 1932; 2nd ed. 1954.
Pahl, J.: Über narzisstische Entwicklungslinien während des Katathymen Bilderlebens. In: Leuner, H. (Ed.): Katathymes Bilderleben—Ergebnisse in Theorie und Praxis. Huber, Bern, 1980.
Prindull, E.: Die Manifestation der depressiven Verstimmung im Katathymen Bilderleben. Dissertation in Medicine, Göttingen, 1964.
Pszywyj, A.: Die imaginative Anwendung des Wassers im Katathymen Bilderleben. In: Leuner, H. (Ed.): Katathymes Bilderleben—Ergebnisse in Theorie und Praxis. Huber, Bern, 1983.
Riedel, I.: Der Tagtraum in der schönen Literatur. In: Ausgewählte Vorträge der Zentralen Weiterbildungsseminare der AGKB, Göttingen, 1974.
Rogers, C.R.: Client-centered Therapy. Houghton Mifflin Company, Boston, 1951.
Roth, J.W.: Das Katathyme Bilderleben bei psychosomatischen Frauenkrankheiten und bei Sexualstörungen beiderlei Geschlechts. In: Leuner, H., (Ed.): Katathymes Bilderleben—Ergebnisse in Theorie und Praxis. Huber, Bern, 1980.
Schultz, J.H., Das autogene Training, Luthe, W. (ed): Autogenic Therapy. Thieme-Stratton, New York, 1969, Vol. I, II.
Schultz-Hencke, H.: Lehrbuch der analytischen Psychotherapie. Thieme-Stuttgart 1951; 2nd ed. 1970.
Silberer, H.: Bericht über die Methode, gewisse symbolische Halluzinationserscheinungen hervorzurufen und zu beobachten. J Psychoanal Psychopathol Forsch 1:1, 1909.
Silberer, H.: Symbolik des Erwachens und Schwellensymbolik überhaupt. J Psychoanal Psychopathol Forsch 3:621, 1912.

Singer, J.L., K.S. Pope: The Power of Human Imagination. Plenum Press, New York, 1978.
Spitz, R.: Übertragung und Gegenübertragung. Psyche 10 63, 1956.
Stamm, S.: Die psychodynamische Wirkung der Hypnose im Spiegel des Katathymen Bilderlebens. In: Leuner, H. (Ed.): Katathymes Bilderleben—Ergebnisse in Theorie und Praxis. Huber, Bern, 1983.
Sterba, R.F.: The fate of the ego in analytic therapy. Int J Psychoanal 15:117, 1934.
Stierlin, H.: Conflict and Reconciliation. Doubleday-Anchor, New York, 1968.
Taylor, J.: A personality scale of manifest anxiety. J Abnorm Soc Psychol. 48:285, 1953.
Thomas, K.: Praxis der Selbsthypnose und des autogenen Trainings. Thieme, Stuttgart, 1967; 4th ed. 1976.
Vogt, O. (1896): Zit. n. J.H. Schultz: Die seelische Krankenbehandlung. Fischer, Stuttgart, 1958, p. 168.
Wächter, H.M., V. Pudel: Kurzpsychotherapie von 15 Sitzungen mit dem Katathymen Bilderleben (eine kontrollierte Studie). In: Leuner, H. (Ed.): Katathymes Bilderleben—Ergebnisse in Theorie und Praxis. Huber, Bern, 1983.
Wilke, E.: Katathymes Bilderleben (KB) in der Behandlung der Colitis ulcerosa. vol. 2. Schriftenreihe der AGKB, Eigenverlag AGKB, Göttingen, 1980.
Wolpe, J.: Psychotherapy by Reciprocal Inhibition. Stanford University Press, Stanford, 1958.
Zaro, J.S., R. Barach, D.F. Nedelmann, J.S. Dreiblatt: Einführung für angehende Psychotherapeuten. Enke, Stuttgart, 1980.
Zepf, S.: Das Katathyme Bilderleben in der Erforschung der Psychodynamik des Asthma bronchiale. In: Leuner, H. (Ed.): Katathymes Bilderleben—Ergebnisse in Theorie und Praxis. Huber, Bern, 1983.

Index of the Case Studies in the Text

Number, Page Number, Diagnosis, Purpose of the Example

Index